Web-based Training

Web-based Training

Colin Steed

Gower

© Colin Steed 1999

Published by
Gower Publishing Limited
Gower House
Croft Road
Aldershot
Hampshire GU11 3HR
England

Gower
Old Post Road
Brookfield
Vermont 05036
USA

Colin Steed has asserted his right under the Copyright, Designs and Patents Act 1988 to be identified as the author of this work.

British Library Cataloguing in Publication Data
Steed, Colin
  Web-based training
  1. Employees – Training of 2. Employees – Training of – Computer-assisted instruction
  3. Employees – Training of – Interactive multimedia 4. World Wide Web (Information retrieval system)
  I.Title
  658.3'124'02854678

ISBN 0 566 08103 2

Library of Congress Cataloging-in-Publication Data
Steed, Colin. 1946–
  Web-based training / Colin Steed.
     p.   cm.
  Includes bibliographical references and index.
  ISBN 0–566–08103–2
  1. Employees — Training of — Computer-assisted instruction.
2. World Wide Web (Information retrievel system)   I. Title.
HF5549.5.T7S675 1998
658.3'12404—dc21

98–8749
CIP

Typeset in Great Britain by Wearset, Boldon, Tyne and Wear and printed in Great Britain by MPG Books Ltd, Bodmin.

Contents

List of figures

Acknowledgements

I would like to acknowledge the invaluable help and assistance from both NETg and CBT Systems in compiling Chapter 2, and Elliott Masie, IT research firm IDC, Tim Kilby, of the Web Based Training Information Center, Asymetrix Learning Systems and the American Society for Training and Development (ASTD) for providing much of the data for Chapter 8.

I would also like to acknowledge some people who have been absolutely invaluable to me in compiling this book. My sincere thanks go to Phil Puddefoot (Oracle), Paul Butler, David Holden, Martin Pratt (Peritas), Paul Henry, Angela Kyte, Laura Overton (CBT Systems), John Buttris, Vanessa Buckfield (NETg), Wayne Schaaf (ITCetera), Julie Gibson, Ed Blackhurst, and my publisher Julia Scott, who believed in the subject as strongly as I do.

Thank you to you all. We must always learn something every day. I have learnt how valuable friends and colleagues like you are.

Glossary

ATEC   Authorized Technical Education Centre
CMI   computer-managed instruction
FAQs   Frequently Asked Questions
FTP   File Transfer Protocol
HRD   human resources development
HTML   Hypertext Markup Language
IBT   Internet-based training
ILT   instructor-led training
IS   information systems
IT   information technology
LAN   local area network
OPIE   Online Programming Instruction Environment
SME   small businesses
WAN   wide area network
WBT   Web-based training
WWW   World Wide Web

Introduction

Web-based training – sometimes called Internet-based training or online training – is set to transform the world of education and training. Put simply, Web-based training enables businesses to store instructional materials (including courses, videos, tests and multimedia materials) at a central location which can then be accessed by anyone connected to the Internet or company intranet, anywhere, at any time. And, significantly, it is absolutely irrelevant which computer platform you run the course from.

With Web-based training, teaching and learning can be freed from the boundaries of classrooms and class schedules. Traditional classroom lectures and presentations can become multimedia learning experiences for students, whenever and wherever they want them. Learning resources from your organization can be supplemented or augmented by the learning resources of the world. And, above all, Web-based training can help us to re-focus our institutions from teaching to learning, and from teacher to student.

There are clearly a number of benefits to be had from this exciting new training medium. Though not an exhaustive list, here are some of the key benefits:

- **Effective**: studies show that this form of training is 30 per cent more effective at skills transfer and retention than classroom training.
- **Convenient**: you train in a place and at a time to suit yourself.
- **Price**: you only pay for the tuition, saving on accommodation, subsistence, travel and opportunity.
- **One to one**: during online sessions, you have a private, personal tutor.
- **Support**: during classes, you can network with your classmates and tutor.
- **Exam preparation**: frequent testing before and after course topics, enabling you to go over topics not fully understood.

The Internet and the Web are fast emerging as some of the trainer's most important tools, with the Web becoming the most popular way to access the Internet. The Web is probably the most educational, entertaining and productive tool available today. With full video and audio capabilities and a platform-independent global network in place, the possibilities afforded by the Web for actually delivering staff training and development programmes are boundless.

Today, Web-based training courses and materials are already available. The Masie Center in New York, an independent IT learning and research firm, says that the popularity of the Internet combined with the rise of corporate intranets and the growing ability to deliver audio and video over networks are building the foundation of online learning to an extent where it will become a $1 billion market in the next five years. Masie points out a series of web-based learning options which will be strong competitors to classroom-based instruction:

- Corporations will be able to offer courses for their employees, accessible over their intranets, with employees taking these courses at their desks, from their homes and even when travelling.
- Universities, colleges and training companies will offer training programmes on a 'pay-as-you-learn' basis, with courses costing as little as £10.
- As desktop videoconferencing grows, Web-based training will include live interactions with experts and teachers.
- Just-in-time coaching sessions, where employees can request a 15-minute session on a critical topic, such as how to deal with a difficult colleague.

The success of Web-based training today, however, is difficult to assess. But what is absolutely clear is that new students are enrolling daily, courseware providers are springing up at an increasing speed and more and more courses are becoming available, demonstrating both the acceptance of the medium and that it is an effective way to gain new skills. With the weight of the major software vendors like Microsoft, Lotus and Oracle, to name but a few, behind it, together with the world-wide proliferation of desktop IT, learning through Web-based training can only be set to increase. Significantly, individuals of all ages and experience are completing courses and gaining qualifications and certifications which, for many, would have been impossible owing to the restrictions of time, geography, availability and cost.

Let's have a brief look at two examples of how Web-based training has helped UK organizations. Leading UK IT training provider Peritas recently delivered a Web-based training programme to ICL High Performance Systems through its Peritas Online Web-based training service. The training programme was to re-skill 80 of its enterprise systems engineers as Microsoft Certified Systems Engineers. At its core was a series of Web-based training courses, combined with a small number of classroom-based workshop sessions. Following the training programme, the first-time pass rate was reported to be a very creditable 97 per cent. In another example – full details of which can be found in Chapter 6 – Thames Valley Enterprise has been using Web-based training to deliver PC applications training to the long-term unemployed to help them re-skill and pursue a new career. Some quotations from three of those who had just completed the courses explained how they benefited from the online learning experience:

> It slotted easily into my daily routine. It also helped me to retrain for a new career. Next to winning the National Lottery, being offered my current job after two years of unemployment was the best thing that could have happened to me.

> I found the quick access to my instructor (via the chat facility) quite amazing.

> Online learning has many benefits, the greatest being that I could learn at my own pace. With online learning, you can design your own schedule, spending more time on where you feel you will gain the most benefit.

Whether Web-based training is a viable option for you or your organization is a question that I cannot answer for you. But, I do hope that this book will provide you with all of the facts to make it the starting point of your investigation. It is imperative that those individuals responsible for their organization's staff training and development now make Web-based training literacy their immediate personal goal, and corporate training departments should now be looking towards formulating a development strategy for taking advantage of this exciting new training medium.

This book is designed to explain how the Internet is currently being used to deliver Web-based training to people's desktops. It will show corporate trainers, IT, IS, HRD and other business managers how to use the Internet or company intranet to develop and train employees and improve performance. It outlines the benefits and drawbacks of Web-based training, looks at the cost considerations, examines the elements that make up a Web-based training programme, helps you to design your own Web-based training strategy, looks at what's currently available on the market today and predicts the likely trends for the future. You will also see some positive evaluations of two organizations' trials in using the Web for delivering training courses. By the end of the book, I hope that it will provide you with enough insight and knowledge to help you – and your organization – to be aware of the issues and have a better understanding of the benefits and methods to adopt.

There are some important questions to address before we begin to explore the world of Web-based training: Why should I bother with this new medium? Do I really need to learn about it? Can I justify the time? I've got enough problems getting all of my staff trained with little or no budget. To answer these points in the briefest possible way, I believe that Web-based training is set to revolutionize completely training and development as we know them and that it will have as important an impact on the training business as that of the invention of the personal computer over 15 years ago. If you're not convinced now, then perhaps you're in the wrong job, or reading the wrong book.

So let's get started, and firstly look at the evolution of the Internet/World Wide Web (which from now on I'll refer to as the Web) and Web-based training (which from now on I'll refer to as WBT), and explore the issues, uses and value of using the Web for staff training and development.

Chapter 1

Why Web-based training?

Today business is confronting problems of enormous proportion. Nearly every business on both sides of the Atlantic is facing shrinking budgets and scarce resources. Yet, the competition is becoming increasingly fierce, forcing business to find ways to get higher-quality products to the market place faster than ever before and with fewer resources at their disposal. These problems are not, however, just on a national level. With the ease of world-wide travel and the rapidly increasing advances in communication technology, more and more companies are becoming multinational, global enterprises.

As the world continues to change, business, industry, education and government alike are finding it increasingly difficult to keep their work-forces competitive and current. For modern business to stay competitive and financially healthy in today's global market, training and education are playing an increasingly important role. However, if they are to compete, survive and prosper, all businesses in the modern world have little choice but to substantially increase their commitment to staff training and development. They need to acquire greater sophistication and more cost-effective and durable means of delivering and distributing training to the workforce.

Continuous corporate learning and training are needed to support:

- new products
- new job skills
- advanced education in technical and non-technical subjects
- management skills and development
- customer service
- corporate education.

As the millennium approaches, a successful organization will be one that learns continuously and quickly. These drivers are dictating a demand for changes in the ways in which the workforce is trained. The new jobs being created by service-oriented economies require higher levels of skill,

**Need for change in
training delivery**

■ **Acceleration of technology change**

■ **The growing skills gap**

■ **Increased demand for training**

■ **Increased demands on productivity**

■ **Reduced amount of time for training**

■ **Increased need for innovations in training and
learning on demand**

Figure 1.1   Need for change in training delivery

increased flexibility and an increased ability to deal with change (see Figure
1.1). The rapidly changing workforce is only part of the dilemma. The other
factor is the even more radical change which is already apparent in the
nature of the work being undertaken in the workplace. The economy is
shifting from a manufacturing base to a service base – with some 70 per
cent of the gross national product in the form of services rather than goods
– and service businesses are information-based. This substantially increases
the need for training and retraining.

So, faced with a shrinking workforce and a rapidly increasing skills short-
age, where are the new skilled workers going to come from? These new
skilled workers will have to come from the current workforce; but they will
have to be retrained. Not only do the skills of low-skilled employees need
to be increased, employees in jobs requiring high skill levels are demanding
continuous retraining. Knowing how to do today's job is not enough. As
technology explodes and reshapes the workplace, today's job skills will
become obsolete when replaced by tomorrow's job requiring a complete
new set of skills. In today's rapidly changing, global service-oriented business environment, continuous training will become mandatory in any organization that plans to remain competitive, successful and in business. Our
organizations will need to transform into learning organizations.

Distance learning: the key to future learning

Distance learning is an idea whose time has now come. It is not a new idea – far from it; correspondence courses and programmed instruction workbooks have been around and in use for many years. But today, a variety of sophisticated communication technologies provide both instructor and learner with numerous ways to participate in learning at a distance. Distance learning is now becoming a widely recognized key to meeting the challenge of delivering more training to more people on more subjects with higher impact and effectiveness, and in a much more cost-effective way.

So just what is distance learning? Basically, distance learning comprises the following characteristics:

- **Distance between learner and instructor.** The distance learning strategy is often given other names (distance teaching, distance education, open learning, distributed education, and so on). All of these terms refer to some form of instruction in which the learner and instructor are physically separated from one another.
- **Independent or group study.** Distance learning may be set up to have learners participating either individually or in groups, or in a combination of both.
- **Delivery options.** Instruction may be provided in a variety of media, from printed materials, audio cassettes, video tape, computer-based training programs, CD-ROMs, to live satellite audio and videoconferences.

Distance learning delivery options

Printed materials

The printed format has been used extensively as the early classic distance learning format. Printed textbooks and training manuals have allowed learners to add to their knowledge for many generations.

Audio cassettes

Audio tapes have long been a much used medium for delivering instruction. Many of the world's linguists learned to speak a second language through their use. Today, audio cassettes can be purchased on a variety of topics, from art to zoology.

Video tape

The growth in the quality of inexpensive video tape and the general low-cost availability of VCRs has made video tape an attractive medium for distance learning. Videos can be used to allow students to hear and see an instructor's lecture. Until recently, many thousands of students have gained Open University degrees from videotaped TV broadcasts.

Personal computers

Personal computers provide an excellent means to engage individual learners in active problem-solving in a realistic way. Well-designed training via a PC is ideal for addressing some types of learning objectives but developing computer-based training (CBT) materials is time-consuming and costly. Perhaps for this reason, many early developers of computer-based instruction produced what were termed 'page-turners' in which the computer presented screen after screen of sequential text; the learner's only interaction was to instruct the computer to go to the next screen. Fortunately, this is very much a thing of the past and today's modern CBT programs provide some of the most advanced training delivery mediums.

Electronic communication

The comparatively recent advances in communications technology have enabled widely separated groups to communicate through the telephone. This has enabled the instructor to interact with learners through 'audio conferences' and this has, more recently, been enhanced by the addition of video pictures and sound through satellite technology: videoconferences. But it is, without any doubt, the emergence of the Internet which is offering the most exciting challenges to traditional distance learning delivery. We shall be looking at the Internet and its spin-off, the corporate intranet, in detail later in this chapter.

There is, however, no single medium which is best for delivering distance learning. All have their advantages, disadvantages, uses and limitations, but it is generally accepted that the best distance learning experiences combine a variety of media, selected for different purposes. The need for and the benefits of distance learning are clear. But, inevitably, there are challenges that need to be addressed at board level. Today's boardrooms and classrooms are generally ill-equipped to keep pace with the projected rate of change of skill obsolescence. Further, the imposition of time, distance and other constraints on workers and learners will create a strong demand for more efficient and expedient ways to distribute necessary information. The need today is for more innovative technological systems that can reach great numbers of people with vast amounts of information under a variety of conditions. The challenge ahead is to provide systems, given the current and future state of the technology, allied to the needs of business and the workforce.

What is the Internet?

Nothing has captured the interest and imagination of educators around the world as much as the Internet and the World Wide Web. The phenomenal popularity of the Internet and the unprecedented rapid adoption of Internet technologies to implement corporate intranets and extranets are creating a tremendous opportunity to provide learning materials and services in a convenient, easy-to-use and engaging manner. So, what are the Internet and the World Wide Web?

The Internet is neither a company, nor a software system, nor a service. It is not owned by anyone. It is simply a generic name given to a global network of computer networks. It is not new. It was created in 1969 in the US Defense Department as a fallback for communications in case of a nuclear attack on the USA. The Internet enables information to be passed around even if one network or group of networks is out of action. Figure 1.2 provides a visual explanation. Let's say that the computer network connection between New York (A) and Chicago (C) was destroyed. With the Internet, New York could still route information to Chicago by routing it via (B). It's that simple. Likewise, Chicago (C) could access Dallas via D or F, or G and E, or B and H (see Figure 1.2).

Since its birth, the Internet has grown dramatically – today's estimate is of 40 million users – with an annual growth rate of 10 per cent. The Internet is now a world-wide network, with over 50 000 networks located in over 150 countries with Internet connections, with users from government, research institutions, universities, companies, private organizations, schools and individual homes. In fact, it's difficult today to find someone who does not use or does not know about the Internet. Factors which have contributed to the popularity of the Internet include:

- Access to vast, actively maintained, online repositories of information.
- Global availability at relatively low cost.
- Engaging multimedia, platform-independent, user interface.
- Intuitive navigation through point and click hyperlinks.
- Extensive information indexing and mapping by an array of search engines.

THE RATIONALE BEHIND
THE EARLY INTERNET (ARPANET)

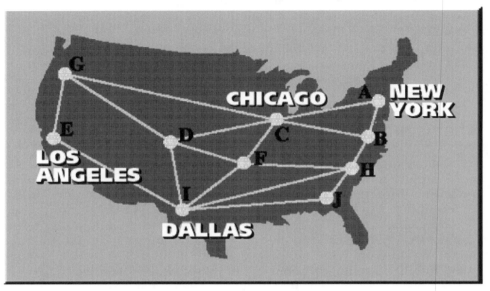

Figure 1.2   The concept of the Internet

- Support for real-time communications between individuals and groups (e-mail, chat, conferencing).
- Relatively simple and low-cost content publishing to a world-wide audience.

While the majority of users use the Internet for e-mail, its popularity really exploded with the introduction of the World Wide Web. The Web represents an unstructured network of millions of computer sites throughout the world. It was invented in 1990 by British physicist Tim Berners-Lee and was first used to publish documents (scientific papers) so that they could be used by other scientists in their research. It was basically an online document publishing system using the electronic distribution facilities of the Internet. The Web uses a facility called hypertext which allows the reader to click their mouse on a highlighted phrase or reference which would then take them to another Web site with information on that subject, a kind of online referencing system. The beauty of the system is that the user does not need to know where the site is located or what the file was called. Apart from the traditional text documents, the Web can also incorporate graphics, audio, animation and video sequences.

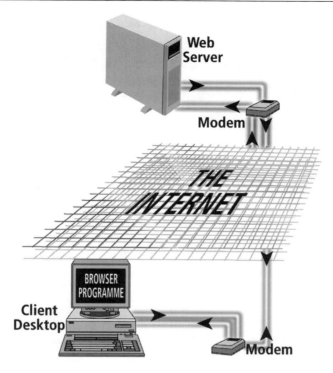

Figure 1.3   How the Web works

The Web has a client/server architecture. This means that the client program running on your computer (your Web browser) requests information from a server program running on another computer somewhere on the Internet. The server program then sends back the requested information over the Internet to your browser program, which interprets it and displays the data on your screen (see Figure 1.3).

The client computer

To access the Web, you need a client computer. It must be connected to the Internet and have loaded on the desktop computer a piece of software called a Web browser. This is a standard piece of software available for all computer platforms which can display the documents and perform the hypertext links. The most popular Web browsers today are Netscape Navigator and Microsoft Internet Explorer (see Figure 1.4 for an example of Microsoft Internet Explorer). This software can be downloaded from the Internet and is generally available free. The Internet connection can either be hard-wired, or it can be a dial-up telephone connection via a modem to

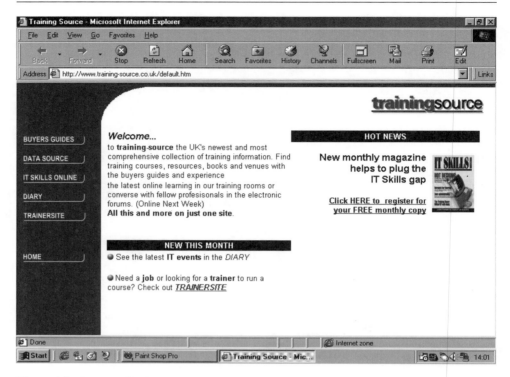

Figure 1.4   Internet Explorer

an Internet Service Provider (ISP). You are most likely to have the latter connection.

The server computer

To deliver content on the Web you need a server computer, where the actual text, graphics, audio, video, and so on, is stored. It has requirements similar to those of the client computer: it must be connected to the Internet and must be able to run a Web server program. Note that you can also set up your own server to run a Web site over your local area network without connecting to the Internet. This is what we call an intranet (we shall cover that in more detail later). In this book we shall be looking at various training sites which offer courses over the Web. These will all be running on a Web server machine – the location does not matter. All you need to connect to them is a Web address, such as *www.peritas.com* (for example).

Why use the Internet for training?

While looking at the Internet as a new addition to your training delivery options, one of the first questions that you will probably ask yourself is: Is it worth it? I'm sure that you have training methods that produce satisfactory results already, so why change? Let's take a look at some of the many benefits provided by WBT and consider how it can improve both the methods and the amount of training and development that can be enjoyed at your establishment.

An article on the Web by Thomas Fox McManus, from the University of Texas at Austin, gives a good explanation of the advantages and disadvantages of the Web.

> The Internet can deliver video – but not as quickly as videotape, CD-ROM or television. It can carry real-time personal interaction – but not as well as telephone or videoconferencing. It can display textual information – but not as easy to read or as convenient to use as a book or magazine. So why then should we use the Internet?

According to McManus, the Internet has two real overriding advantages over all of the other media:

- The Internet combines advantages of other media so that it conveys video and sound better than a book, is more interactive than an audio or video tape and, unlike CD-ROM, it can link people from around the world, and more cost-effectively.
- The Internet is also a vast resource of information. It is, arguably, the largest and most diverse source of information in the world today. It is possible to incorporate the wealth of information available on the Internet in your courses. For instance, if you are designing a course on Renaissance art history, you can include links to the Vatican Library and the Louvre, as well as to the Art History exhibit at the Australian National University, and so on. This sort of immediate access to information and resources cannot be found on any other medium.

But to make the real case for using the Internet/Web in education, we should begin with the criteria to assess its present impact and potential contribution. McManus stresses that for any technology to be worthwhile educationally, we need to ask three questions:

- Does it make learning more accessible?
- Does it promote improved learning?
- Does it accomplish both of the above points while containing, if not reducing, the cost of training?

So let's look at the three aspects. Can the Web pass the test?

Making learning more accessible

Each of us probably has a different interpretation of what 'access to learning' means, although most will agree that it means making education more attainable by more people by providing learning opportunities in the workplace, home, college or school. The Web is made for education. Its accessibility is one of its main assets, if not the main asset.

Some of the world's best universities and higher education colleges are providing opportunities to students who are unable to attend campus. Until recently, they relied on correspondence, traditional print instruction materials and perhaps audio or video tapes. That's all starting to change now as educators capitalize on using Web-based technology. The Open University, based in Milton Keynes, England, is a prime example of a dedicated distance education institution that uses the Web to support its mission of providing accessible education. The Open University has been acknowledged as a leader in world-wide distance education since it was founded in 1969. It has some 200 000 students around the world studying over 300 different courses. In 1994 it experimented with offering an advanced psychology course using the Web. The course was so successful that the following year it offered two computer science courses via the Web; and it now intends to continue to expand its list of offerings.

City University, in Bellevue, Washington, USA, is another dedicated distance learning institution. It operates with the mission of 'making education available to all who desire it without interrupting commitments to work and home'. Recently, they established their Education Resource and Online Academic Degree System to take advantage of Web-based technology to offer their programmes. At present they provide online an MBA degree programme and a Bachelor of Science in computer systems. Through the university's Web site, students around the world apply to the university, register for courses and complete course work electronically. They can also send questions and assignments to their tutors and participate in specialized live forums.

An example of traditional institutions using the Web as the backbone of their distance learning efforts is the University of Massachusetts Dartmouth Division of Computing Education. Its Web-based CyberEd full-credit undergraduate and graduate courses make full use of the Web complete with images, sound and video, to present material, test, communicate among students and faculty, and submit assignments. Its goal is to 'create a distance learning environment that rivals the traditional classroom environment in the quality and content of the learning experience . . . to encourage a new educational paradigm in which the instructor is no longer regarded as the sole source of all knowledge'. Reports by participants and visitors posted at its Web site suggest CyberEd is well on its way to achieving its goal.

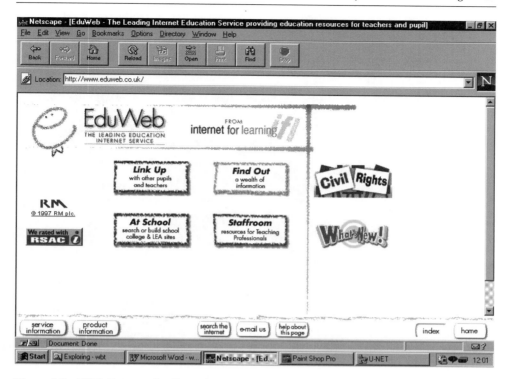

Figure 1.5   RM's Internet for Learning EduWeb

As the list of accredited colleges and universities extending access to their programmes to students using the Web grows, a new kind of institution – the virtual university – is emerging to challenge the established ones by providing universal access to online courses and degrees. While not accredited, these 'virtual' institutions are blazing the trail in what will no doubt become the common way to study in the near future.

The Web is also transforming the school curriculum. Technically, students and parents now have the same access to information resources as the schools. This has started to result in tremendous change in the way that our schools work on both sides of the Atlantic.

With UK schools now offered free access to the Internet, free Web browsers from Microsoft, and with specialized Internet for Schools networks such as RM's Internet for Learning Eduweb (www.eduweb.co.uk) (see Figure 1.5) and BT's CampusWorld (www.campus.bt.com) (see Figure 1.6) fully operational, school students are becoming familiar with the rich source of information and learning possibilities offered. The UK Government has also recently launched a new initiative, UK Net Year, which is

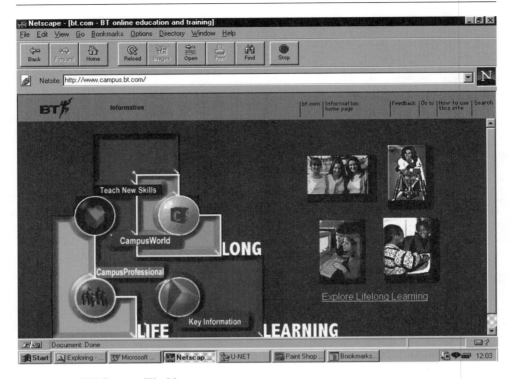

Figure 1.6   BT CampusWorld

aimed at connecting all 32 000 of the UK's schools to the Internet, as well as dramatically reducing telephone call charges for Internet access.

Let us first have a look at two schools who are already making use of the Internet, Cherwell School in Oxford and Tendring Technology College in Essex.

Cherwell School

Cherwell School started out like many other schools in the UK, with one computer linked to a standard modem for Internet access. This lasted for about 12 months before the school opted to extend its Internet provision to a 22-station networked IT room, including four workstations in the staff room and one in the library (see Figure 1.7). All staff have access to the Internet and around one-third have their own personal e-mail address. Students are introduced to the Internet in Year 9 (age 13/14) IT lessons, as well as using it in particular parts of the school curriculum. From Year 11

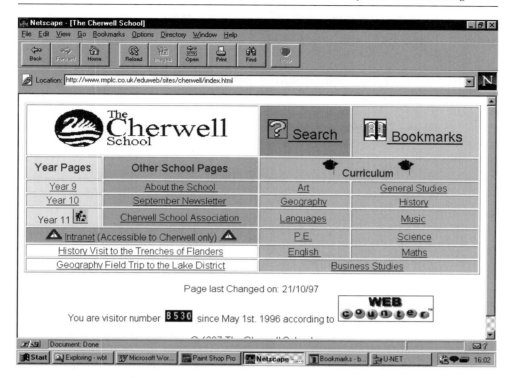

Figure 1.7   The Internet at Cherwell School, Oxford

(age 15/16), students make increased use of the Internet for research and for creating Web pages.

Cherwell has used Internet for Learning's EduWeb area to create its own Web site which holds information about the school, including the school prospectus and exam results, as well as being used as a launch point to locate useful information for both staff and students. The site was created by students and staff and currently contains pages for history, geography, maths, languages, PE, science and art. Each department develops its own pages according to its needs, but a common feature is the hypertext links to 'sites of interest' identified by each department as being relevant to the National Curriculum.

It became clear to the school quite quickly that the Internet was of more value to certain curriculum areas than to others. Geography was identified as one of the more focused areas and is used in a Year 9 project on Population and Development. South Africa was chosen as an example of a developing country, where contrasts in wealth and development within the country itself could be found. The students were supplied with a worksheet which asked them to carry out a number of tasks to gather information from different sources in order to ask a series of questions. They had to:

- visit *The Times* newspaper archives and look at current issues in the *South African Mail and Guardian* newspaper;
- visit Web sites with other useful links, such as the ANC homepage; and
- look at the Web page of a small farm school in rural South Africa and assess how similar or different life at the school is compared to life at Cherwell.

Success was a key part of the project, so students were given clear direction about what to use the Internet for, rather than simply being told to find out something about South Africa. This meant extra preparatory work for the teacher to preview sites, checking that they provided relevant information and drawing up the worksheet, with guidance on how to access the sites.

Evaluating the effectiveness of the lesson, it was found that the approach taken allowed students of all abilities to answer the questions and complete the task, while allowing students to access 'live' Web sites to see up-to-date facts and figures. Having used the Internet to support and extend students' learning, the school is in no doubt that the costs involved (about £1 500 per annum for ISDN call charges for the whole school) are a necessary expense. Martin Roberts, head teacher at Cherwell, commented on the school's use of IT in the curriculum: 'Skills in and confidence about using IT and the Internet are of critical importance to pupils who will be adults in the 21st century. Schools must become involved.'

Tendring Technology College

Students at Tendring Technology College, Essex, have been using the Internet to gather data on a range of diverse subjects. From the students' perspective, they have found the research fun and exciting, while the teaching staff have been able to teach the students research skills, normally seen as rather a 'dull' activity. Some of the research projects have included:

- History: researching into fashion in the 1920s and the life of Henry Ford.
- Geography: collecting meteorological data and national statistics.
- Science: interacting with the NASA site and collecting data.
- PE: collecting data relating to a variety of sports.
- IT: exploring Microsoft, IBM and other IT manufacturers' pages.

In researching the various topics, both in teacher-led and personal time, the students have benefited from the wealth of subjects covered in the Internet for Learning Pathways area. Not only has this provided a stepping stone to other sites, but it has also reduced the time that can be spent just searching the Web. Many of the students have also registered for the Netpals service, which provides an e-mail based pen-pals service throughout the world for schoolchildren. Additionally, their teachers are making use of the numerous educational forums to discuss topical educational issues with colleagues around the country.

Promoting improved learning

As we have seen, there is plenty of evidence that the Web is a valuable means to increase accessibility of learning. Evidence for how it can promote improved learning, however, is not as forthcoming. According to Ron Owston's research paper on the subject (*The Teaching Web: A Guide to the World Wide Web for all Teachers*) there is an ongoing debate in the instructional design literature about whether there are any unique attributes of any media that can promote improved learning. This debate stems from the observation that, after more than 50 years of research on instructional media, no consistent significant effects from any medium on learning have been demonstrated. Some researchers argue that no effect can possibly be demonstrated because any improvement in learning that may accrue will come from the instructional design, not the medium that delivers the instruction. Others contend that the match of delivery mechanism to an individual's learning style is a primary factor in determining the improvement.

So we cannot simply ask: Do students learn better with the Web as compared with traditional classroom instruction? Owston argues that we have to realize that no medium is likely to improve learning in a significant way when it is used to deliver instruction. However, he argues that there are at least three distinct learning advantages to Web use which are discussed below.

The Web appeals to students' learning mode

One of the primary learning advantages of Web use is that it appeals very much to the way students now prefer to learn. For today's students the computer is an integral part of their world and they tend to be visual learners to a greater extent than previous generations because their world is rich in visual stimuli: today's younger generation expect videos with every CD released; the television is a norm; video/computer games are more popular than ever before; and reference books are being replaced with CD-ROMs such as Encarta.

Try this simple experiment. Explain in simple terms what the Internet is to your child. Then test them on their comprehension of the concept. Next, show them a simple diagram or video on the subject. You should find that the comprehension of the second method is much better. Now add interactivity into the equation and you will find that this is by far the 'most interesting' method for them; they simply enjoy visualizing and interacting, and therefore will find learning much more enjoyable and hence will learn better.

The Web provides for flexible learning

We saw previously that accessibility provided by the Web is an effective vehicle to help students gain an education without being on campus. A growing number of institutions now want to provide their regular, full-time students greater flexibility in accessing their courses as well. When you browse through courses listed today, you will discover many courses where staff have dramatically reduced the amount of face-to-face contact between instructor and student, or in some cases, entirely eliminated it. Instead, they provide Web-based study projects and online activities that students can access at their own convenience: putting student reading matter on the Web, debate carried out in 'virtual conversations', and the tutor broadcasting news and class discussion forums using e-mail and Internet 'chat' facilities. While some may decry the loss of face-to-face contact between tutor and student, it is not hard to find teaching staff who believe the quality of interaction and learning that takes place online is actually superior. According to Owston:

> They argue that interaction is more thoughtful and considered when students have the chance to think about their responses to questions and discussion topics before posting them to an electronic public forum. These faculties also contend that students who are shy or uncomfortable about participating in class discussions do not feel that way in online forums.

Interaction where participants contribute to forums at different times is called *asynchronous* communication. The Web provides facilities to permit *synchronous* communication which allows participants to carry out live conversations and discussions. Additionally, live video can be used to create a learning environment that simulates a live classroom because students can both see and hear each other. This virtual classroom allows students to take part in the class from any Internet connection in the world. The technology to do this is still in its infancy but rapid progress is currently being made in its development.

The Web has had an effect in schools too. According to Owston's research, when computers are introduced into school classrooms, teachers inevitably change their teaching style to allow students greater autonomy in controlling their learning.

They tend to shift their style of teaching from didactic to a more project-based approach. Teachers in the Apple Classrooms of Tomorrow project, which placed large numbers of computers in classrooms across the US, are just one group who have reported these kinds of changes. The Web is a tool that fits well with this new learning environment. It empowers students to become part of the Internet community and to take advantage of the wealth of learning opportunities available through the Internet without having to master arcane computer commands.

The Web enables new kinds of learning

Business leaders are now calling upon our schools, colleges and universities to graduate a different kind of student than those of a generation ago. This is in response to the challenges posed by the new global economy, where the knowledge and skills of a nation's workforce are key to its competitive success. Among the skills called for are critical thinking, problem solving, written communication and the ability to work collaboratively. Owston stresses:

> In the hands of able teachers, the Web can play a prominent role in fostering the development of these skills required. Teachers can encourage students to explore the Web with the goal of having them weigh evidence, judge authenticity of data, compare different viewpoints on issues, analyse and synthesise diverse sources of information, and construct their own understanding of the topic or issue at hand. By so doing, teachers will be well on their way to having students develop critical thinking and problem solving skills. Students can develop written communication skills using the Web. The theory is that when students have a real audience to write to – with a real purpose in writing to them – they will become more conscious of their vocabulary, syntax and grammar. Online work provides this authenticity. E-mail, electronic reply forms and Internet newsgroup readers are part of most Web browsing tools today so students do not have to leave the Web to carry out online writing. Teachers who design projects or assignments that incorporate this feature of the Web will be giving their students an ideal opportunity to develop their writing skills.

Finally, teachers can also foster development of collaborative skills on the Web. This is done by structuring group projects where group members are in different geographical locations yet have a common goal to reach or problem to solve.

Containing the costs of education

Now that we have seen the Web can promote greater access to education and improved learning we need to consider the cost of doing it. Research has revealed that the Web can actually lead to decreased per capita costs for training. According to a recent article in *Computerworld* magazine, the McDonald's Corporation in the USA has recently cut its training costs by almost one-fifth and confidently expects this to be further reduced once the company's intranet infrastructure is established. According to the learning manager of the company's IS department: 'The savings will be even greater because we can make the training available to more people.'

In the education sector, the UK Government has launched a major initiative to help the UK's 32 000 schools access the Internet for little cost. UK NetYear is an ongoing high-profile programme led by private/public sector partnership, designed to raise awareness of the potential of the Internet as an educational tool. At the launch of the initiative at the Labour Party Conference in Brighton in 1997, Mr Blair promised that by the year 2002, every one of the UK's 32 000 schools will have modern computers, the educational programs to go on them, the teachers skilled to teach, the pupils skilled to use them, connected to the Internet for free and with telephone call charges cut to as little as £1 per pupil per year.

UK NetYear will motivate local communities and businesses to become involved in the process, not only in sponsorship and fundraising but also directly, by mobilizing volunteers within IT-literate workforces to provide guidance for schools. Chairman of UK NetYear, and chairman of IT training company Peritas, David Wimpress said that he believes that the effective use of information and communication technology could transform the UK educational system. He argues that by working together, the Government, the education sector, business and the community can help to develop the new skills and new approach to take the UK forward.

So a strong case for using the Web in education and training exists in all of the three main areas discussed:

- Does it increase access to learning?
- Does it promote improved learning?
- Does it contain the costs of education?

So now let's look at our businesses. Are they ready to use the Internet and the Web for staff training and development?

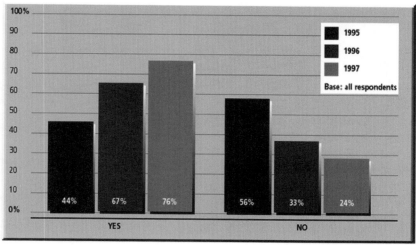

Figure 1.8   The Internet at work

Corporate use of the Internet

The rapid growth of the Internet and corporate intranet has been remarkable. According to the AST's IT Barometer Survey 1997, the past year has seen a continuation in the adoption of the Internet by corporate organizations, with 76 per cent now making use of its various facilities (up from 67 per cent the previous year and 44 per cent in 1995) (see Figure 1.8). In the same time there has been an across the board drop in the level of concern by corporates over various areas of Internet usage (see Figure 1.9). The research reveals that concern about members of staff using the Internet for purposes not connected to their work has fallen fastest which indicates that the novelty of the Internet is beginning to wear off and staff are now, for the most part, using it to aid them in their work rather than for entertainment.

In spite of the scepticism voiced by IT directors in last year's survey, when almost half said that having a Web site was not important to the future success of the business, the phenomenon of the corporate Web home page has continued to gain momentum (see Figure 1.10). The past year has seen the number of corporates with a Web site leap from 23 per cent to 43 per cent. Of those that do not have one, 73 per cent are now considering developing a Web presence.

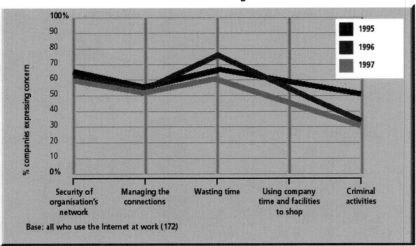

Figure 1.9   Concerns over Internet usage

Another major research programme (The Durlacher Quarterly Internet Report, 1997) reveals a continuing strong growth in the corporate Internet market and predicts that this will continue at over 10 per cent per month for at least the next two years. Over 85 per cent of large UK corporates now have some form of Internet connection and this is expected to increase to 92 per cent within the next 12 months. Purchasing and other transactions on the Internet is being carried out by a third of UK corporates. But it is not just large corporations who are using the Internet. In the case of UK SMEs (small businesses), 39 per cent are currently connected, with 20 per cent indicating that they will be online within 12 months.

Corporate use of the intranet

An intranet is a restricted and secure Internet, where companies can use technology popularized by the Internet, such as e-mail, Web pages, browsers and servers, to create internal closed networks accessible to only the company's employees. In effect, an intranet is an internal Internet. It may be defined as: *'An internal Web site which the company employs to disseminate information and services throughout the enterprise.'* Or alternatively: *'A closed communication system within an organization which allows people to access information from a central source using a Web browser.'*

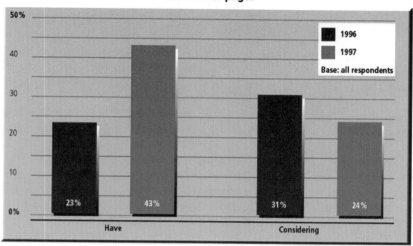

Corporates with/considering Web Home pages

Source: AST IT Barometer Survey 1997

Figure 1.10   The corporate use of the Internet

These services can include e-mail messaging, staff training, staff notices, corporate information, telephone directories, ordering supplies, personnel information, staff records, health and safety messages, company procedures, staff announcements, and so on. The costs are offset on printing and paper expenses and the company not having to buy and keep up-to-date many different versions of applications to suit different computer platforms.

AST's IT Barometer study also reveals that 25 per cent of UK corporates have already implemented an intranet. Of those who had installed an intranet, 27 per cent had done so in the past three months and a further 22 per cent during the past six months (see Figure 1.11). So the number of UK corporates utilizing an intranet very nearly doubled in the six months preceding the AST 1997 survey. The Durlacher report also revealed that some 60 per cent of large UK companies have installed some form of corporate intranet and this has serious implications for the expected explosion in the use of Web-based training.

Current intranet users agree that some of the drawbacks associated with using the Internet do not apply to an intranet. The intranet manager of one of the UK's largest multinationals said that his firm's intranet was 'reliable, fast and secure. We've got graphics, video clips and sound. Things like speed are problems on the Internet but not with an intranet.' A spokesman for Sun Microsystems points out that applications development on an intranet should be easier than in traditional programming environments

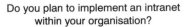

Do you plan to implement an intranet
within your organisation?

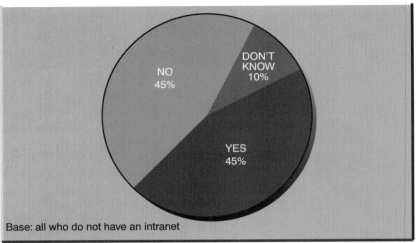

Source: AST IT Barometer Survey 1997

Figure 1.11   Implementing an intranet

because Web applications currently rely on two relatively simple standards: Web browsers and HTML (Hypertext Markup Language). Being based on platform-independent standards, Web sites should be relatively easy to maintain.

Many companies are using connections between their intranet and the Internet to share information and transact business in a secure manner with their partners, suppliers and customers. Under these circumstances, companies are in effect extending access to their intranet-based applications to permit controlled access by known users. This accessibility service is called an extranet. Companies that have connections from their corporate intranet to the Internet do have some valid concerns about security. They must ensure that company confidential information does not cross the boundary between the closed corporate network and the wide open public Internet. This can be accomplished by erecting 'electronic fences' with 'proxy servers' and 'firewalls' between their intranet and the global Internet.

The AST IT Barometer Survey found that the momentum that intranet technology has picked up to date is unlikely to abate in the near future, with 52 per cent of those intending to implement an intranet stating that they intend to do so in the next year. When prompted to say which of the benefits offered by an intranet were the most important, it was the fact that it allows common access to information that came out as the front runner (see Figure 1.12). Following this, all with quite similar ratings, were the facilitation of communication, inter-operation with current networks, and time saving.

Durlacher estimates that the UK intranet market will be worth some £5.5bn within four years, growing from just £80m recorded in the early part of 1997. It is this rapid take-up of corporate intranets which will facilitate the expected explosion in Web-based training in the near future. Corporate intranets, extranets and the Internet form a rich infrastructure for the realization of a comprehensive learning environment, where individuals can have access to:

- interactive self-paced instruction;
- skills assessment;
- instructor-led training information and registration;
- reference materials;
- online communication with subject matter experts, instructors and colleagues; and
- individualized learning plan management systems.

With such an online learning environment, individuals can develop customized learning plans and navigate through available learning resources without concern over where and how those resources are provided. Learners can access their training plans and learning resources at any time, and

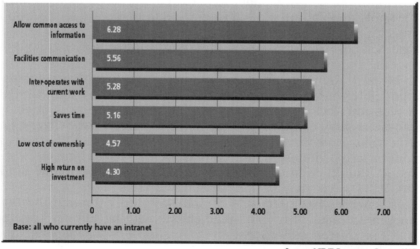

Source: AST IT Barometer Survey 1997

Figure 1.12   The benefits of an intranet

anywhere. As learning resources are updated and added to, they become immediately available to all authorized learners.

Why Web-based training?

There is no doubt that the best environment to learn anything is in the classroom. The classroom is the perfect place to learn because students have the opportunity to talk, interact with and learn from both the tutor and the other students on the course. You listen to the tutor, practise what has been explained, and if you have a problem, discuss it with the tutor. The classroom is an environment that we are all used to and comfortable with; it's what we were all brought up with since our nursery school days. But the reality is that the classroom environment does have a few problems associated with it. Notably, it is becoming increasingly expensive both in terms of money and time away from the workplace, and the tutor is unable to teach at a pace that suits every individual on the course.

During the past few years, self-paced, self-study materials have progressed enormously in terms of learning effectiveness. But the down-side of using self-paced materials, whether it's a self-paced teach-yourself workbook, video or multimedia CD-ROM, is that it relies on the individual to be highly motivated, with the required self-discipline to get the task completed. There is simply no tutor or colleague to whom you can say: 'Can you tell me how to do this – the CD doesn't explain it' or 'My PC does not do what the book says it should when I do this'. So although self-paced learning is another ideal method of training delivery, the reality is that it requires too much self-discipline, requires people to be highly motivated, and does not supply a tutor or colleague help/interaction service. So if we could combine the best of the classroom with the best of the self-paced self-study methods, we would have the ideal platform for learning. And that is just what the exciting new medium of WBT brings.

Web-based training is an innovative approach to distance learning in which computer-based training (CBT) is transformed by the technologies of the Web, the Internet and corporate intranets. Advances in computer network technology can now provide an ideal vehicle for delivering training to individuals anywhere in the world at any time. WBT programs allow companies and individuals to receive – and deliver – real-time, networkable multimedia (audio, video, animation and data) directly to the students' desktop. WBT is instruction that is delivered via a Web browser (such as Microsoft Internet Explorer or Netscape Navigator) through the Internet or corporate intranet. It offers online classes with facilities for interacting with a live instructor and other students or simply as independent study in which the student works on their own with, perhaps, contact through e-mail and real-time 'chat' with the tutor and other students.

WBT courses may draw on Web-based resources such as text (lecture notes, case studies, assignments, tests), or they may be sophisticated computer-based training courseware, including audio, video, animation and graphics. Already, Web-based training material and courses of all kinds are available, ranging from little more than a syllabus to managerial skills to sophisticated technical courses on computer programming. Some courses are free while others have some fee attached. No doubt, WBT training course providers will soon employ mentors or counsellors to be available online, to interview students, help them with course prerequisites and recommend which course is right for them.

Uses and value of the Web in training

The Web will probably soon become the most popular medium for the delivery of distance learning materials. Its relatively inexpensive nature, vast resource base and rapidly growing popularity in the consumer market make it likely that it will be available in the majority of households in the not too distant future. New waves of schoolchildren now use the Internet as part of the school curriculum for carrying out research assignments, and it is now becoming the norm for all new computers to be sold as already configured to access the Internet. Look in the local high street store today and you will see an 'Internet Ready' sticker prominently displayed as a selling point. Commercial providers of Internet connection services, in fierce competition for new consumers, are starting to force down the cost of Internet access.

The software required for developing training materials on the Web, combined with the software necessary to receive them, are easy to use and are often free. Perhaps the only factor which is stopping the further increase in Internet use is the cost of telephone line usage. Although the cost is only that of a local call – approximately 4p a minute – it is still a factor when carrying out any lengthy, serious work over the Web. However, it will probably not be too long before an enterprising cable or satellite company sees the value of offering free local calls (as in the USA). Then we really will see WBT become as normal as watching an educational TV programme.

The Web can be used simply as a method of transmitting Web-based training materials to the student's computer so that they can be used 'off-line', that is, when not logged on to the Internet. So, for example, the student would connect to the Web to download the course materials and disconnect to actually use the materials on his/her computer. The Web can also be used to act as an online (that is, while connected) instructional medium. While some technical issues still exist which influence the speed of transmission of materials – especially large video files, for example – the Web is capable of delivering text, graphics, animation, audio and video. We shall explore this subject of transmission speeds later.

New advances in Web browser programs (the software needed to access and interact with the Web) are making it possible to deliver computer-based training programs online with many of the features previously only available offline. For example, the browser's Frame technology makes it possible to split a screen into multiple windows, so facilitating simultaneous viewing of related materials (see Figure 1.13). This allows the courseware author to leave an explanatory graphic or video in one window while explanatory text is displayed in another, and a menu of topics displayed in another. In short, the Web is a viable, popular and growing medium which is here to stay and is an increasingly important instructional delivery tool.

Benefits and drawbacks of WBT

Let's look at some of the main benefits and some obvious drawbacks of Web-based training. The majority of them are, of course, applicable to any self-study training, although some are obviously applicable to WBT programmes only. We shall look at the various benefits and drawbacks from

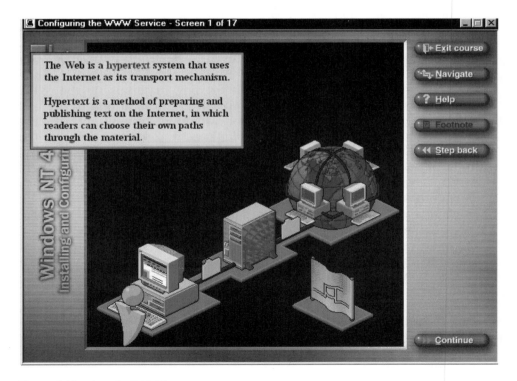

Figure 1.13   A typical WBT program

two different viewpoints: as a user and manager of WBT, and as a company or department providing WBT to its users.

Benefits for the WBT user/manager

- **Reduced training costs per head.** The cost of using an interactive WBT programme is significantly less than traditional classroom training. While it is expensive to develop interactive programmes, delivery cost per course is significantly lower per trainee, typically by 20–25 per cent. Additionally, travel, accommodation or subsistence costs can be eliminated.
- **Learning gains.** Studies have shown that interactive versions of training programmes increase the learner's understanding of the course material by as much as 56 per cent over classroom versions. WBT combines the best of self-paced, self-study training with the best of classroom training in that a course tutor is available and interaction with other course participants is encouraged.
- **Consistency of presentation.** Course material is presented in exactly the same way to the same standard every time. The training manager can ensure that everyone in the company uses the same material, something which is virtually impossible with CD-ROMs or CBT.
- **Constantly up-to-date material.** Because course material can be instantly updated on the Web server with any curricular changes (no matter how large or small) the most up-to-date courseware can be used. The new material will also be available to market much quicker.
- **Timeliness of information delivery.** Take the case where a test is taken in the classroom. Students typically receive the results back in the next class. Using WBT, test results can be delivered back to students within seconds of completion, providing instant feedback. This scenario can also be used for pre- and post-course assessments to measure the student's readiness for the course or its effectiveness.
- **Faster completion of training.** One of the primary benefits of self-paced learning is that it allows the learner to control their learning experience. They can work at a pace that suits them best, as well as bypassing training that is not relevant. Because the programmes are self-paced, they are likely to be completed earlier than a single-paced classroom course. Studies have shown savings of between 30 and 70 per cent in training time. With WBT, the learner can take courses over the Internet in their own home and can even take different parts of a course at different times. In this way, students can really take control over the learning environment.
- **Content retention.** Because of the interactive nature of the presentation, combining multimedia (text, graphics, audio and video) in an interactive environment enables the development of courses

that simulate real-life scenarios and provide immediate feedback. Learners retain more of the course material than with classroom versions of courses; studies have shown a 25–50 per cent higher retention factor.

- **Better utilization of instructors.** In most organizations the best instructors are used most often to conduct the training. With WBT those people can be used for what they are best at: training in the classroom.
- **Affordable technology.** Unlike most new technological innovations, WBT will not require any new significant expenditure on new hardware or software. Most people have access to a desktop (or laptop) computer, a modem and access to a telephone line. All that would be needed is Web browser software (generally free over the Internet) and a dial-up account with an Internet Service Provider like UUNET Pipex, Planet Online, U-Net, CompuServe or AOL. Additionally, different computer platforms can access the same course materials.
- **Control over course management.** You may limit or extend training opportunities to any small or large groups of students. Security codes and passwords allow absolute control by the training manager over who takes what course. Additionally, billing ID, number of course accesses and test results can be monitored and controlled by the training manager. The course tutor can also track students' progress, determining how fast/slow the student is progressing through the material or whether the student is having problems with a particular segment.
- **Training more accessible.** The Internet has opened up a whole new field of training opportunities for anyone who wants to learn. No longer do they have to wait for an available course place. Now they can take a course whenever and wherever it suits them. In addition, the technology for accessing these courses is not important. Since WBT courses are delivered via easy-to-use Web browsers, there are no technical barriers to overcome in order to take a course.

Disadvantages for the WBT user/manager

- **New software and procedures.** Students will need to become familiar with Web browser software and using the Internet.
- **Bandwidth/browser limitations.** Limitations in bandwidth (how much data can be squeezed down the line) may restrict instructional methodologies as performance for sound, animated graphics and video play back can sometimes be painfully slow.

Benefits for the WBT provider

- **Training development costs reduced.** The Internet has introduced a common set of industry standards for developing applications. These include course authoring tools like IBT Author, Asymetrix Toolbook, IconAuthor Net Edition, Java and Hypertext Markup Language (HTML) to build the training course once, knowing that it will run on any computer and on any platform (Windows, Macintosh, Unix). With traditional CBT, it is necessary to develop a different version of a course for every computer platform being targeted.
- **Easy and affordable distribution.** Courses are installed on one computer (the Web server) which students around the world can access through their Web browser. This provides instant distribution to an unlimited number of students, with the advantage of absolutely no packaging, duplication or distribution costs to be incurred by the course producer.
- **Up-to-date content.** With the course residing on one central Web server, courses can be updated instantly.
- **No run-time licences.** Courses published can be delivered without cumbersome run-time licences.

Disadvantages for the WBT provider

Limitations in bandwidth may restrict instructional methodologies as performance for sound, animated graphics and video play back can be painfully slow.

As with all new technology innovations, WBT offers great promise, but comes complete with its own set of challenges. With major advances in the field occurring monthly, it will not be long before it begins to make a major impact in the distribution of training and education.

There is no doubt that network-delivered training, whether it is transmitted over the local area network (LAN), wide area network (WAN), Internet or corporate intranet, is a solution that many companies are going to adopt with increasing frequency. With the abundance of free Web browsers available we now have a platform-independent delivery system which adds to the lure of the Web for training and development. In the USA, the independent Web-based Training Information Center carried out a survey of attitudes of WBT in corporate America which reveals that although less than 20 per cent of companies in the USA currently use WBT, more than 70 per cent plan to incorporate it during the next 12 months.

Box 1.1   Glossary of terms and equipment required

Hardware/software requirements
In order to access Web-based training, you will need certain hardware, software and network connections.

- Firstly, you will need a Pentium (or 486) or Macintosh computer with a minimum of 16 MB RAM. It will probably need a soundcard and a good graphics card. Any computer platform is suitable.
- A fast modem (at least 28.8 bps but preferably 56.6 bps).
- A good printer, capable of printing graphics.
- An Internet connection through an Internet Service Provider (like UUNET Pipex, U-Net, Planet Online, AOL, Compuserve).

Your computer will also need certain software loaded and configured, much of which is available free of charge from the Internet.

- The software supplied by your Internet Service Provider that connects you to the Internet. This includes your connection software, plus programs for e-mail, Telnet and FTP.
- A Web browser program. There are literally dozens of Web browsers available for every platform and operating system. The two most popular Web browsers by far are Netscape Navigator and Microsoft Internet Explorer. Web browser programs are basically configured to display text files and images but you will need to download 'extensions' for each browser that you have loaded if you want to display audio and video files.

What is the Internet?
The Internet is a global network of computer networks. It was created in 1969 in the US Defense Department as a fallback for communications in case of a nuclear attack on the USA. The Internet enables information to be passed around even if one network or group of networks is out of action. While the majority of users use the Internet for e-mail, its popularity really exploded with the introduction of the World Wide Web. The Internet is now a world-wide network, with over 50 000 networks located in over 150 countries with Internet connections, with users from government, research institutions, universities, companies, private organizations and individuals.

What is an intranet?
An intranet is a restricted and secure Internet, where companies can use technology popularized by the Internet – such as e-mail, Web pages, browsers and servers – to create internal closed networks accessible to only the company's employees. In effect, an intranet is

an internal Internet. It may be defined as: 'An internal Web site which the company employs to disseminate information and services throughout the enterprise.' These services can include e-mail messaging, staff training, staff notices, corporate information, telephone directories, ordering supplies, personnel information, staff records, health and safety messages, company procedures, and so on. The costs are offset on printing and paper expenses and the company not having to buy and keep up-to-date many different versions of applications to suit different computer platforms.

What is the Web?

The Web was invented in 1990 by British physicist Tim Berners-Lee and was first used to publish documents (scientific papers) so that they could be used by other scientists in their research. It was basically an online document publishing system using the facilities of the Internet. The Web uses a facility called hypertext. This allows the reader to click their mouse on a highlighted phrase or reference which then takes the user to another Web site with information on that subject, a kind of online referencing system. The beauty of the system is that the user does not need to know where the site is located or what the file was called. The Web represents an unstructured network of millions of computer sites throughout the world. Apart from the traditional text documents, the Web can also incorporate graphics, audio, animation and video sequences.

What is a browser?

A Web browser is a menu and icon-based layman's tool for accessing the Web. Web browser software is loaded on the student's desktop computer and the program provides an interface to the Web. Very little computer knowledge is required once the software has been loaded and configured. The most popular Web browser software are Microsoft Internet Explorer and Netscape Navigator.

What is e-mail?

Electronic mail (e-mail) is the main reason why people want to be connected to the Internet and it is the most frequently used Internet application. E-mail is instant and more efficient to send than normal mail. Sending e-mail is a simple matter of entering the recipient's e-mail address (csteed@dial.pipex.com, for example), typing in the message and clicking the Send button on your e-mail program.

What is FTP?

File Transfer Protocol is a method of transferring files between a remote computer and the client (your desktop computer). To access the remote site you will need a user name and a password; the standard routine is to enter 'anonymous' or 'ftp' for the user name and your e-mail address for the password. Some systems require you to have a personal account on that system in order to download files. To use FTP, you will need a separate FTP program; one is already installed on Windows 95.

What is Telnet?
Telnet lets you connect to a remote computer and operate it as though you were sitting at a directly attached terminal. To access a remote computer, you will need its site address and a password to get in, although some sites will allow anyone to access the machine. To use Telnet, you will need a separate Telnet program; one is already installed on Windows 95.

What is Usenet?
Whereas e-mail offers one-to-one private messages between sender and recipient, Usenet is a one-to-many message service. Usenet is made up of literally thousands of individual Newsgroups (over 24000 exist at present) with subjects ranging from abseiling to xenophobia. You can send messages to a newsgroup that you belong to and read responses from other members.

References and contact details

The AST IT Barometer Survey 1997, published by AST Computer. Web: www.ast.co.uk

The Durlacher Quarterly Internet Report 1997, published by Durlacher. Web: www.durlacher.com

Thomas Fox McManus, *Delivering Instruction on the World Wide Web*, University of Texas at Austin. Web: ccwf.cc.utexas.edu/~mcmanus/wbi.html

Ron Owston, *The Teaching Web: A Guide to the World Wide Web for All Teachers*, York University, California. Web: www.edu.yorku.ca/~rowston/home.html

Web Based Training Information Center. Web: www.webbasedtraining.com

Chapter 2

The learning implications

In this chapter we shall explore the learning issues and implications in WBT/multimedia instructional design. In particular, we shall focus on:

- the benefits and value of WBT/multimedia distance learning systems;
- instructional principles for adult learners; and
- the instructional design methodologies used by two of the major WBT course providers, CBT Systems and NETg.

Benefits and value of WBT/multimedia distance learning systems*

The use of multimedia has, in many ways, been around for decades. A variety of media have been used in the classroom for years. Conferences and seminars have long made effective use of music, lights, slide projectors and video tapes. What differentiates today's multimedia, however, is the combination of multiple media and computer technologies. Computers can now present data, text, sound, graphics and video on the desktop. Computer-based multimedia skill and knowledge applications offer benefits and value difficult to equal in non-technology implementations.

Corporations which use multimedia technologies to improve the performance of their staff to meet strategic business goals generally fall into one of five categories:

- Companies that have invested heavily in IT and want to leverage this investment further.
- Companies that are implementing costly mission-critical applications for which they have made aggressive performance and revenue commitments to their executive management.

*This section was contributed by David C. Forman and Sandra J. Kaplan, NETg.

- Companies that want to improve cost efficiencies and instructional returns from their existing learning programmes, which are predominantly instructor-led.
- Early adopters, or companies tied to progressive and innovative uses of the latest methods and technologies.
- Companies that have heard about the multimedia phenomenon and simply want to explore what it means and how it can help them.

Despite their diverse motivations for exploring multimedia learning systems, these organizations all search for non-labour-intensive ways to augment productivity and profitability. Technology has been identified as a significant means to these ends, and multimedia-based learning systems are seen as a key guarantee that technology investments will produce intended business results. Let's look at the two main areas of advantage offered by such systems: organizational and instructional.

Organizational advantages

Today's business edge depends upon the ability to respond quickly to change, whether it stems from economic, regulatory or competitive pressures. Organizations that wish to adapt rapidly to new environments confront well-documented hurdles. Some of these include:

- **The volume and velocity, or rate of change, of information.** It is estimated that 10 000 scientific articles are written each day, and that the sum total of information doubles every five years.
- **Reductions in product life cycles.** With new research and information come new products. IBM produces smaller, faster chips every two years. The swift, world-wide dissemination of information means that, to remain competitive, new products must reach markets faster than ever before.
- **The downsizing and decentralizing of lean organizations in the 1990s.** Fewer employees remain, and those who do are tasked with cross-functional responsibilities increasingly performed as team members, rather than individually, and with less managerial support. To add to this complexity, individuals and teams are frequently geographically dispersed, increasing the need for standardization and collaboration.
- **Mismatch between job requirements and entry-level worker skill/knowledge.** Organizations have a dwindling supply of skilled applicants from which to recruit. Many new workers will be the product of our declining school system. Literacy and graduation rates are down at a time when jobs are often more complex and team as opposed to individual performance is critical. There is a lack of connection between our education and economic systems.

All of these issues can be categorized into the Three C's: Consistency, Competence and Currency. First, is consistent information being received by all employees in the company, local to or remote from headquarters? Performing well clearly depends on the quality of available information. If information is missing or workers receive variable information and instructions, then inconsistent performance levels are assured.

Second, is the workforce competent, or ready, to perform? Do they know where to find and how to retrieve critical information? More importantly, do they know what to do with that information to perform faster, smarter and with fewer errors? With a broader range of responsibilities and less managerial support, competence has become more difficult to achieve. Third, is the workforce current, keeping pace with new information and products? Yesterday's product catalogue cannot meet tomorrow's business plan. How quickly can the organization and its personnel respond to changing business realities? Can the organization sustain high performance levels? Multimedia learning systems can help organizations cope with each of the Three C's.

- **Consistency.** Multimedia learning systems, be they instructional or informational, offer the same content presented in the same manner each and every time an application is used. Program providers are assured of getting a standardized message out to their frequently geographically dispersed audience. Reducing inconsistencies in the message makes it more likely that programmes will yield intended results and less likely that there will be errors or rework due to poorly covered content. Furthermore, the quality of the information is higher (that is, it is not merely textual), fostering attention and the likelihood that critical messages will be received.
- **Competence.** Multimedia learning systems permit users to see, hear and interact with instruction and information at their own pace. Learners can repeat or revisit realistic scenarios as often as they like. In many cases, needed data and explanations are at their fingertips for use during real-time interactions with customers and colleagues. Furthermore, computers offer a variety of efficient mechanisms for monitoring and measuring knowledge and skill acquisition and tracking areas in need of remediation or improved explanation.
- **Currency.** Perhaps one of the greatest advantages that multimedia learning systems provide is the rapid distribution of timely information. Should information content change, whether it is a new procedure for repairing a piece of equipment, a new health and safety regulation or a new price list, it can be quickly and efficiently downloaded to local workstations or made available via diskette or CD-ROM on non-networked learning stations. The delays and overheads of cascading seminars, printing and distributing volumes of updates and revisions, or videotaping and distributing addenda are avoided. Further, programme

providers have built-in mechanisms to assure that critical messages have been heard by user populations.

It is apparent that computers themselves can take a fair share of credit for many of these advantages, given their raw speed, storage capacity, geographical reach and fingertip accessibility. However, multimedia adds the critical dimensions of high information quality and high appeal, providing the extra 'bandwidth' that motivates workers to transfer knowledge and skill into on-the-job performance.

Instructional advantages

From early computer-based training (CBT) 'page turners' – predominantly text and simplistic ASCII graphics – to analogue interactive video instruction multimedia systems, to the latest all-digital multimedia implementations, instructional methods continue to improve. Enabling technologies which underpin these improvements include: lower-cost, more powerful processors; faster, higher-capacity networks; greater amounts of low-cost storage; feature-rich operating environments; and more intuitive graphical user interfaces. In areas as diverse as interpersonal skills, procedural training, knowledge of facts or development of intellectual abilities, multimedia learning systems have proven benefits and value. Described below are their main instructional features, followed by research-based benefits information.

Multiple information modes

As the name implies, multimedia learning systems communicate through the use of a variety of modalities, including audio, scanned images, bit-mapped computer graphics, animation, text and motion video. Regardless of the delivery method, experts agree that appealing to more of the learner's senses enhances attention, motivation to learn and retention of material. Learners see, hear and do, confirming wisdom that has existed for centuries (see Figure 2.1).

Training when and where needed

There is often significant scheduling and throughput problems with classroom-based training. Classes may not be available when they are needed. And for large numbers of students, it may simply take too long for training to occur in blocks of classroom time. IBM, for example, estimated it would take 18 years to upgrade the skill levels at one manufacturing plant using community college instructors. Several factors make scheduling

Appealing to learner's senses

" If you tell me, I will listen,
If you show me I will see,
If you let me experience
I will learn"

Lao Tzu

Figure 2.1 The learner's senses

less a concern for multimedia learning systems located in learning centres. First, courses are always available and can be installed on systems in a matter of minutes. Second, technology-based training significantly compresses learning 'seat time', so learners can move through course work more quickly. Third, learners can spend as much or as little time as they can afford at one session: bookmark features allow them to return to courses without repeating material that has already been mastered, accelerating material completion. Of course, for multimedia learning systems located on the desktop, delays and inconvenience are no longer an issue.

Learner control of pace and direction

The issue of who controls the learning experience has a profound effect on the instructional outcome. Again, contrast multimedia learning systems with the workshop, or instructor-led, experience. Workshops are designed to appeal to the broadest common audience. Material has to be covered in the prescribed time, and there is little flexibility for learners to diverge from the content or flow of information dictated by the instructor's guides. The branching strategies designed into effective multimedia learning systems allow for varying degrees of flexibility, from complete discovery learning to highly guided and forced choices. As noted earlier, learners can stop or resume at their convenience. They can review material, observe models and practise responses as frequently as they see fit, without the peer pressure of appearing to be 'slow' or interruptive. Furthermore, with the advent of new hypertext, hypermedia and underlying database technologies, learners will have ever-increasing opportunities to chart the paths and avenues of their own learning adventures. Learners are in control; they can make their own choices.

Instructional principles for adult learners*

Key elements can make a dramatic difference in the effective design and delivery of instruction to adult learners. Building these elements into training programmes will make learners want to participate in the first place, stay with the programme once they've started it, feel satisfied and confident as they progress, and leave the programme with a storehouse of new knowledge and skills that they can use on the job or retain and apply to future situations. These elements can be divided into three categories:

- **Motivational.** Humanistic psychologists tell us that the way people feel about an endeavour influences their commitment to it. If they feel secure, respected, esteemed, empowered or in charge, they are likely to make an investment in it. If they feel threatened, anxious, hostile or demeaned, they are likely to resist.
- **Information processing.** Cognitive psychologists tell us that information is more likely to be acquired, retained and retrieved for future use if it is learner-constructed, meaningful, relevant, builds on prior knowledge, is logically organized in 'learnable chunks' and has built-in or learner-generated memory devices to assist in retention and use of the information for the future. Poorly organized course materials delivered to passive learners hinder learning; well-organized course materials delivered to active, engaged learners will enhance it.
- **Behaviour change.** Behavioural psychologists tell us that behaviour change is brought about by learning experiences that include these elements:
  - Observation and imitation of role models
  - Guided, spaced practice with specific feedback on pros and cons of performance
  - Positive reinforcement for efforts
  - Practice in applying and using the new learning in a variety of situations.

  Without these opportunities for modelling, guided practice, feedback and reinforcement, and transfer of training, the new learning is not likely to last very long.

There is some overlap between these categories, and appropriate instructional strategies may accomplish several of these goals (motivation, information processing, behaviour change) simultaneously.

*This section was contributed by Dorman Woodall, NETg.

Current training methodologies

Good instructional design strategy facilitates the development of self-contained, clearly defined, well-structured learning modules that teach technology skills and concepts clearly and comprehensively. We now look at two companies at the forefront of providing quality multimedia-based training programmes over the Web – CBT Systems and NETg – to see how they have applied modern-day training methodologies into their training programmes.

CBT Systems' training methodology

CBT Systems' training methodology is based on well-established media-based training principles (Alessi and Trollip, 1991; Gagne *et al.*, 1988; cited in www. cbtsys.com), which, in turn, are drawn from the general concepts and principles of traditional cognitive theory (Bruner, 1960; Solso, 1984; cited in www.cbtsys.com). Over recent years, educational theorists have come to favour the cognitive approach, and current research is increasingly based within the framework of the cognitive theory model.

The cognitive approach

Essentially, the cognitive approach focuses on the learner and the learning process, particularly on the way in which the learner receives, organizes and retains information. Educational cognitive theorists attribute a large degree of autonomy and initiative to the learner, and believe that successful learning depends, to a significant extent, on the attitude, motivation and participation of the learner. The following instructional principles and techniques are central to the cognitive approach to training:

- Instruction must be motivating, both cognitively and affectively.
- The learner is an active participant in the learning environment (both intellectual and psychomotor involvement is required).
- Learning is achieved by applying and adapting prior knowledge and experience to new situations.
- The sequence of instruction is logical and organized, and is tailored to the needs and profile of the learner.
- Positive, timely and individualized feedback is continually supplied.
- The learner is continually assessed; students know how well they are doing both during and after instruction.
- The learner is in control of the pace and sequence of instruction; however, sufficient advisement strategies, which help the learner make appropriate training path decisions, are provided at critical junctures.

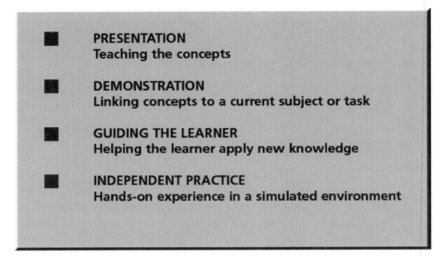

Figure 2.2   Key steps to learning

Four key steps to learning

The cognitive approach focuses on the mental processes involved in learning. This approach results in the development of highly interactive courseware that is conducive to learning: a context in which the learner is motivated and constructively and actively involved (see Figure 2.2). The four key phases of the skills training model are:

- Presentation: teaching concepts.
- Demonstration: linking concepts to a current subject or task.
- Guiding the learner: helping the learner apply new knowledge.
- Independent practice: hands-on experience in a simulated environment.

During the first phase, you present the information to the student, introducing and teaching the concepts and theory. The second phase involves demonstrating how these concepts relate to the application or programming language under discussion.

These two phases are usually termed 'instructor-centred'; essentially, the information is presented and the learner is an observer. But even during these instructor-centred phases, CBT Systems use interactive devices, such as *en-route* 'discovery' questioning, to involve the learner with the narrative as much as possible. During the third phase, they introduce students to the workings of the application, and demonstrate how its features can be used productively. During the fourth phase, students are encouraged to perform real-life tasks in a hands-on interactive session in a simulated environment. In the fourth phase, the focus is on the learner, with the instructor assuming the role of observer, providing appropriate feedback when the learner performs each task. The four-phased model is a logical approach to teaching practical skills. This approach is also widely accepted as a highly effective computer-based training method.

Training structures

CBT Systems' courses are divided into units, each of which develops a broad learning theme. Units are subdivided into topics, consisting of one or more learning points (see Figure 2.3). Owing to the demands of the medium (where only a limited amount of text can be presented on screen at a time), units, topics and individual screens are as discrete and self-contained as possible. Each unit is preceded by a set of relevant and measurable learning objectives, in which the outcome of the instruction is clearly stated in terms of student performance.

Courses must be tightly structured, with clearly developing narratives and forward movement. Each conceptual learning point is explained once and the text moves on to the next point in linear programmatic fashion. It is a learner-paced training method, and although the text is transient, students have control over the pace of the information they receive. Those

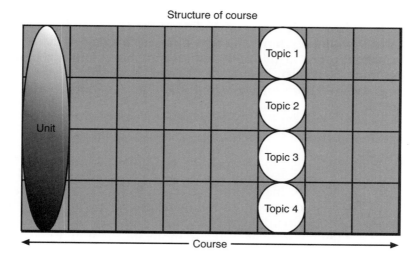

Figure 2.3   CBT Systems' courses: units and topics

who are ready to move on to the next point are not held back by unnecessarily long explanations or repetition; those who wish to go over points again can do so using a 'step back' navigational facility. Supplementary information is presented in footnotes, which the student can access when necessary.

At a higher level, courses are logically structured and organized within curricula, with clearly defined training paths. Curriculum planners set the courses in context, illustrating how each course relates to others and allowing students to trace their training sequence. The testing facility at each curriculum, course and unit level gives the student an accurate gauge of learning progress at each level. This is a flexible, learner-centred approach that puts the student in control and gives computer-based training a powerful edge over other learning methods.

Assessment

Student learning is assessed mainly through the use of tests, which are an essential part of the instructional process. Test results provide information about the level of learning, the quality of teaching and future instructional needs. Tests are a means of guiding instruction, giving students an accurate gauge of their learning progress. Tests also have an important role in preparing students for certification exams; several curricula in the CBT Systems' library map directly to ILT certification paths (such as Novell CNA, CNE; Microsoft MCSE; Lotus CLP). Test questions are matched to the learning objectives for each unit. The generation of useful tests flows from a clear understanding of the target audience's needs and the corresponding learning objectives designed to meet those needs. Students can take a test at the unit, course and curriculum level, and all levels are scored. Test questions are randomized, ensuring that the student is presented with a representative but different assessment with each attempt.

Learner participation

CBT Systems' courses are highly interactive, and while it is their training policy to hold the student's attention with clearly written and well-presented material, they do not view students as passive recipients of information. Instead, they try to engage them, motivate them and make them active participants in their own learning. Students interact with CBT Systems' courses in two ways: through answering course 'discovery' questions and through performing hands-on procedural simulation and coding exercises (see Figure 2.4).

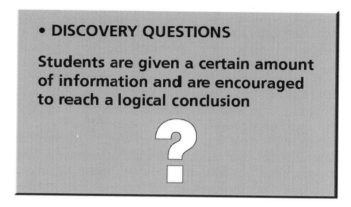

Figure 2.4   CBT Systems' courses: discovery questions

Discovery course questions

It is widely accepted that embedding questions throughout instructional text is a highly effective computer-based training method. As part of their strategy to encourage active learner participation in their courses, discovery questions, in which students are encouraged to think critically and figure things out for themselves, are at the core of CBT Systems' training methodology, and are used liberally throughout the course text. By being invited to anticipate the right answer or simply to give an opinion, students are much more actively involved in their own learning.

Discovery questions are based on inductive or deductive reasoning: students are given a certain amount of information and are encouraged to reach a logical conclusion. The learning point of each question is always reinforced in the text immediately following a question. This is a more effective training method than simply asking students to repeat something they have already learned. When students make the effort to work out a conclusion themselves, they are more likely to retain the information. Questions also add a forward momentum to the course narrative; students feel that the text is progressing and that they are helping to unfold each learning point.

Discovery questions are fully integrated into the text so that they do not interrupt the flow of the narrative. They concentrate on the important learning points in the text, focusing the student's attention on that material. CBT Systems maximizes the opportunities for including discovery questions by using a variety of question types. Simpler question types ask the student's opinion or ask the student to judge whether a statement is true or false. Complex questions include user-input fill-in-the-blank questions, which encourage students to type in their response, and multiple-choice questions that ask students to choose one or more correct options. Multiple-choice questions use plausible foils which present a challenge to the student; when the answer is not obvious, the student needs to make an effort to work out the correct option or options.

Course questions do not have to rely on material that has already been presented in the CBT Systems course. Except for certain end-user courses, they assume that students who take their courses have a fairly sound background in the appropriate area of computer technology, and that they should be able to apply that knowledge in coming to the correct conclusions. Questions that ask the student to guess the answer are avoided, as they feel that guesswork has little educational merit. Course questions are worded sensitively so that students do not feel that they are being tested on their knowledge of the course content. Question stems are phrased encouragingly; for example, 'Which do you think is the correct option?' and 'See if you can choose the right answer'. However, answering course questions is not compulsory; the student has the option to cancel the question at any time.

Discovery questions are not used to assess students, but to give them the opportunity to use their existing knowledge and cognitive skills to reach a reasoned conclusion. When students answer correctly, they receive affirmation and a sense of making progress. Regardless of whether the answer is correct or incorrect, students always receive sensitive feedback which is essential to the effectiveness of training.

Hands-on interactivity

CBT Systems' courses offer each student the opportunity to gain invaluable hands-on experience performing critical job-related tasks. Their hands-on exercises offer the student a thorough interactive practice session pertinent to the learning points covered previously in the course. They have developed two types of hands-on exercise: simulation exercises and coding exercises. In both types of exercise, students are guided through performing software tasks in simulated applications, so possible errors are anticipated and helpful, sensitive feedback is supplied. They view feedback as a critical component of hands-on exercises and most current theorists support this view.

Simulation exercises

Computer-based training is an excellent medium for teaching students how to perform practical computer-based tasks; for example, how to set up a print queue in NetWare or replicate a database in Lotus Notes. Other computer-based training methods adopt a step-based approach to simulations, compelling students to perform the constituent parts of a task in a particular order, an order that may not actually be required by the software itself. CBT Systems, on the other hand, recognizes that a task may be accomplished successfully in a variety of ways. Their hands-on simulations are constructed with this principle in mind, concentrating on the task and giving students the flexibility to choose their own methods of reaching the correct solution. This task-based approach is particularly effective when, say, the student is to fill in several dialog box fields which can be completed in any order.

In simulation exercises, CBT Systems rebuilds the application environment authentically; they do not just present a series of bitmaps and hotspots. This approach ensures that the interface incorporates all the functionality required to carry out a task. Students can practise the task as often as necessary; they can also choose to view a step-by-step demonstration of the task. These exercises provide the learner with the authentic look and feel of the live application and more confidence when it comes to moving from the simulated environment to the real software.

The NETg Skill Builder® philosophy

NETg takes the position that the adult learner has a set of unique work-related needs that must be met if the instruction is to be accepted. These needs grow out of the adult learner's work environment and have been identified in the growing body of research on the adult learner. From this research NETg had developed a list of principles which are aimed at making its Skill Builder courses both acceptable and relevant to this important population. The main adult learning principles covered in all NETg Skill Builders are: learner control, time sensitivity, real-world application and concrete examples.

Learner control

Adult learners want to control their learning environment. This includes controlling the pace, content, appearance, presentation and modalities of the course whenever possible. NETg addresses these concerns by providing learners with the maximum amount of control possible over their learning environment. The courses provide learner control in the following areas:

- Selectable installation options for feedback levels and functional options.
- Branching for sequence control and individual needs.
- Menu control for content selection.
- Emphasis pointer options and audio and visual presentation options (all selectable).

These features are all under the control of learners in the form of the course map, where they may pick and choose the specific topics they wish to learn. These choices can be from a presentation order menu, an alphabetical topic menu or a listing of new software features, when appropriate. Learners may choose which emphasis pointers are most helpful to their learning. This may include a pointer containing text relevant to the item being emphasized and adjacent to it. In CD-ROM based courses, learners also have total freedom to receive instruction through sound only, text only or both sound and text. These options can be selected from a menu available at all times.

Time sensitivity

Adult learners have specific time constraints for their learning goals. Interactive courseware addresses this requirement by allowing learners to set their own pace and select the content they wish to pursue. Thus, learners are able to meet timeframe requirements rather than have a set schedule forced upon them. NETg's instruction is unit-based and allows learners to select only the material they need to learn at any given time, progressing at their own pace. In addition, courses with the Learner Management option selected will record what learners have already covered and where in the course they were upon exiting the course. Learners will then be returned to that same point when re-entering the course later, allowing learners to spread training over a period of time most convenient for them. A third key feature implemented in Skill Builder 4.5 is the ability of the course to administer a pre-test, determine precisely which units or topics learners need to experience, and provide instruction focusing on only that content. This feature reduces the amount of training time required for learners who have prior learning regarding some of the lessons within a course.

Real-world applications

Most adult learners have a goal in mind when they start training. They have a specific need to be filled or a certain task to learn. NETg courseware is designed to present instruction in a scenario with which the learner can identify and from which they can generalize, applying their new knowledge in an immediate and practical manner.

Concrete examples

Adult learners tend to want concrete, real-world examples of the value of the learned task. In many ways, this is an extension of the concept of real-world examples listed above. Thus, NETg scenarios are realistic and require learners to accomplish tasks relevant to their world and easily extended to their tasks. NETg presents realistic spreadsheet tasks using Excel and realistic word processing tasks using Word. Client/server programming courses present realistic client/server programming techniques and solutions. It is neither practical nor cost-effective to teach 'make-work' tasks in today's training environment. The goal is to enhance the transfer of learning from the instruction to the job site with a minimum of effort, and have learners back as productive team members as quickly as possible. Concrete, example-based, realistic training makes this possible.

Instructional objectives

In order for the learner to walk away from NETg courses with a direct and verifiable set of skills, these skills must be stated as instructional outcomes or objectives. These objectives not only become the basis of how the instruction is organized and how learning outcomes are assessed, but also provide the learner with a means for organizing their efforts in meeting the objectives. NETg uses the methodology developed by Robert Mager in the preparation of instructional objectives for all of its Skill Builder courses.

In his book, *Preparing Instructional Objectives*, Mager states that 'Objectives are useful tools in the design, implementation, and evaluation of instruction'. For NETg instructional objectives form the major building blocks of a Skill Builder (design). In turn, these objectives also determine the type of exercises or instructional instances that are needed in order for the learner to achieve mastery (implementation). Finally, the objectives allow the creation of test items which ensure that the objectives have been achieved (assessment). All Skill Builder instructional objectives have the following qualities:

- They must make clear to the learner what he or she is expected to do. There must be no ambiguity; consequently, objectives should avoid outcome statements that are open to interpretations, such as: 'To understand . . .', 'To really appreciate . . .', 'To believe . . .' Clearly stated outcomes which are not subject to interpretation will say: 'To solve . . .', 'To identify . . .', 'To construct . . .'
- The instructional objective should describe the conditions under which the performance is to occur. Using their unambiguous 'stem' objectives that describe their conditions would be: 'To solve with the aid of Excel's macro language . . .', 'To identify without the aid of documentation . . .', 'Given a list of constraints, construct . . .'
- Good instructional objectives must describe measurable performance criteria so that the learner knows when he or she has achieved mastery. Their 'stem' objectives with performance criteria added would read: 'To solve with the aid of Excel's macro language five problems at an accuracy level of 80 per cent . . .', 'To identify without the aid of documenta-

tion the three key components of a spreadsheet cell . . .', 'Given a list of constraints, construct a shell sort routine that successfully re-orders the provided sample data . . .'

Linking objectives to assessment

If the rules of creating good instructional objectives are followed, assessment can be easily linked to test items which determine two very important conditions: prior learning and mastery. All learners come to the instructional event with prior knowledge. To the extent that we can ascertain this existing base of knowledge, we can concentrate on what the learner does not know, rather than waste his or her time (not to mention the client's money) on what they already know. This can be accomplished by pre-testing the learner prior to the instruction using test items linked to the specific instructional objectives. The result of pre-testing is instruction that is customized to the learner's needs.

Once these needs have been covered in the instruction, post-test items must determine if the associated set of objectives have been mastered. Since these test items are linked to instructional objectives which include measurable performance criteria, the learner knows when he or she has achieved mastery. Depending on whether mastery has been reached, the learner either ends the instruction or moves on to review items until mastery has been achieved. All NETg Skill Builders contain post-testing. Skill Builders built in 1996/97 will have both pre-testing and post-testing.

Multiple domains

Learning is categorized into several different types called domains. The three major domains addressed in NETg's design methodology are affective, cognitive and psychomotor.

Affective domain
Information in the affective domain is oriented primarily towards feelings, beliefs and emotions. Using an affective model to understand why people learn gives a motivational basis for learning. An affective model provides a way to motivate learners to commit themselves to a learning experience. When creating instructional instances, NETg uses an affective domain model developed by John Keller of Florida State University. This model is called ARCS (see Figure 2.5) and is briefly described below.

According to the ARCS model, before learners can learn, they must be attending to the information presented. The first step of Keller's model is to gain the learner's attention using any of a wide variety of methods. Motion, animation, sound, colour and change are all effective means of gaining attention. It should be noted that, once gained, attention does tend

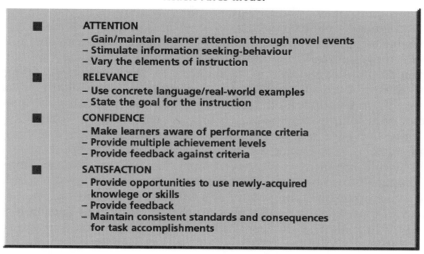

Kellers ARCS Model

- **ATTENTION**
  - Gain/maintain learner attention through novel events
  - Stimulate information seeking-behaviour
  - Vary the elements of instruction
- **RELEVANCE**
  - Use concrete language/real-world examples
  - State the goal for the instruction
- **CONFIDENCE**
  - Make learners aware of performance criteria
  - Provide multiple achievement levels
  - Provide feedback against criteria
- **SATISFACTION**
  - Provide opportunities to use newly-acquired knowlege or skills
  - Provide feedback
  - Maintain consistent standards and consequences for task accomplishments

Figure 2.5   The ARCS model

to wander, and has to be regained periodically and with each new instructional sequence. From the first screen of a Skill Builder course, NETg captures the learner's attention using graphics and colour. In the CD-ROM versions, motion and audio are part of the attention-gaining mechanism as well. In an ongoing effort to recapture and hold learners' attention, changes of screen images, audio in CD-ROM based courses and background information in case-based instruction all occur frequently, and always occur as topics change.

Having gained the learner's attention, they must be made aware of exactly why this knowledge is important to them. Learners who know they are going to receive useful training which will improve their job performance will make greater efforts to learn and will retain information longer. In many of the desktop courses, learners are exposed to a realistic business situation where they are asked to accomplish tasks which closely mirror what they are expected to accomplish in their own work environment. Thus, a spreadsheet course may use the development of a budget to teach critical aspects of the application to learners whose jobs include the development of budgets for their departments. In more technically oriented courses, examples and exercises tend to focus on specific tasks common to all users of the target application, teaching learners how to accomplish tasks they will perform when working with the application. Examples include teaching the management of network security, or teaching a learner how to create an 'OK' button in Visual Basic.

The ARCS model states that once learners have had the opportunity to learn the desired information, it is necessary to let them practise what they have learned in a safe, non-threatening environment. This practise (guided and non-guided) builds confidence in their ability to demonstrate the knowledge acquired. Once learners have been taught the concepts and procedures, they must have an opportunity to practise skills they are learning in order to build confidence in their ability to use those skills. NETg uses simulations and Quick Quizzes to meet this aspect of learners' needs, allowing them to apply their knowledge to prove to themselves that they can indeed accomplish the tasks.

Because NETg is teaching learners how to use software and programming languages, it has made a conscious decision to simulate the live application. While requiring more development time to create, the simulated environment provides a safe place for practising new skills, allowing learners to make errors without penalty and with the maximum amount of feedback. NETg uses simulation to prevent the learners from getting lost in a procedure or making mistakes which can cause confusion and disorientation. Learners who make errors in a non-simulated environment are not going to have their confidence increased; rather, confidence may be reduced because of their perceived failure to accomplish their tasks. This can be a most unpleasant experience for novices, leaving them with a sense of doubt about their ability to complete the assigned task, instead of the sense of accomplishment the exercise was intended to provide.

Once learners have confidence in their ability to demonstrate their knowledge, they are offered a chance to prove that knowledge in an evaluation situation. Successful evaluations result in learners' satisfaction in their ability to learn and perform. Satisfied learners confident in their own proven ability are more likely to accept, internalize and use the information or knowledge just acquired. This final element of the ARCS model is found within NETg courses in the use of four components: feedback, simulations, Quick Quizzes and the Mastery Test. Feelings of accomplishment after receiving helpful feedback, successfully completing a simulation or a Quick Quiz are the first layer of satisfaction experienced by learners. The ultimate feeling of satisfaction comes with the successful completion of the Mastery Test, the main indication that the instructional objectives for that unit have been achieved.

Cognitive domain

By cognitive, we are referring to those types of knowledge, skills and competencies which are essential to the learning of a particular new task or set of skills. Information in the cognitive domain may be simple or complex, unique or highly interrelated, but cognitive information consists of things we know from an essentially pure knowledge point of view. It is in this domain that the learner develops problem-solving skills based upon prerequisite or prior learning.

Work by Miller on short-term memory indicates that most learners are capable of dealing with seven items (plus or minus two) of information at the same time. This is a major consideration in the design of information the learner receives. NETg take care to limit the number of items presented on-screen, and limit procedural steps to groups of not more than seven steps at one time. Based on concepts taken from information processing theory, they combine smaller pieces of information into larger meaningful pieces of information. This allows them to increase the amount of information presented to the learner. An example would be treating the nine-digit social security number as three pieces of information instead of nine (a three-digit number, a two-digit number and a four-digit number).

A cognitive design model focuses on how instructional instances are presented and how they relate to other types of knowledge. A commonly accepted cognitive design model used in NETg's Skill Builder product is Bloom's taxonomy (a continuum of knowledge complexity), which identifies the six types of cognitive information (see Figure 2.6). NETg uses the cognitive model to determine the level of expertise and depth of knowledge that must be developed in learners. The model is used to sequence and relate instruction, as well as to guide the language of the instructional objectives. A description of the levels of Bloom's taxonomy and how they are implemented in NETg's Skill Builder is presented below.

1. Knowledge. The knowledge level deals with facts. Performances associated with this level include objectives associated with listing, labelling, defining and selecting. Because information at this level is essentially

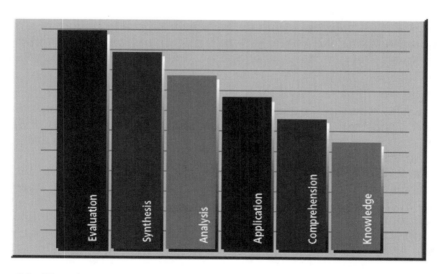

Figure 2.6   Bloom's taxonomy

comprehension of facts and background, the knowledge level is most often presented within NETg courses using things like orientation screens and exploratory learning, pointing out the components of a screen or where special controls are located. While some mention of the use of detailed procedural steps needed to invoke an action is not uncommon, it is more usual to teach a high-level description of the purpose.

2. Comprehension. Comprehension deals with understanding facts. Performances associated with comprehension include objectives associated with interpreting, translating, restating and explaining. NETg uses instructional instances presented throughout the course to provide learners with opportunities to develop their knowledge at the comprehension level. Exercises and simulations give learners opportunities to integrate their knowledge, while Quick Quizzes encourage them to make connections between facts in order to answer questions posed to them.

3. Application. Application deals with being able to apply the knowledge and understanding of the previous levels. Performances associated with this level include objectives associated with illustrating, calculating, solving and demonstrating. The majority of NETg instruction falls into this category because most of their courses deal with procedural tasks; consequently, students are given the opportunity to actually apply their knowledge to a specific task through the use of simulations throughout the course. These simulations provide practice in applying the facts, allowing learners to demonstrate comprehension which results in practical knowledge of how information and concepts are actually applied in real situations. Again, NETg's use of simulation is intended to provide learners with a safe environment in which to practise their new skills. This environment allows learners to make errors without penalties and builds their confidence by showing that they are able to accomplish the tasks.

4. Analysis. Analysis requires the use of the skills developed in the previous steps and then determining why something is the way it is. Performances associated with this level include things like comparing and contrasting, stating conclusions, diagramming and detecting errors. The analysis level is generally the highest level of Bloom's taxonomy learners will encounter in a NETg Skill Builder. This level pushes the student to extend their understanding from the 'how' of knowledge to the 'why'. Exercises and simulations may ask learners to do something they have not seen in specific detail which is a logical extension of information already learned but in a slightly different context. In some cases, a multiple-choice Quick Quiz can be used to offer learners a written description of a situation analogous to something already learned but which differs in detail. Asking them to decide upon the correct response based on analysis of the situation and the content of the available responses is an example of this level of cognitive learning.

5. Synthesis. Synthesis deals with the use of knowledge developed from previous levels to create new understanding of information and its relationship to other facts or information. Performances associated with this level include integrating, generalizing, designing and constructing. Synthesis is difficult to present in most computer-based methodologies. NETg uses the actual instruction to lead learners to make connections between facts and information they have acquired, and then allows them to experience the results of those connections through exercises and simulations. This is especially true in courses dealing with technically oriented materials, such as in the client/server curriculum. In these courses, learners are taught specific procedures (creating properties and methods for an object in object-oriented programming) and then asked to create objects which incorporate learning from several different places into a single task.

6. Evaluation. Evaluation is the highest level of the taxonomy. It involves the ability to make judgements and assessments using the skills developed in the previous levels. Performances associated with this level include judging, assessing, applying standards and evaluating. An example of this evaluation level would be to list criteria for selecting one of several operating systems, then provide learners with several situations which combine different criteria, and finally ask them to select the preferred operating system. Learners must first analyse the particular situation, determine (synthesize) an optimum system based on their knowledge and then evaluate the offered choices to determine if their optimum system is offered. If not, learners must review the offered systems, perform another analysis of the situation and attempt to synthesize another solution supported by their knowledge and matching an offered solution.

Psychomotor domain
The psychomotor domain is primarily concerned with the use and acquisition of muscular or motor skills, such as the use of a mouse or the eye–hand co-ordination for an interface. The consideration of psychomotor skills is most evident in the design and development of the Skill Builder interface. Every time a change is made to this interface, it undergoes extensive testing in the Bell South Usability Lab. In order to ensure the clearest and most consistent interface possible, representatives of NETg's target audience use the interface while every detail of their experience is observed, documented and evaluated by the Usability Lab's expert staff. The data that is collected assures the client that the learner audience will receive the clearest and most easy to use interface possible.

Multiple modalities

Learners are different in terms of preferences and abilities; they also use different combinations of 'input channels' for acquiring and processing information. A generally recognized principle of instruction is that the more channels of information input used, the greater the probability that learning will be acquired and retained. NETg typically uses the following four modalities or channels to provide instructional input to the learner: auditory, visual, tactile and kinaesthetic.

- **Auditory.** The auditory modality is most commonly recognized as the ability to process aural (sound) information and integrate it into one's mental map or knowledge domain. NETg's use of the auditory modality includes such things as tones which inform learners that their actions are correct or incorrect. In NETg's CD-ROM Skill Builder, musical themes announce that learners have moved to the mastery test or are about to leave the course. Of course, the narration, provided as an option on CD-ROM courses, is a key auditory element.
- **Visual.** The visual modality is most commonly recognized as the ability to process visual data such as pictures, graphics, text, and so on. This information is seen, understood and integrated by learners into their knowledge domain. The visual modality is the most common method of providing input to learners. The text, along with screen captures of the application, graphics and use of colour, are the primary visual components of the course.
- **Tactile and kinaesthetic.** These two modalities are minor channels of instruction in NETg courses. The tactile and kinaesthetic modalities are most commonly recognized as the ability to process and integrate information acquired through the sense of touch and movement. Information is presented so that learners feel a stimulus or a response, which is interpreted and integrated in to their knowledge domain. An example would be clicking on a mouse button (tactile) and the moving of the mouse (kinaesthetic).

Modularity

Using the principles already discussed, NETg has created modular components of instruction. Under Skill Builder 4.5, these modules exist at the lesson level. Each lesson contains one or more lesson objectives, an independent mini-scenario and unique test items. This stand-alone structure allows NETg to extract lessons from a unit or course and recombine them into a new, customized learning solution on demand, creating the instruction a learner requires.

References and contact details

David C. Forman and Sandra J. Kaplan, *Benefit and Value of Multimedia Learning Systems.*

Dorman Woodall, *Instructional Principles for Adult Learners.*

CBT Systems
Web: www.cbtsys.com

NETg
Web: www.netg.com

Chapter 3

WBT in practice

In this chapter we shall explore some of the different types of WBT courses that are currently live on the Internet. This will provide you with an example of WBT in practice and help you to understand the power of the learning possibilities of WBT, as well as providing a sound overview of the types of WBT courses that are being used today. We shall be looking at a description of the site, how the programme works, with associated screen shots to give you a feel of the WBT programme being discussed. I do recommend that you take some time out to have a look at the programmes for yourself as this will aid your appreciation of the opportunities available to develop your own internal WBT programmes with little or no cost to the organization. I have provided the Web site addresses of all of the sites mentioned so that you can easily log on to them and use them without charge. Before we look at particular courses and their facilities, it is wise to outline the basic elements that can make up a typical WBT programme.

The elements of WBT

There are basically four distinct elements that make up today's Web-based training programmes: general communication, online reference, testing and assessment, distribution and delivery of multimedia. We shall explore each one separately and show examples of how an element is used within a training programme. But it is worth remembering that the four elements may or may not all be used in a WBT programme. Obviously, it depends on the nature of the training programme which elements are used and so please bear in mind that just because a programme does not include all four does not mean that it is not a good programme.

General communication

The Internet provides excellent facilities for communication between students and tutors. Electronic mail (e-mail) can be used by tutors to distribute course schedules, homework, notices, assignments and tests, while students can use it to register for courses, ask questions and communicate with the tutor as well as other students on the course. At a more advanced level, it provides online 'chat' facilities where students and tutors can discuss matters in real-time using their keyboards. Additionally, tutors can converse with individual or groups of students, or students can communicate with other students. In some training programmes, a concept called 'virtual workshops' is used where a guest speaker provides information to a group of students and then responds to their questions, much like attending a traditional seminar or workshop. The only difference, obviously, is that the students are all in different locations.

Figure 3.1　Website of Beatles memorabilia

Online reference

By using their Web browsers, students can explore the vast resource that makes up the Web. In so doing, the student can 'bookmark' or retain the reference of the information for future use. Take, for example, a course on The Music of the Beatles. Here, students can search for sites of information on the Beatles for use in their course. For example, they may be able to find sites in libraries or museums throughout the world which contain Beatles memorabilia, lyrics to Lennon–McCartney songs, Beatles discographies, photographs, fan sites, audio tracks, video clips, song manuscripts, and so on (see Figure 3.1).

Testing and assessment

Computer-based testing has long been a preferred method for assessing students. Using the Internet for testing and assessment can go further by completely automating the process of retrieving exams and returning back marked assessments. The computerized testing and assessment facility has long been the foundation of the UK's Open University and many online education sites today have facilities for pre- and post-course assessments. A good site to see pre- and post-course tests and assessments is Question Mark Computing's Web site (www.qmark.com).

Distribution and delivery of multimedia

Students can, on an as-needed or just-in-time basis, download computer-based training courses – or just single course modules or topics – to their desktop computers. Because students can access single course modules or even just topics of a course rather than whole courses, much time lost going over training that is not necessary can be eliminated. A good site to download different CBT vendors' courses is Oracle's OLA site (www.ola-emea.oracle.co.uk). To access CBT programmes on your desktop you will also generally need to download a specific plug-in program for your Web browser; these are generally available free-of-charge from the site you are downloading the course from.

Multimedia training programmes can be delivered over the Internet to the student's desktop in either an offline or online mode. Offline download has the advantage that the student is only logged into the Internet while the course download is taking place. Once downloaded on to the student's desktop computer, the course may be taken at any time convenient to the student. The disadvantage to this, however, is that because the student is offline, he or she is unable to take advantage of the online facilities available with the tutor. In effect, the offline download facility is no better than purchasing a CD-ROM, unless it is used as coursework for which the student then goes online for communication with other students and the tutor on a regular basis.

However, the real cutting edge of WBT is the delivery of interactive multimedia in real-time via the Internet: the online mode. This has really only been made possible recently with the advent of new programming tools such as Sun's Java and Macromedia's Shockwave, as well as the new Web browser plug-in programs which facilitate the streaming of data down the line. These tools enable students to experience interactive lessons complete with sound, animation, graphics and full motion video.

However, while multimedia over the Internet is now possible, it is not always practical. The speed of most modems in the field today makes the display of complex animations and playback of full motion video unbearably slow. But, hope is on the horizon. During the past six months new advances in technology have already begun to eliminate this hitherto large problem which is discussed in more detail later. Let's now look at some of the available WBT programmes and see how some use all of the four elements outlined, while others – just as effective for their purpose – may utilize only one or two of the elements discussed.

WBT programmes: text and graphics courses

The majority of WBT courses available at the moment comprise pages of textual information with assorted explanatory graphics, such as diagrams, charts and icons. They are similar to reading a textbook and, as such, are not interactive with the learner. The way that these training programmes score over a traditional textbook is in their ability to jump from links in the text to other pages. Some of these simple WBT training programmes also include some contact with an adviser through the use of e-mail.

University of Plymouth: Welcome to Online Learning

The University of Plymouth offers many courses online. It has recently introduced a WBT course for new or potential students who are about to embark on a distance learning programme from the university. As a prerequisite, the university has developed a short course – Welcome to Online Learning – which covers: Learning Online, Computing Tips, Support, Tips for Studying and About the Course. Figure 3.2 shows the opening screen. The course is completely text-based and, although it could make some use of explanatory graphics, such as diagrams and charts, it does fulfil a useful purpose of getting new students familiar with the online learning environment.

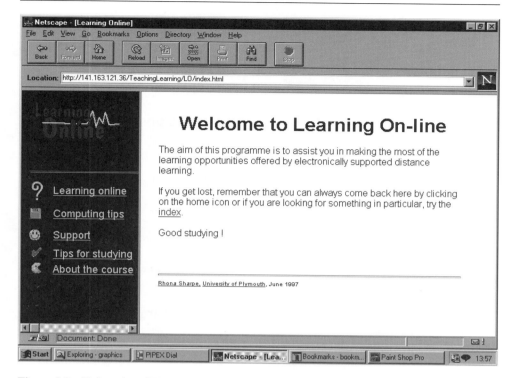

Figure 3.2   University of Plymouth: Welcome to Learning On-line

Figure 3.3 shows one of the topics, Computing Tips. Within Computing Tips, the sub-topics (Saving Your Work, Electronic Filing, Backing Up, Customizing Your Interface, Browsing the WWW, What is E-mail?, Computer Conferencing) are shown on the left-hand bar. For a more interactive use of online learning, we'll now look at two sites which are good examples of how WBT can provide that essential ingredient: interaction with the student. You can find the site at 141.163.121.36/TeachingLearning/learning.html.

WBT programmes: interactive courses

Interactivity is the key to learning. There is no doubt that people learn most effectively by interacting both with the instruction and the tutor. A good explanation of interactivity was given to me recently. This was that interactivity is like a conversation between two people. It is not, however, one person answering the questions of another person, but simply a series

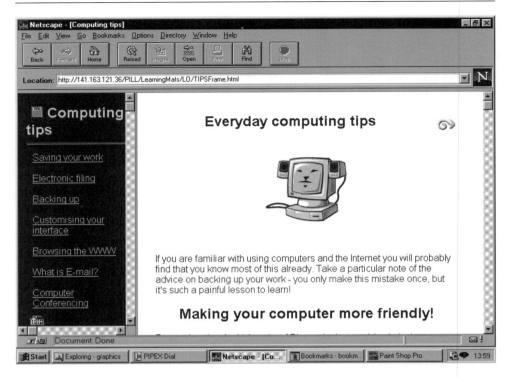

Figure 3.3   Welcome to Online Learning: Computing Tips

of responses, as each one acts upon the other. Interactivity will improve the learning experience. WBT programmes that ask the student to do nothing more than read a series of screens are much less effective than those that check that learning is taking place, track a student's progress and provide remedial strategies in an encouraging and effective manner.

The Web, as a platform-independent medium, is the answer to the trainer's prayers in as much as it can combine real interactivity with the benefits provided by multimedia distance learning with the traditional classroom. Of course, one of the main dangers is that the WBT instructional designers concentrate solely on the technology and forget about the interactivity. This is where standards in online training will become of the utmost importance in the next few years.

The following WBT training programmes are examples of those which are primarily simple text and graphics courses, but have been enhanced by the addition of some level of interaction. Once again, I have provided the Web site addresses and suggest that you explore the sites yourself. All courses offer a free trial.

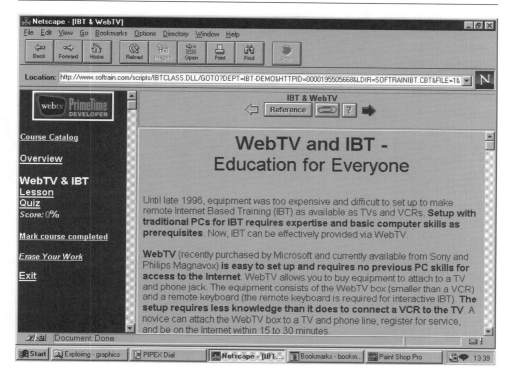

Figure 3.4   The SofTrain Consultancy site

SofTrain Consultancy: WebTV training programme

The SofTrain Consultancy Inc. (see Figure 3.4) site is an example of simply giving information and employing interaction with the student by giving feedback through a post-course test and feeding the results back immediately. Not only does the feedback show the student what has been answered correctly, but, just as importantly, explains the correct answer if the incorrect one has been given. The SofTrain site can be found at: www.softrain.com.

The course is on the topic of WebTV and Internet-based training (IBT). The actual course is a series of textual pages, but the interesting part comes at the end of the course. Here, you are given the option of taking a post-course test. There are five questions to answer and you are given feedback on whether your responses are correct or not. Hints are given for each answer which is incorrect. You are given ten minutes to complete the questions. An example of the first test question is given in Figure 3.5. The questions are simple multiple choice, although there are only two choices! You click on the answer you think is the correct one, and the result is

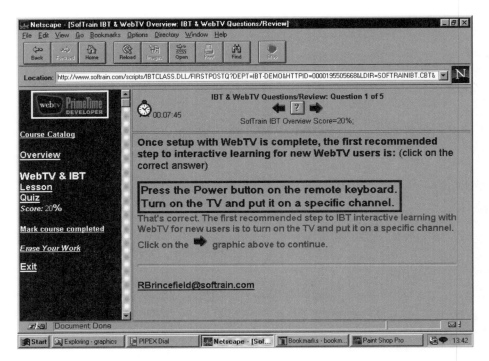

Figure 3.5   WebTV test question

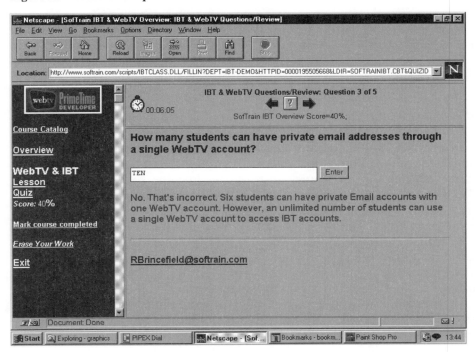

Figure 3.6   Test question feedback

immediately displayed on the screen underneath the question. Figure 3.6 shows an example of the feedback given on an incorrect answer.

Randysoft Software

The Randysoft Software site (www.randysoft.com/demo.shtml) (see Figure 3.7) is another very good use of simple interactive WBT. Here, you will find a series of short tutorials which are aimed at teaching HTML, CGI Scripting, JavaScript, Perl, C++ and other programming languages such as UNIX Shell (see Figure 3.8). These courses are much more interactive than the previous ones mentioned. They utilize a simulated programming environment called OPIE (Online Programming Instruction Environment) which lets the user actually enter program code into an open text area (window), submit the code and then instantly see on screen the results. Assessment is carried out in real-time, which provides information to the student on what, if anything, they have done incorrectly. Taking the HTML Beginners Course as an example, after clicking the Use Opie! button a new

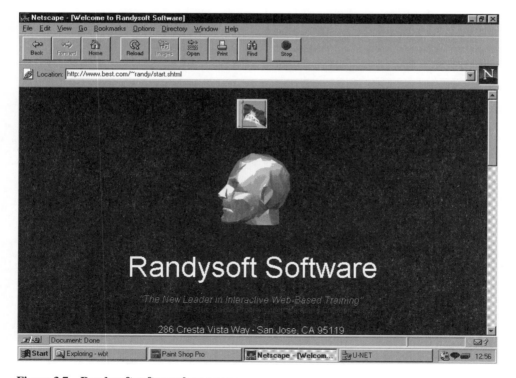

Figure 3.7   Randysoft software home page

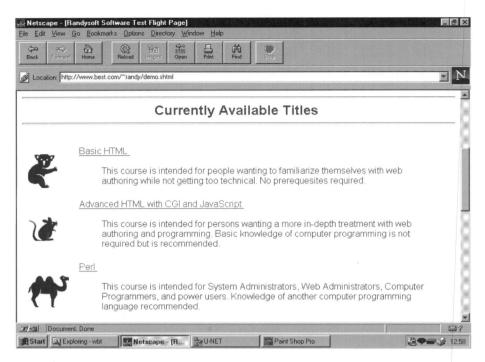

Figure 3.8   Randysoft currently available titles

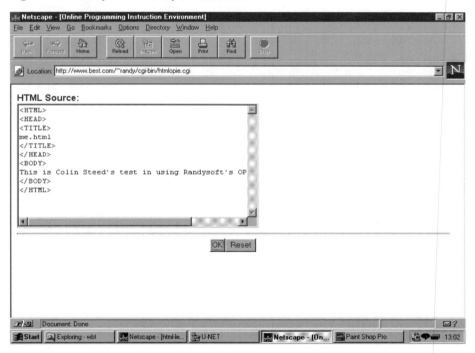

Figure 3.9   Randysoft HTML Beginners Course

window was opened in the browser. I was then instructed to enter some HTML code and text into the window (see Figure 3.9) and then clicked the OK button. The result of my coding was shown immediately in a new window output by OPIE. It's a great way to learn. Many of Randysoft's customers set up their own private Web servers. They then load the Randysoft material and make it available only to their department or group using the Web server access control. One customer outlined the benefits his company (Hewlett-Packard) had gained from using the Randysoft WBT.

> We were surprised by the speed with which the students completed the online lessons. Given all the time used in a lecture class with introductions, breaks and stopping for questions, we figured that a lecture day is about six hours of information. These students covered the same material in about three.

Marshall University School of Medicine's Interactive Patient

If you have any aspirations to become a doctor, or would like to see a 'fun' site offering interactive text and graphics, then visit Marshall University's The Interactive Patient (medicus.marshall.edu/medicus.htm) (see Figure 3.10). This program, from the Marshall University School of Medicine, allows the user to simulate a 'patient' who has come to you with a medical problem. This excellent teaching tool is aimed at physicians, residents and medical students. Your job is to interact with the patient, asking exploratory questions, requesting additional history, performing a physical exam and reviewing lab data and X-rays. Although I did not get that far, at the end of the session the user is encouraged to submit a diagnosis and a treatment plan based on the information provided. All submitted answers are evaluated and feedback is provided. The main thing that it taught me was that I should not give up the day job!

While all of the WBT programmes outlined above offer a valuable insight into the world of online learning, they are pretty basic and do not fully utilize the rich array of possibilities offered by WBT. They could all be dramatically improved with the introduction of various graphic and multi-media elements (including animation, audio and video) to improve the learning possibilities afforded by today's WBT programmes. Although they are not the best examples of WBT (we'll cover some later in the chapter), I have included them as good examples of how, with little or no resources or development cost, it is possible to create WBT. So, do have a look at the sites and try them out yourself. They will serve you well in your investigation of WBT and help you to appreciate fully the systems that I'll describe in much more depth below.

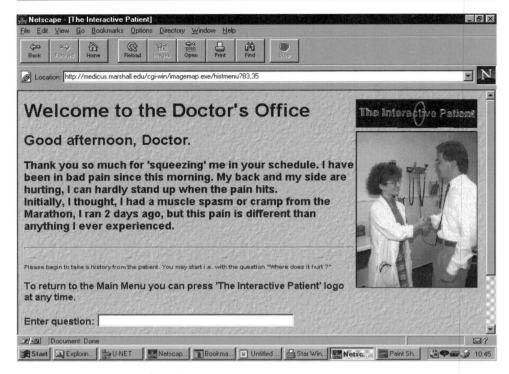

Figure 3.10   Marshall University's The Interactive Patient

WBT programmes: interactive multimedia

As mentioned in the earlier chapters, WBT combines all of the advantages of the traditional classroom-based courses with those of multimedia, distance education. By adding multimedia to WBT training programmes, we can enhance and upgrade the learning environment. By including video, sound and animation in the programmes, the instructional designer can improve the effectiveness for learning by encouraging students to learn with more than just their visual sense. Interactive multimedia also opens the way for conversion of video-based training to the Web.

However, at present, the limitations of bandwidth are holding up the development of this area on the Web. As the 'limited bandwidth' problem is gradually eased, and eventually solved, then watch for an explosion in the use of WBT, for this is the only issue restricting WBT at present. My prediction is that it will be solved, and relatively soon. Having seen the results of Street Technologies' proprietary video streaming today (see Figure 3.11), I have little doubt that, by the turn of the century, the band-

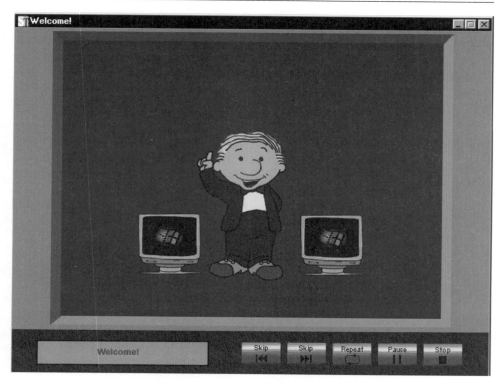

Figure 3.11   Street Technologies' streaming demonstration

width limitation problem will have been almost, if not totally, eliminated. There is an excellent demonstration of effective streaming on Street's site (www.streetinc.com). You will need to download their proprietary plug-in, but it is all explained on the site, and the experience is well worth it. Let's now look at the core of what's available by looking at a couple of sites that make good use of WBT facilities, including audio, video, animation, messaging and conferencing.

LearnItOnline

One of the best sites around for getting started with WBT is the Learn-ItOnline site from Logical Operations (now Ziff-Davis Education). The site can be found at www.learnitonline.com.

This site provides hands-on, interactive training. The training programmes provided are mainly on desktop applications, including Microsoft Office, Lotus Notes and the most popular Web browsers (Internet

Explorer, Netscape Navigator and Communicator). The site allows you to take a free trial of some of the training programmes, allowing you full access to a course, although only some modules of the course are available under the free trial offer. There is an excellent annual subscription to the site of $69.95. Considering that there are some 20 courses currently available and you can have unlimited access to the entire list of courses for your 12 months' subscription, this represents outstanding value for money.

To get started, you firstly need to register as a Free Trial participant, whereupon you will be sent a temporary login name and password (valid for a month). Additionally you will need to download a special free plug-in program for your Web browser. Downloading the plug-in is simple and takes about three minutes. Once downloaded, you simply close your Web browser, click on the file (learn.exe) using your Windows Explorer and follow the on-screen set-up instructions. Before you start your LearnItOnline tutorial, it would be useful to look at how to navigate around the course, and become familiar with the various graphics and icons.

Navigation

Once you have started the tutorial, you will see a dialogue box in the bottom right-hand corner of the screen (see Figure 3.12). This is where the course communicates with you throughout the tutorial and where you

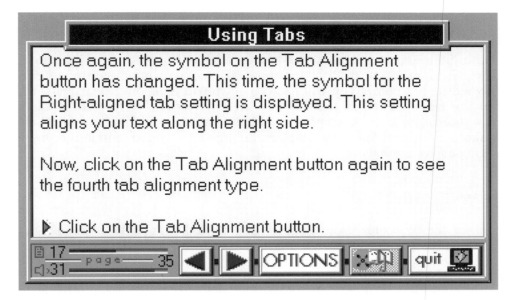

Figure 3.12   LearnItOnline: dialogue box

control the flow of the tutorial and determine its overall status. The gauge tells you the total number of text and audio pages that are available (35 in this example), how many pages of audio have been received by you already (31), and what text page you are currently on (17). The Back button takes you back to the previous step and the Forward button advances you forward to the next step in the tutorial.

Clicking the Options button will display a menu with additional user options, such as switching between Preview and Performance modes, restarting the tutorial, accessing help and turning Audio on and off. The Media button is currently not available. In the future LearnItOnline will introduce additional media enhancements, such as video, and they will be accessible by clicking this button. Clicking the Quit button will allow you to end the tutorial prior to its natural completion.

Training instructions

Training text and instructions appear in the dialogue box above the navigation bar. This is where the teaching takes place. In addition to conceptual information and instruction, you will see visual clues to indicate the actions you need to perform, or to clarify the topic being discussed. A green pointer in the dialogue box indicates that you are being asked to perform a hands-on task (such as, say, 'Click on the Tab Alignment Button'). A red pointer will be displayed on the screen to highlight and encourage you to observe a particular item. At various times throughout the tutorial, you will be asked to perform various hands-on tasks. Because you are working in a simulated environment, the tutorials will act like the actual software application with one very important exception: if you make a mistake there is no harm done, it is a simulation of the software. In fact, the LearnItOnline Assistant will let you know that you have made an error, and will give you the option to try again or let the Assistant show you how to do it.

Completion

When you complete the module, you will see a Congratulations dialogue box appear on the screen. If you wish to take the tutorial again, you simply click the Restart button. If you do not wish to take it again, click the Finish button and you will receive a Points to Remember page, which highlights the important learning points.

Taking a course

Once you have received your login name and password, and have downloaded the Learnflow plug-in, you are ready to begin the online learning experience. We shall walk through a basic course, Word 7.0 level 1. Once

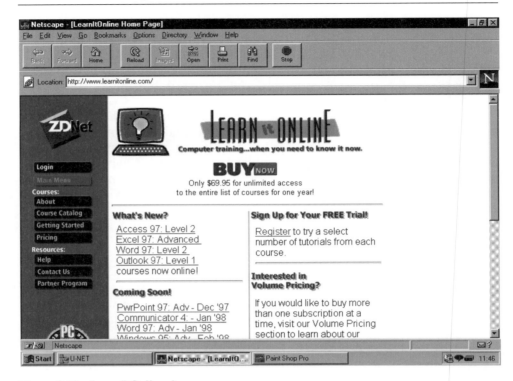

Figure 3.13   LearnItOnline: home page

you have accessed the LearnItOnline site (www.learnitonline.com) you will
be presented with the LearnItOnline home page (see Figure 3.13). You
need to click on the Login button, enter your User Name and Password
and click the Submit button to take you into the courses area (see Figure
3.14). Click the Take a Course button on the left-hand panel. Here, you
will see a list of courses currently available (see Figure 3.15). On the course
catalogue page scroll down to Word 7.0 Level 1 and click on it. Here, you'll
find a complete outline for the course. Notice that the course comprises a
list of subjects and within them a list of modules. The topics and modules in
the Word 7.0 Level 1 course are given in Box 3.1.

Let's try the first one, Introduction to Word for Windows. Next to the
module is a Taken box which acts as a reminder to you which modules you
have already taken. In this case, all boxes are empty (see Figure 3.16).
When you click on the module you wish to take, it will automatically start
to download. Once a certain amount has been streamed down to your
desktop the tutorial begins. The module took around two minutes to
stream down before the tutorial commenced. The tutorial takes you
through the first module, expertly narrating the various parts of the tool-

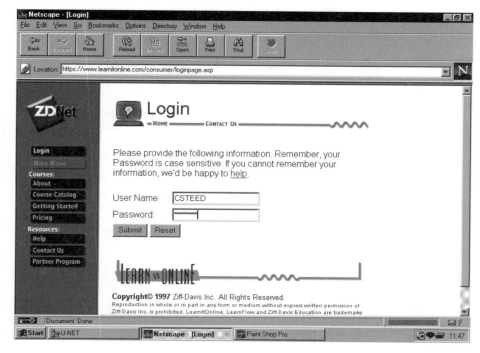

Figure 3.14   LearnItOnline: login page

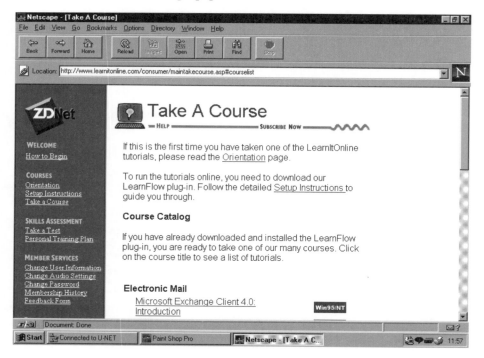

Figure 3.15   LearnItOnline: courses

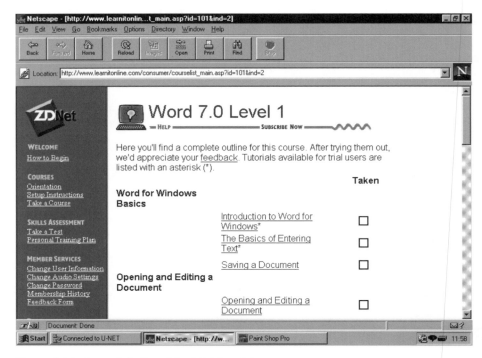

Figure 3.16   LearnItOnline: Word 7.0 Level 1 course

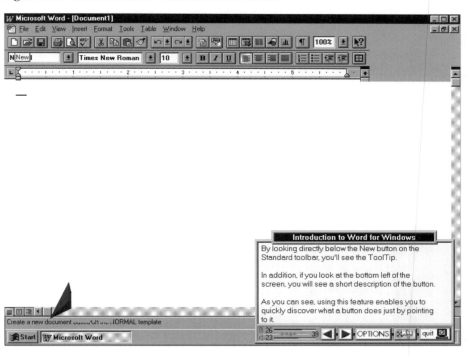

Figure 3.17   LearnItOnline: tutorial

Box 3.1   Word 7.0 Level 1 course content

Word for Windows Basics
Introduction to Word for Windows
The Basics of Entering Text
Saving a Document

Opening and Editing a Document
Opening and Editing a Document
Using the AutoCorrect Command
Previewing and Printing a Document
Creating a New Document

Navigating in Word for Windows
Scrolling a Document
Navigating a Document

Additional Editing Techniques
Techniques for Selecting Text
The Edit, Replace Command
Using the Undo Button
Moving and Copying Text
Editing in Print Preview

Character Formatting
Character Formatting
Changing Fonts and Font Sizes

Paragraph Formatting
Paragraph Formatting
Paragraph Borders and Shading
Indents, Numbered Lists and Bulleted Lists
Line Breaks and Line Spacing

Introduction to Tabs and Tables
Using Tabs
Introduction to Tables
Using the Table AutoFormat Command

Controlling Page Appearance
Headers and Footers
Changing Margins
Inserting Page Breaks

Proofing Tools
Using the Spelling Checker
Using the Thesaurus
Using the Grammar Checker

Inserting Files and Graphics
Inserting Files into a Document

bars, and so on, with the red pointer highlighting the areas and various hands-on tasks being performed. Note in Figure 3.17, the dialogue box with the red pointer highlights the point being discussed.

Once the module has been completed, a list of points to remember is displayed (see Figure 3.18) followed by the Course Record screen, showing that the first module has now been completed (see Figure 3.19).

Let's have a more in-depth look at another module in the course. This time we shall take the module on The Edit, Replace Command, which shows more of the hands-on work that is undertaken. Figure 3.20 shows the opening page to the Edit, Replace Command module, outlining the topics covered in the module. In the screen shown (Figure 3.20) you are presented with a Word document and are told to click on the Edit/Replace command which presents the Replace dialogue box at the top of the screen. The nar-

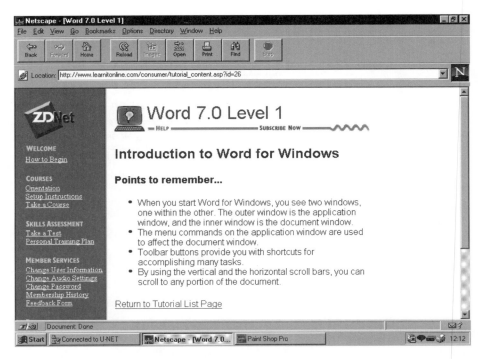

Figure 3.18   LearnItOnline: points to remember

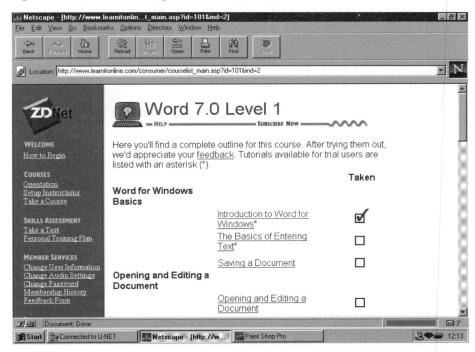

Figure 3.19   LearnItOnline: course record screen

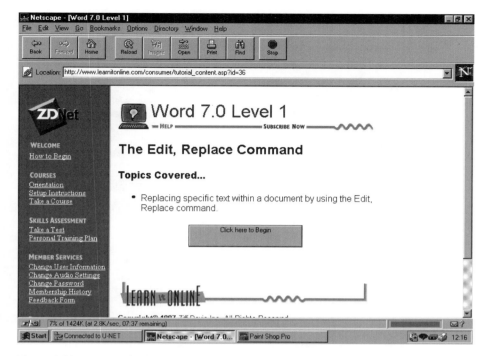

Figure 3.20   LearnItOnline: the Edit, Replace Command module

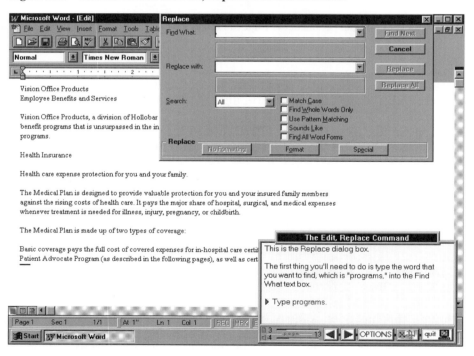

Figure 3.21   LearnItOnline: the Find command

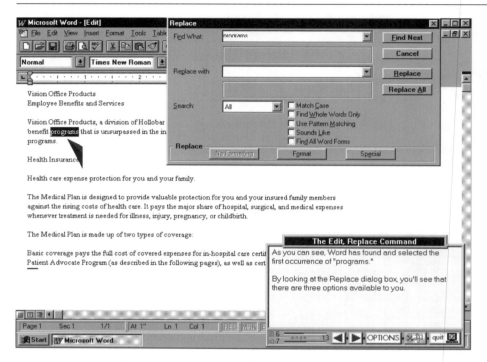

Figure 3.22   LearnItOnline: results of the Find command

ration says to enter the word 'programs' in the Find What box (see Figure 3.21). Here you follow the instruction and click Find Next on the Replace dialogue box.

The next screen (see Figure 3.22) shows you the results. Note the red pointer highlighting the word that you are searching for. The narration, shown in the dialogue box at the bottom of the screen, explains the results, and the following screens show you the results of finding and replacing text. It covers all of the various options and search criteria, each one getting you to enter the information on the screen and displaying the results with an explanation of what has happened. At the completion of the module, a Congratulations dialogue box appears (see Figure 3.23) giving the option of going through the module again or finishing it. By clicking on Quit, you are then presented with a Points To Remember screen (see Figure 3.24) which lists the salient points to remember for the Edit, Replace Command.

Although this has been a fairly basic walk through of the LearnItOnline learning environment, it will show just how simple the training programmes are to use, and additionally, how good training can be carried out using WBT in a cost-effective and time-effective manner.

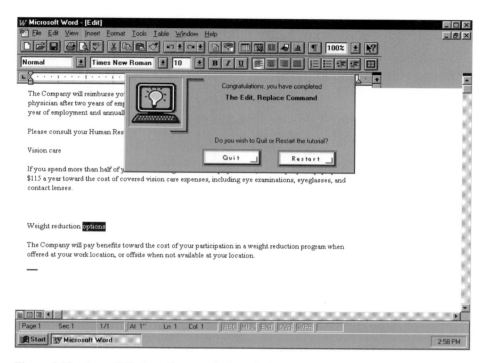

Figure 3.23   LearnItOnline: Congratulations dialogue box

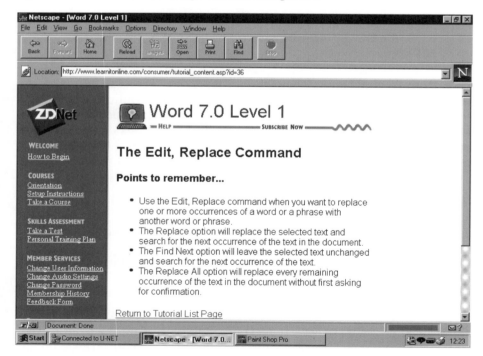

Figure 3.24   LearnItOnline: Points to Remember screen

The resources required are minimal. I used a P100 Pentium with sound card, connected to a 28.8 modem and a standard dial-up account with an Internet Service Provider. Nothing special there. The time taken to download WBT – a constant criticism from some observers – was minimal, especially bearing in mind that I downloaded the full option of audio narration with the course. The two modules used here were streamed down in less than four minutes each. There are other excellent features on the site apart from the actual course programmes. The Skills Assessment facility consists of multiple choice tests for most of the courses on the site. Each test contains between 15 and 35 questions. Once you complete the test, you can then view your Personal Training Plan, which lists all the tutorials within a course indicating those recommended for you to take, based on your Skills Assessment test score.

Although LearnItOnline does not use all of the elements available to today's WBT systems – online tutors, chatrooms, individual module online testing and video, for example – it accomplishes its aims and objectives well. And that is important to remember. You do not have to have all the 'bells and whistles' available at your disposal to achieve a sound learning platform. Let's now have a look at two sites which go one step further, and make use of multimedia elements such as streamed audio, animation and video to accomplish their learning goals: DigitalThink and the Oracle Simulator.

DigitalThink

The site from DigitalThink (www.digitalthink.com) goes further than the LearnItOnline site in as much as it provides interactive online communication between tutor and students, as well as an area where students can communicate together. Let's now look at some of the facilities of the excellent DigitalThink site to explore how it all works.

The DigitalThink site comprises two areas: the Orientation area and the Course area. In the Orientation area you can:

● read descriptions of the current and upcoming courses, learn about the instructors and register for courses;
● preview course syllabuses and become acquainted with the course before you make the decision to purchase it;
● learn about the tools available on the site to help you learn online;
● contact the people who manage the site; and
● take a free trial course, Smart Searching: The Power of Simple Searches.

The Course area is where you take your courses and interact with other students, instructors and tutors. The area is open to registered students only. Here, you will find:

- your personal locker page, with links to your classes, instructors, tutors and online classmates;
- course lessons, complete with colour graphics, hypertext and audio;
- interactive quizzes;
- hands-on exercises;
- course-specific discussion boards;
- live, instructor-led chat sessions; and
- help, via e-mail.

How it works

An example of a DigitalThink course page is shown in Figure 3.25. Note the navigational toolbar in the left-hand frame; I'll explain more about that later. As you proceed through your course, new lessons, hands-on exer-

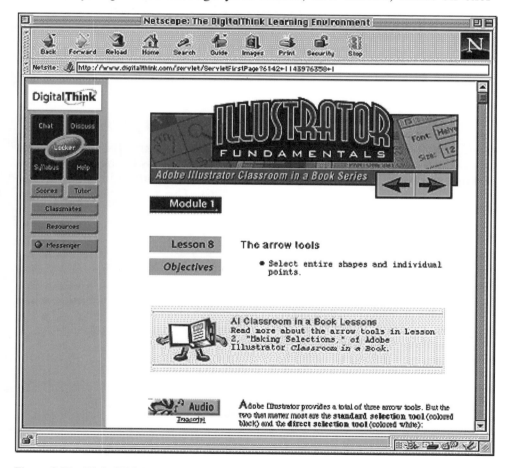

Figure 3.25   DigitalThink course page

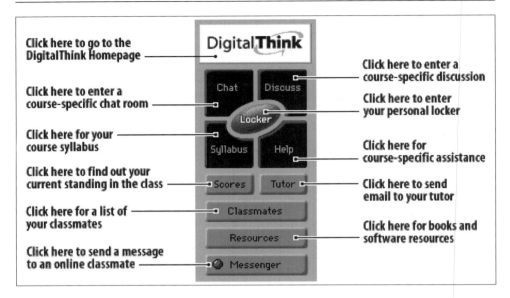

Click here to go to the
DigitalThink Homepage

Click here to enter a
course-specific chat room

Click here for your
course syllabus

Click here to find out your
current standing in the class

Click here for a list of
your classmates

Click here to send a message
to an online classmate

Click here to enter a
course-specific discussion

Click here to enter
your personal locker

Click here for
course-specific assistance

Click here to send
email to your tutor

Click here for books and
software resources

Figure 3.26   DigitalThink toolbar

cises, interactive quizzes and other materials will appear on the screen. The DigitalThink toolbar provides you with one click access to the features you will use while taking the course. The toolbar will be your guide everywhere you go in the Course area (see Figure 3.26). The toolbar comprises the following options:

- **Chat**: this will take you to a specific chatroom.
- **Discuss**: click to enter a course-specific discussion.
- **Locker**: enter your personal locker page.
- **Syllabus**: obtain the syllabus of your course.
- **Help**: ask for course-specific assistance.
- **Scores**: find out your current standing in the class.
- **Tutor**: send e-mail to your tutor.
- **Classmates**: find a list of your online classmates.
- **Resources**: find out what books and software resources are available for your course.
- **Messenger**: send a message to an online classmate.

Let's now see what the screens look like, with a description of how you would use them.

Syllabus
Click on the Syllabus button and you will see where you are in the course,

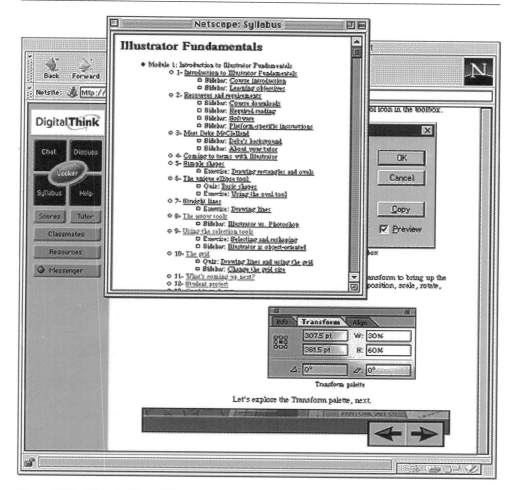

Figure 3.27   DigitalThink Syllabus

which topics you have completed and which topics are still to be taken (see Figure 3.27). Your course syllabus provides two key functions:

- You will always know where you are in a course; a red arrow points to the current topic you are taking.
- The syllabus provides you with a way to skip directly to the course topics that interest you most. To move to another topic, simply click on it.

Personal locker

The Locker page is your gateway to your courses, classmates and personal profile (see Figure 3.28). Your Locker contains links to:

- the courses you are currently enrolled in;
- the last page you viewed in a course, so you can continue from where you left off;
- your classmates;
- your quiz scores;
- your student profile page, where you can describe yourself to your classmates; and
- your personal registration information.

Classmates

You can access your Classmates page from your Locker as soon as you have registered for a course. The classmates page lists all of the students who are enrolled in your course, as well as the module each student has

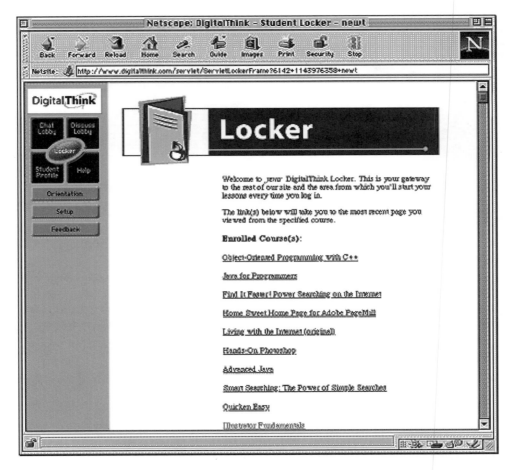

Figure 3.28   DigitalThink Locker page

most recently completed (see Figure 3.29). E-mail links are provided to allow you to communicate with other students.

Chat

When you take your online course, it is valuable to be able to chat with other students on the course. The more you contribute, the more value you will receive from the online learning experience. The Chat facility provides an excellent way to contribute your opinions or ask questions of your class-mates or instructors (see Figure 3.30). Chatting takes place in areas organized by course name, so you do not end up chatting about a topic that you have no interest in. Other students in the chat areas will share your interest in the course topic, and you will find some interesting opinions presented by your classmates.

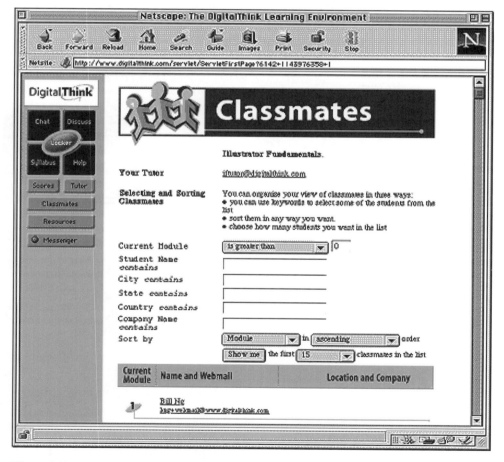

Figure 3.29   DigitalThink Classmates page

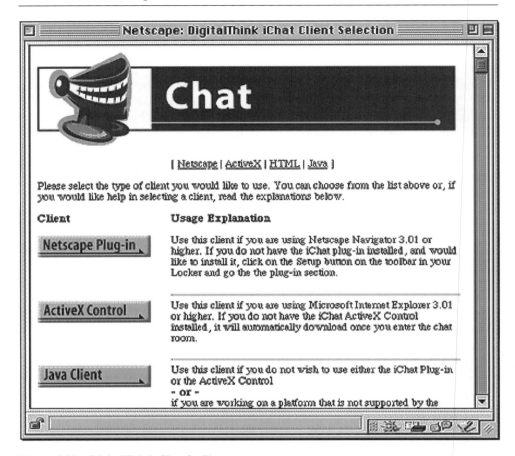

Figure 3.30   DigitalThink Chat facility

Participating in a chat session is simple: type in your comments, and track the chat in a separate window on-screen. You can introduce yourself, chat with everyone in the chat area, or just one individual and enjoy real-time communication with classmates from around the world. DigitalThink will be introducing special hosted seminars in the chat area in the near future.

Discussion
The Discussion area allows you to post messages to your classmates, tutors and instructors (see Figure 3.31). Unlike chat sessions, discussions do not require you to be logged-in at the same time as other participants. So, you can post messages at any time, and when a classmate logs in to the site, they will be able to pick up your message. Additionally, you can check back to see new postings on the topic by your classmates, instructor or tutor.

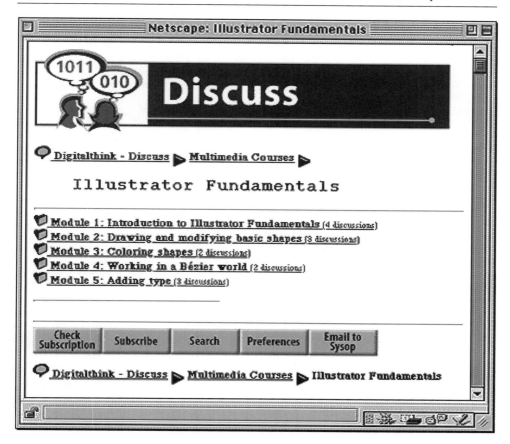

Figure 3.31   DigitalThink Discussion area

Messenger
The Messenger enables you to communicate with students, tutors and instructors who are online taking the same course as you. You activate the Messenger by clicking the Messaging button on the toolbar. To send a message, simply select the recipient(s) from the list of online students, type in the message and click the Send button. The recipient(s) you have chosen will be notified by an audio and visual alert (see Figure 3.32). Similar to chat sessions, the Messenger adds a level of online instant collaboration and course/community interaction.

Resources
The Resources page provides you with access to the course materials that you will need to complete the course. Materials outlined include books, software, shareware, downloadable files your course may require and

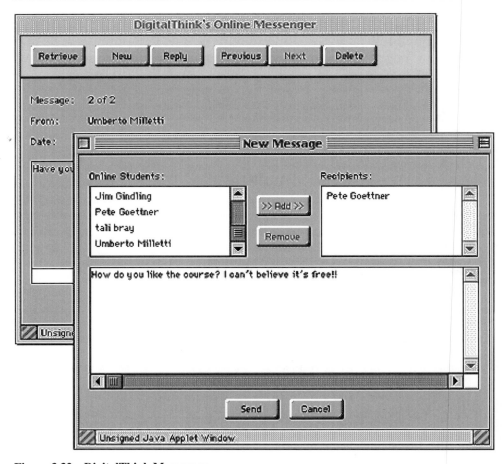

Figure 3.32   DigitalThink Messenger

course-specific FAQs (frequently asked questions). The bookstore and software store can take payment by credit card online or via fax (see Figure 3.33).

Digital Think is certainly an excellent site, utilizing many features available to WBT programmes. The courses are all IT based, including C++ Programming, Certification (Java and NT), Design and Publishing (Illustrator, Photoshop, Pagemaker), Internet Literacy, Java Programming, Perl Programming and an interesting course on Enjoying Wine! Course prices are around $300.

The Oracle Simulator

Software simulation provides an excellent way of learning and practising new skills in a completely risk-free environment. Students can see the results of their actions, gaining confidence all the time, as well as learning from their mistakes. Audio- and video-based conferencing and guidance also provide realistic ways of learning. And all this is now possible. An excellent example of one of these latest WBT simulations is an interactive tool for database administrators to develop their skills through various simulated scenarios which emulate real-life situations. The Oracle Simulator also demonstrates the power of the new Java programming language as a development tool for WBT systems.

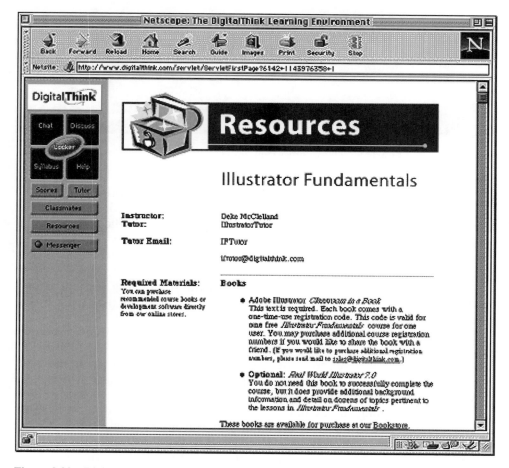

Figure 3.33   DigitalThink Resources page

Figure 3.34   The Oracle Simulator: office simulation

The simulations take place in a fictitious company's hotline office (see Figure 3.34). The student acts as the Hotline contact in order to carry out the associated back-up and recovery tasks. Within the office, the student has access to customer files, a computer terminal, reference books, a telephone and a letter from the on-call adviser. The student can access any object by clicking on it. Click on the drawer and you are presented with a drawer of customer files. By clicking on any file folder, the student is presented with the customer's profile and a list of situations that exist in the customer's database environment (see Figure 3.35).

There is a colour-coded list of database administration situations, from relatively simple to solve, through moderately challenging, to difficult. The Overview provides a synopsis of each situation. By clicking on the telephone you will receive a message from the customer, outlining the basic problem with the database. Additionally, the customer sends the student an e-mail, containing the actual error messages from the database at fault. By clicking on the computer terminal, you can interact with your on-call expert (using videoconferencing), interact with your customer through the e-mail and/or videoconference, and view a log of the information you have received from the expert and the customer (see Figure 3.36).

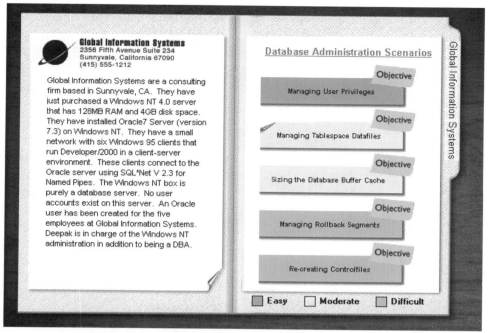

Figure 3.35 Office simulation: customer details

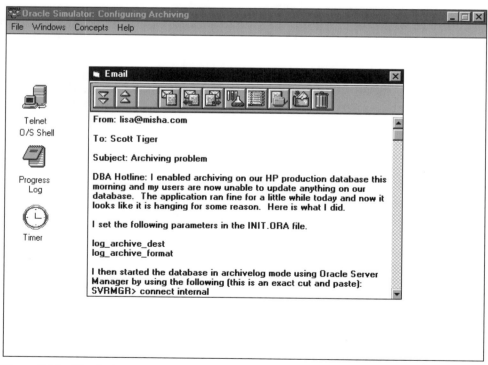

Figure 3.36 The Oracle Simulator: e-mail

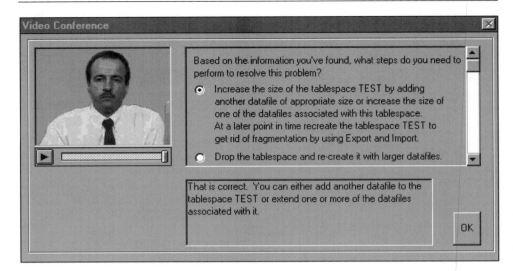

Figure 3.37   The Oracle Simulator: videoconferencing

As you solve the database problem, your on-call adviser guides you through various choices and through a series of desktop videoconferences (see Figure 3.37). A progress log screen records all your interactions with both your adviser and your customer. You can also keep track of the amount of time it takes you to solve a customer's problem by using the Timer window. On each screen, the simulation traps user actions, such as double clicks, menu selections and command selections, and either carries out the action or provides instructional feedback if the action is incorrect. Additionally, cue cards are displayed to guide you through the optimum solution. Throughout your progression through the many paths of the simulation, it keeps track of all of the steps that you have taken to solve the problem.

The Oracle Simulator is a first-class example of the way simulation can aid the learning process, and the company must be congratulated on an excellent online learning tool. Expect to see many more of these simulation tools on the market in the near future.

Chapter 4

What's currently available? Integrated curriculum management systems

The Web provides the potential to revolutionize training and education to the same degree as it has revolutionized access to information and communications for users around the globe. However, a number of issues need to be addressed if the Web is to be applied successfully to deliver a positive and effective learning experience for learners.

To effectively harness the power of the Web, a distributed learning environment must be more than just a course authoring and delivery system. It must be more than CBT delivered over the Web. The most powerful aspects of classroom-based training are based on the invaluable interaction between the instructor and students. Students can ask questions directly of their instructor, submit exercises and get individual attention. Clearly, the communication and collaboration aspects of classroom-based instruction provide crucial support mechanisms for learners, and any Web-based training must do the same. With technology-based training, such as CBT or CD-ROM, the major benefits to the student are the ability to work at their own pace, in their own time and in a location of their choosing. Multimedia technologies have significantly enhanced the sophistication of the course material to help engage and challenge the learner, and, once again, any Web-based training must do the same.

The concept which underlies the WBT systems today is guided learning. It is based on combining the collaborative aspects of classroom-based training with the self-paced and more flexible nature of CBT. Guided learning is based on three fundamental ideas:

- An integrated learning environment
- Content management
- Class management.

This chapter outlines integrated curriculum management and course delivery systems designed to run on a company intranet or to be used as a platform for training providers to offer their courses either online or via a company intranet. These systems are complete training management, administration and course delivery systems and are generally made up of integrated modules: listing courses, defining courses available for different students, registration, tracking usage, hosting 'chat' areas and facilitating tutor/student communication.

This chapter does not provide details of all of the available systems, but it does comprise the majority of the major players; there is a full list of sites in the Appendix. Under each system I have provided contact information to enable you to obtain further details from the system provider. The systems described in this chapter are:

- LearningSpace (Lotus)
- Oracle Learning Architecture (Oracle)
- DLE, Distance Learning Environment (Pathlore)
- TopClass (WBT Systems)
- CBTCampus (CBT Systems)
- SkillVantage Manager (NETg)
- Symposium (Centra Software)
- LOIS (Knowledgesoft)
- Enterprise Learning Centre (Gartner)
- Librarian (Asymetrix).

LearningSpace

The Lotus Institute developed LearningSpace (see Figure 4.1) following extensive research into distance learning and the use of technology. Originally released in September 1996, Learning Space has been specifically designed to support any time, any place, instructor-led and collaborative learning programmes for the Web or Lotus Notes.

LearningSpace is 'learner-centred' because students can explore and navigate to information based on their interests, as well as their levels of competency. They can work individually, at their own pace, in their own time. LearningSpace is 'learning team centred' because students collaborate in problem-solving activities, discussions and exercises which result in the creation of new knowledge. This new knowledge is captured and stored in LearningSpace. LearningSpace is designed to support the delivery of a course in which students do not meet face-to-face, as well as to augment those course offerings which do include some face-to-face interaction. The suite of five interconnected Lotus Notes databases provide a flexible, dynamic environment for developing, deploying and delivering courses, as well as supporting and augmenting classroom training.

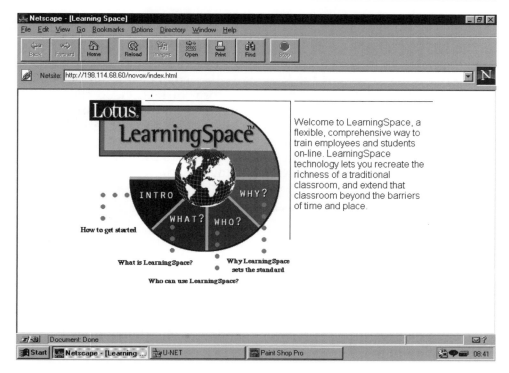

Figure 4.1   LearningSpace

The LearningSpace modules

The LearningSpace application comprises interconnected modules, each of which is a Lotus Notes database. Students receive the Schedule, MediaCenter, CourseRoom and Profiles modules. Instructors and instructional designers receive these four modules plus the Assessment Manager module.

Schedule

The Schedule is a central module for participants to navigate through course materials. It presents the instructional design and structure for the course as created by an instructor. From here students are presented with learning objectives and applicable deadlines as they navigate to course materials and exercises, take tests and quizzes and participate in surveys. The Schedule may be designed for a self-paced course or structured around specific time frames (e.g. containing modules to be completed each week).

MediaCenter

An instructor or course designer creates the MediaCenter, the shared knowledge base which includes all course-related content, as well as access to external sources such as the Web and other content repositories. Information in the MediaCenter can take the form of text, video clips, multimedia, CBT, graphics, spreadsheets, simulations, and so on. LearningSpace provides the ability to create keyword taxonomies for categorization and searching. The MediaCenter can also contain additional information beyond assigned course content to allow students to explore intuitively and learn in a way that is consistent with individual learning styles and needs.

CourseRoom

The CourseRoom is an interactive, facilitated environment in which students have discussions among themselves and with the instructor, as well as collaborate on team tasks and assignments. The CourseRoom provides for public and private discussions and enables collaborative learning that is both participant-to-participant and instructor-to-participant. The CourseRoom supports asynchronous collaboration through Notes replication and is being extended to support synchronous collaboration through whiteboard applications and videoconferencing.

Profiles

The Profiles module is a collection of student and instructor descriptions which includes contact information, photographs and information about education, experience and interests. This application allows students to create a personal 'home page' of information about themselves and to identify other students with similar interests and objectives.

Assessment Manager

The Assessment Manager is an evaluation tool for instructors to test privately, review and grade and give feedback on participant performance. Quizzes, exams and surveys are posted in the Schedule for students and are e-mailed back into the Assessment Manager module for private review by the instructors.

Simulation of a LearningSpace course as a student

The modules of LearningSpace provide for a wide variety of learning experiences because the tool can be adapted to the course content, the instructor's course design and the learning styles of students. To appreciate how the technical architecture of LearningSpace can accommodate various learning experiences, we will follow a simulated course from the perspectives of a student and an instructor.

First, we will follow the experiences of Jim, a student on that course. Jim works full time and chooses to participate in a distributed course because he prefers not to take time away from his family and other personal responsibilities to attend classes at a scheduled time and place. Jim is beginning a new course in LearningSpace being offered by a university several hours away. He starts in the course Schedule (A in Figure 4.2) by playing the instructor's video clip of introduction materials. He then browses the Schedule module to gain a complete understanding of the course learning objectives and expectations. One of the first entries in the Schedule directs Jim to the Profiles module where he is instructed to edit his profile.

Jim navigates to the Profiles module (B) and finds his name under the participant category. When he opens his profile, he clicks on the 'Edit Your Profile' button. From there he enters his contact information, education, work experience, and his interests. He also adds a picture of himself and writes about his interests. Jim navigates back to the Schedule module (C), goes to the Personal Progress view and marks this task complete. He subsequently moves to the next document, which instructs him to read an article

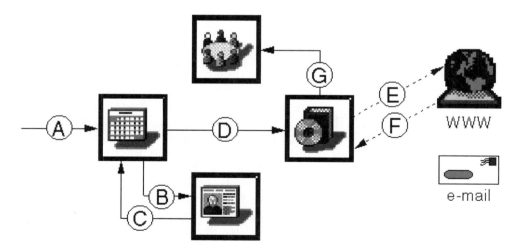

Figure 4.2   LearningSpace: beginning a new course

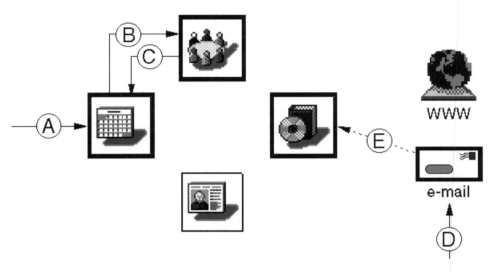

Figure 4.3   LearningSpace: assignments

and watch a video clip in the MediaCenter (D). He links to the MediaCenter and completes his assignment. While in the MediaCenter, Jim would like to learn more about a specific topic area. He clicks on the WWW SmartIcon and accesses the Web for additional information (E). While browsing on the Web, Jim finds information that he thinks his fellow students would also be interested in reading. He copies the first page of the Web site including the hot links. He goes back into the MediaCenter (F), navigates to the CourseRoom (G) and 'Starts a Discussion'. Jim pastes in the captured Web page to share the information in the CourseRoom with his fellow students. Jim 'leaves' the LearningSpace environment and plans to complete the next exercise the following day on his return flight from a meeting.

Once *en route*, Jim re-enters the Schedule (A in figure 4.3) where he left his last completed task. The next assignment is a group project with a team that has been established by the instructor. He reads the objectives of the group project and finds the name of the team in which he will participate. He notices that the 'View Related Discussion' button appears at the top of the screen indicating that a discussion about this document exists in the CourseRoom (B). He clicks on the button to view the current discussion. He finds several documents, one of which was entered by a fellow team member. He opens the document and reads his team-mate's ideas. He clicks on the 'Comment' button and adds his suggestions and ideas. He also notices a document which was entered by the instructor, which he reads. Jim has several questions and creates a comment on the instructor's document requesting a response to his questions. Before leaving the

CourseRoom, Jim decides to read some of the other discussions that are taking place within the team as well as those for all students, and adds a few more comments to these discussions.

Jim then re-enters the Schedule module (C) to complete his first quiz. He opens the document and clicks on the 'Start Here' button to begin. He completes the questions, which include true–false, multiple choice and several short answer questions and clicks on the 'Submit to Instructor' button. When Jim returns home, he connects and sends his additions to the server and receives additional information entered by other members of the course. A few days later Jim's quiz is returned via e-mail (D). The returned, graded quiz displays the correct answers, Jim's answers and an explanation of the differences between the two. He also receives an annotation from the instructor about areas in which he excelled and those on which he may want to spend more time. The instructor has included a link to content in the MediaCenter, and following this link (E), Jim begins his work on the next segment of the course.

Simulation of a LearningSpace course as an instructor

We will now follow the experiences of Mary, the instructor for Jim's course. Before the course began, Mary designed the course and entered content into the Schedule and MediaCenter modules for all her students to access. Now that the students have begun the course, Mary serves as the facilitator for CourseRoom discussions. In preparing the course, Mary defined the course learning objectives as she would if she were teaching face to face. She established a structure for the class and outlined a variety of individual and group assignments which could be mapped to measures of success. She also obtained copyright permission for all content she chose to distribute in LearningSpace.

After planning the course, Mary entered LearningSpace and created a Course Profile by filling in a form in the Schedule (A in Figure 4.4). She entered an overview description of the course, and chose to divide the course into several units, each of which could be completed over a one-week period. Mary then entered the MediaCenter module (B) and clicked on the button labelled 'Create MediaCenter Object'. She filled in the title, source and author fields, added appropriate keywords to make the document easy to locate in the future and then inserted the text of the journal article she would like her students to read, copying and pasting it from the journal's Web site.

She next clicked on the 'Create Related Schedule Entry' button (C) and filled in fields for the Schedule assignment such as name of assignment, unit name and due date, and created a link back to the new MediaCenter entry. Mary's students will now know what to read when, and will have immediate access to the article with a click of the mouse. Mary repeated this

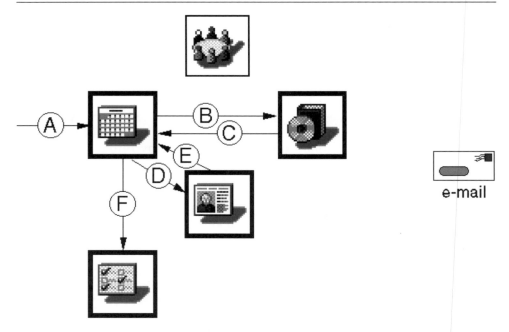

Figure 4.4   LearningSpace: planning a course

process for each individual assignment in the course. Some of the assignments Mary designed for her students are collaborative. To create these assignments, Mary went to the Schedule module and clicked on the 'Create Entry' button. She filled in fields describing the assignment and due date, and wrote the questions for students to discuss or work on as a team.

To support the distributed team assignments, Mary went to the Profiles module (D), browsed the student profiles and then assigned students to diverse teams. At the end of each unit, Mary's students will have worked individually and collaboratively towards meeting the learning objectives for the course. After summarizing the learning objectives for each unit in the Schedule (E), Mary designed a variety of assessments in the Assessment Manager module (F), including surveys, self-tests and exams for Jim and others to test their new knowledge.

Now that Mary has developed the course and Jim and his classmates have begun to work through each unit, Mary serves as facilitator in the course. She thoughtfully chooses when to intervene in a student discussion to add a comment or pose a probing question (A in Figure 4.5). Through e-mail (B), she inquires privately of a student whether he feels comfortable joining the conversation when his participation seems limited. On other occasions, Mary decides not to contribute to a discussion to enable students to struggle through a difficult problem on their own.

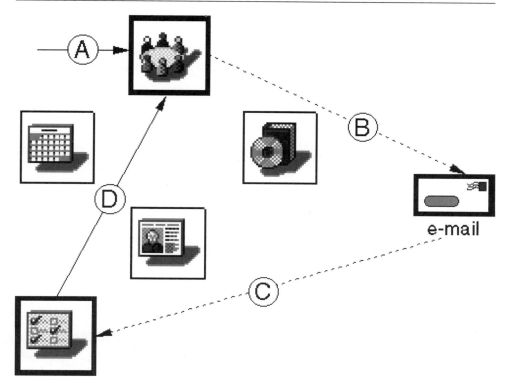

Figure 4.5   LearningSpace: facilitating a course

Noticing a difference of opinion among students discussing an issue, she creates a survey in the Assessment Manager (C) to explore the source of the various perspectives. Reviewing the private answers to the survey, she then submits a summary of the findings for the entire class in the Course-Room (D). By developing this course and facilitating it in LearningSpace, Mary feels connected to the diverse learning needs of her students, without ever meeting them face to face.

System requirements

LearningSpace requires Lotus Notes Release 4.1 software and appropriate hardware as outlined below.

Server requirements

Any certified server configuration as outlined in the Notes Server 4.1 documentation or as found on the Web site at //www.lotus.com/ntsdoc96/29ca.htm.

Client requirements

Recommendations are 75 MHz 486 processor, 16 MB RAM, VGA with 256 colour support, 40 MB of free disk space before installing Notes, more depending on the content of the course, and Lotus Notes Release 4.1 Client or Desktop. Optional additional hardware: 28.8 modem for dial-up connectivity and multimedia capability.

Contact details

Web: www.lotus.com

OLA, Oracle Learning Architecture

OLA (see Figure 4.6) is an online learning environment which integrates Oracle's leading-edge database and Internet/intranet technology with sound education principles to provide customer-specific education solutions. OLA supports the delivery of training and educational materials to users over networks such as the Internet, a corporate intranet or a university or school network. OLA offers an end-to-end education solution, from design and development of educational content to delivery and deployment of the content.

The OLA infrastructure incorporates state-of-the-art learning capabilities and is expandable to accommodate growth and innovation. It is a repository-based education delivery infrastructure which combines Oracle's WebServer, relational database technology, video servers and network technology with the most up-to-date multimedia education products and services. The technical infrastructure and products are combined to deliver 'learning on demand' education which can be delivered anywhere, anytime, using the most appropriate delivery platform for the learner.

Figure 4.6   Oracle Learning Architecture (OLE)

OLA: a two-tiered approach

The total education opportunity is to address not only the corporate IT training gap, but also general education automation. Oracle believes that the training gap can be addressed by the following:

- Initially offering an OLA Internet Service that provides course content addressing corporate IT developer, administrator and user topics, as well as soft-skills areas, such as management skills and writing skills. This breadth of course content would enable OLA to deliver a complete training solution for corporate enterprises, departments, workgroups and individuals. The OLA service would be serving the role of an electronic education brokerage. This is covered in Chapter 5 on Curriculum Delivery Sites.
- Offering the OLA product, which provides customers with an enterprise-wide education and training development, delivery and administration platform. This product would establish OLA as a licensed software application and development environment which would broaden account reach and use of Oracle's core technology.

OLA provides a rich set of administration, reporting, content and interactivity features:

1. **Administration**:
   - content management
   - user profile management and tracking
   - access security at combined user/course level
   - user self-registration
   - automated royalty calculation and record keeping.
2. **Reporting**:
   - user group usage reporting
   - user comments
   - broad administrative reporting.
3. **Content media types**:
   - combinations of text, graphics and audio.
4. **Course navigation**:
   - multiple navigation options
   - customized course path based on user competency
   - book marking/placeholder.
5. **Content subject matter**:
   - Oracle technology, database-related subjects, Unix, C/S architecture and programming, networking, selected applications.
6. **Interactivity**:
   - online access to instructors
   - competency feedback via skills testing
   - product simulation
   - course and curriculum tracking.

Service architecture and component technologies

OLA uses the Oracle WebServer, automated order processing and the Oracle7 relational database technology to provide robust security and scalability for supporting thousands of users and terabytes of content. Its key architectural components include: course content and porting filters, content management, course structure and control, and course delivery.

Course content

OLA provides a framework for deploying content from many courseware providers. The course profile (title, author, objectives, prerequisites, etc.) is maintained in the Oracle7 database. The flexibility of OLA's architecture permits storage and retrieval of course content in numerous ways:

- **Learning objects**: for OLA course components (text, sound, images) and course grammar stored independently.
- **Legacy content**: courses stored in native authoring in flat file system language and (HTML or Java) downloaded to clients.

Content management

The OLA service manages content in two areas:

- Physical storage of courses and course elements in a file system organized by source of content (primarily by vendor).
- Tracking and control through Learning Objects stored in OLA's Oracle7 database. This allows OLA to control access and relationships between courses and users.

Course structure and control utilities enable the addition and removal of courses, and editing course profiles.

Course structure and control

OLA's course structure and control features include administration tools, billing, reporting and user interface.

Administrative tools

- Facilitate creation and maintenance of user accounts and administrative accounts: super user, site-wide, editor, vendor, Education Sales Rep (ESR).
- Enable environment and site configuration.
- Administer and moderate comments and bulletin boards.

Billing

There are convenient options both for corporations to purchase multi-user and multi-title licences, and for individual purchasers to order courses.

Reports

Several types of reports can be created showing course and user statistics. Full support for custom reports is also available.

User interface

The OLA service will have a user interface conforming to the Oracle Applications Web standards, and will provide users with easy and intuitive navigational capabilities to access desired information. Online help is available from within the environment.

Content delivery

At initial service availability, content delivery is supported by standard Web file types, including HTML and Java applets, and served via the Oracle WebServer to standard Web browser clients.

OLA product vision

OLA as a product will provide customers with an end-to-end education solution; a development, delivery and administration platform. This product would establish OLA as a licensed software application and development environment that would broaden account reach and use of Oracle's core technology. In addition, OLA will establish the standard for all education and training delivery, both over the Internet and over enterprise intranets. Beyond the corporate IT segment, Oracle Education is leading the way in defining standards for Internet-based instructional design, course authoring and course delivery. These standards are equally applicable across content from IT to 'edutainment' for pre-school children.

Oracle has created a draft guideline for Learning Objects, and is working with industry experts and influencers to refine the guideline and obtain industry support. This would permit:

- Learning Objects to play freely across multiple education server platforms.
- Learning Objects to be presented via multiple instructional design environments.
- Learning Object brokers to provide standard retrieval and routing services.

By providing online education standards leadership, Oracle can:

- provide the core technology upon which online education is based;
- enable a wealth of online education content development that is playable over the Web; and
- further stimulate online education demand by enabling the development and delivery of a higher quality of content, Learning Objects.

New capabilities of OLA

The OLA product would include a richer set of capabilities than that of the OLA service:

- Course content authoring and conversion environment based on CORBA compliant Learning Objects and Oracle8 objects.
- Student assessment and tracking through standardized authoring mechanisms and course interfaces.
- Content management where multimedia course elements and instructional design are stored and manipulated independently, enabling easy reuse and adaptation.

Course content and authoring

A course content authoring environment is being developed that will enable rapid multimedia course development utilizing the Oracle Universal Server for network deployment.

Content management

The OLA product will manage content in two areas:

- Physical storage of courses and course elements in multimedia file systems, such as Oracle's Media Data Store (MDS).
- Tracking and control through Learning Objects stored in the Oracle database and supported by inherent object-based technologies. This allows OLA to control access and relationships of courses and users.

Course structure and control

Via the OLA product, Oracle Education plans to extend the Learning Objects model to a full object-based implementation, incorporating CORBA compliant object technologies as supported in Oracle Universal Server's family of products.

Course delivery

In addition to utilizing Oracle WebServer for HTML course delivery, the OLA Product will extend the range of client types and transport protocols supported for receiving and delivering courses. This can potentially provide leverage for Oracle Media Net, delivering courses over a variety of network types to a variety of multimedia clients, including the NC (NetworkComputer).

Content from A to Z

OLA is an 'open' system allowing content providers to choose authoring tools and utilities necessary to develop content for OLA: a basic authoring system for courseware development, as well as templates and specialized tools for course developers. This not only enables students to receive a wider variety of education, but also provides a marketplace for customer-developed education content. In other words, as students, customers can benefit from using OLA; they can also reap financial rewards from providing content for others to use.

In the short term, OLA content will comprise Oracle and Alliance Partner CBT courses which have been converted to run on the Internet. OLA CBT courses test student skills along the way, with interactive questions that give immediate feedback. Also, features such as online help, glossaries and indexes provide students with additional support. Soon OLA will provide processes to convert other Oracle training, including instructor-led and Oracle Channel training, as well as the availability of a process to convert any content – text, audio or video – to run on OLA.

Contact details

Web: ola.oracle.com

DLE, Distance Learning Environment

A leading provider of distance learning and computer-based training technologies, Pathlore Software, launched its Distance Learning Environment (DLE) in 1997 (see Figure 4.7). With DLE, Pathlore has created an open systems standard which unites both self-paced and virtual classroom training. It also supports the delivery of multimedia instruction over an organization's existing network infrastructure.

DLE is an architecture specifically designed to support the network delivery of both self-paced and virtual classroom training. It provides the open, integrated strategy demanded by today's competitive business, uses existing networks to train large numbers of employees simultaneously and at a cost significantly below traditional training methods. At the heart of the DLE architecture is the capability for network delivery of computer-

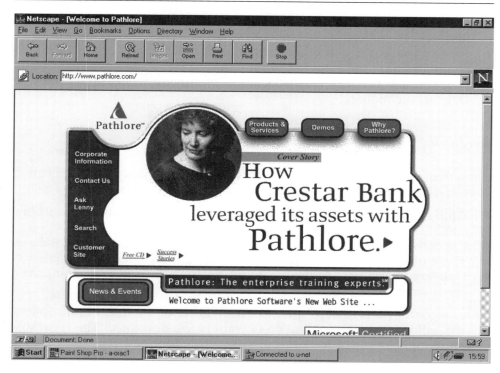

Figure 4.7   Distance Learning Environment (DLE)

based training using the Internet, intranets and other client/server networks. In addition, networks can now deliver self-paced instruction combined with instructor-led video broadcast events, often known as the virtual
classroom, to the student desktop, and all without specialized videoconferencing equipment.

DLE supports a variety of technologies, including chat-rooms, electronic
whiteboards, audioconferencing and videoconferencing. By merging both
self-paced and virtual classroom training, students and their instructors no
longer need to be on the same physical campus. With DLE, the company
network is now the campus and the classroom is each student's desktop.
Three main features make this architecture different from all other training
software currently available:

● DLE is a complete distance learning environment which unifies training
   application services such as authoring, student administration,
   computer-managed instruction (CMI) and interactive multimedia using
   standard relational database technology, and DLE incorporates the use
   of both self-paced and virtual classroom instructional technology.

- DLE is designed to deliver instruction to the company enterprise over networks including the Internet, intranets and client/server networks.
- Among the features of DLE is a platform-independent approach which eliminates the need to re-author courseware when an organization chooses new delivery networks, such as moving from client/server to Internet technology.

Architectural model

The architectural model for DLE is divided into three layers: Application Services, Executive Services and Delivery Services:

- **Application Services**: consists of a set of software tools used by authors, administrators and students.
- **Executive Services**: manages data objects in a relational database. These objects include courseware, student scoring and multimedia.
- **Delivery Services**: delivers online instruction over a company's client/server network or the Internet.

Course content and media are stored in DLE as platform-independent objects, allowing presentation on a variety of desktops. This portable design eliminates concerns regarding when to adopt new technology, such as Network Computers or NetPCs.

With DLE, Pathlore Software is delivering a foundation, not just a product, which manages all aspects of network-delivered learning. By adopting the Distance Learning Environment, any organization can implement distance learning using the most appropriate virtual classroom and CBT technologies. Pathlore has already released two DLE-enabled products: Phoenix Internet and Phoenix for Windows. All Phoenix distance learning products integrate enterprise delivery, authoring, administration and computer-managed instruction (CMI).

Phoenix Internet and Phoenix for Windows, however, were designed and developed from the DLE architectural model. Phoenix for Windows is targeted at the client/server enterprise training market, while Phoenix Internet is targeted at the organizational intranet and Internet markets. While the Pathlore name is new, the company has nearly 20 years' experience in the requirements of delivering centrally administered online training: through both the development of CBT products, and implementing services provided by the company's Professional Services Group.

Contact details

Web: www.pathlore.com

TopClass

TopClass is a software program designed to manage the delivery of instruction via the Web or a corporate intranet (see Figure 4.8). It was developed at the University College Dublin, Ireland, and is distributed by WBT Systems. TopClass was originally called WEST (Web Educational Support Tools) but has now been renamed. Although TopClass can be used with any communication network that uses TCP/IP, it is most frequently used on the Web.

TopClass creates an environment to provide enabling tools for the creation, delivery and management of training over the Web. It emulates the instructor-led environment of personalized and supported training by providing bulletin boards for course notices, e-mail for submission and correction and conference forum areas for discussion groups. It also offers the instructor the facility to take standard courses and tailor them for each student on a dynamic basis depending on the student's progress. TopClass emulates the instructor-led environment of personalized and supported training by providing:

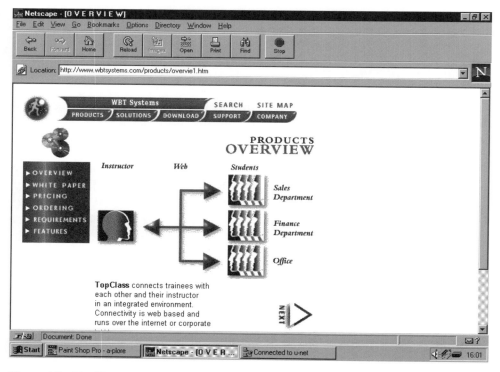

Figure 4.8   TopClass

- Bulletin board systems for course announcements.
- E-mail for submitting course exercises, allowing instructors to correct submissions and returning the results back to the student.
- Automated grading of exercises with multiple question types.
- Conference forum areas for discussion groups, allowing students and instructors to collaborate.
- A facility to customize standard course material to each student's needs and progress.

TopClass uses a central database to store and manage all information on users, classes, courses, submissions, and so on. It manages the information for each course. The TopClass server maintains a current record of the students, and the assigned tutors, classes and course material. This, together with the built-in conferencing and messaging system, makes TopClass a fully supported and personalized learning environment.

Administrators have their own interface which allows the management of the environment, including classes, courses and students. They can assign instructors and create and maintain courses. Instructors can manage classes, courses, class announcements and assign materials, create and edit courses, correct submitted coursework and perform automated course testing. Students can register for courses, send and receive messages to and from instructors, as well as discussing issues and any problems with the instructor through the conferencing facility.

System requirements

To operate your own training environment using TopClass, it is necessary to either purchase a computer system to be used as a Web server or develop a collaborative relationship with an agency that has a Web server which will permit the installation of the TopClass server software. Obviously, access to the Internet is also required. Decisions will also need to be made about the purchase of licences for using TopClass. Licences can either be obtained through the purchase of permanent licences, an annual subscription or an annual fee.

Contact details

Web: www.wbtsystems.com

CBTCampus

CBTCampus (see Figure 4.9), from CBT Systems, is a powerful new training and learning environment which enables you to deliver training wherever and however it's needed, whether running live across the Internet or across a local area network (LAN). CBTCampus combines ease of use with great flexibility for both students and administrators in one integrated environment.

For managers and administrators, CBTCampus provides a simple drag-and-drop interface, making it easy to provide training to employees wherever they are, as well as to record their progress and test results. Managers can also process students' requests for additional training courses. You may also include other training material in the system, such as courseware developed by your organization or from other vendors, presentations or materials for instructor-led training courses. No matter which method you choose to take a course, from a CD, a LAN or over the Internet, CBTCampus delivers the same consistent interface for all registration activities and for all CBT Systems courseware. With CBTCampus, you can take courses via the Internet, a corporate intranet, your hard disk, a CD or a LAN. And

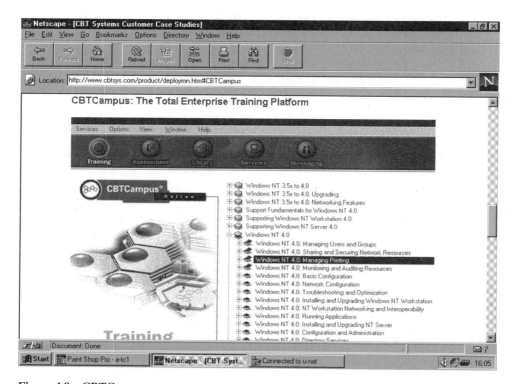

Figure 4.9   CBTCampus

if you've been working offline, you can easily replicate your offline and online records, so you know exactly how much progress you've made.

CBTCampus is robust (full transaction recovery is built in), scalable and modular, allowing you to choose which parts of the system you require. For example, if you use only Web deployment, then you needn't worry about the other components. The system's platform independence means that all courses can be stored on most Web server and LAN server platforms, and that courses can be run on most major client-side platforms (Windows 3.x, Windows 95, Windows NT, and OS/2), and through a browser using a browser plug-in.

Components of CBTCampus

- **CBTCampus Server**. Tracks the relationship among data such as: students' names, ID codes, progress, test results and details of available curricula and courses. You can have several CBTCampus servers in various locations. This arrangement can be most beneficial if you have autonomous learning centres around a country or the globe.
- **CBTCampus Course Server**. Either a Web or LAN server is used to store the courses. You can also have more than one course server in various locations, to optimize performance.
- **CBTCampus Administration Package**. The software application (usually installed on the training administrator's computer) allows for the registering of students, tracking their progress, making courses available and carrying out other administrative tasks. This is a secure, password-protected environment.
- **CBTCampus Student Environment**. Here, the student can study details of the curricula and courses available, take a course online, take tests, request additional courses from the administrator and download courses to a hard disk drive or to floppy disks. The student environment is also secure and password-protected.

The campus tour

For students, CBTCampus offers a single intuitive interface that reflects the structure of a virtual campus. The student can use any or all of the five centres:

- Training Center
- Assessment Center
- Library
- Services Center
- Messaging Center.

These Centers give students and their managers access to a range of facilities, allowing them to plan their study programmes, take courses online, download courses, request courses from the administrator and take tests. Students can switch easily between Centers to carry out different tasks.

The Training Center

The Training Center lists the courses available for the student to take online. These courses have been installed by the training administrator and are accessible by the student. The training administrator can give individual students access to certain courses. Alternatively, the administrator can load self-registration courses, to which students obtain access by themselves. The different Centers in CBTCampus share a certain amount of functionality. For example, it is possible to see a list of available courses in both the Training Center and the Library. Similarly, students can launch a course from a number of Centers. This gives students greater flexibility, as they can access information from a number of different points.

To take a course, the student selects it and clicks the Take Course button. The course is then launched and the student can begin. Selecting the course title and clicking the Progress button allows the student to check their progress through the course. A progress report opens, detailing the units that the student has already completed. If a student would rather not run the course from the network, they can select it and click the Download button. Courses can be downloaded to a local hard disk drive or to floppy disks. This means the student can study from a remote location without the costs associated with accessing a remote network by modem. Downloading the course to a laptop or to floppy disks allows the student to take the course home or on the road.

The Assessment Center

When students want to test their knowledge after completing a course or curriculum, they switch to the Assessment Center. To take a course test in the Assessment Center, the student selects the course and clicks the Take Test button. A curriculum test is made up of questions from each course in that curriculum. To take a curriculum test, the student selects the curriculum and clicks the Take Test button. Many students will use the Assessment Center to take pre-tests. Pre-tests may be taken before studying a course to help students assess their knowledge of the material. If a student scores well in the pre-test, for example, they may decide to take a more advanced course instead.

The Library

In the Library, the student sees a list of study material available. This list can include CBT Systems courses, non-CBT Systems courses, custom curricula and additional training material (such as presentations, course handouts, administrative documents and instructor-led material). The list includes not only the titles that the administrator has made available to the student, but also features the full list of titles in the CBT Systems library. Different icons next to the titles are used to distinguish between courses that are available to take online and those that are not.

Below the main window are buttons which the student can use to carry out a variety of tasks. For example, if the student sees a course on the list which is relevant to their study but has not been made available, the student can select the course and click the Course Request button. A form then opens in which the student gives details of the course request, including the preferred delivery method of the course. When the student completes this form, it is sent electronically to the training administrator, who can view and process all student requests from within one window. This feature helps administrators keep their library up-to-date with relevant courseware.

By clicking the course Info button, students can see detailed information about the course, including the topics covered, the number of hours of study that are entailed, and so on. Students can view the courses by curriculum, as well as in a full list of courses. This information helps students to plan their study, as they can clearly see which courses are related and those that are named for a given certification. Additionally, students may expand any curriculum to see the courses it contains. To see the relationship between courses and curricula in the Library, the student clicks the Catalog button. This opens the CBT Systems catalogue, which clearly illustrates, using hypertext links, how courses and curricula are interrelated. This catalogue is a useful tool for planning a study programme.

The Services Center

Several functions are available to students in the Services Center. The first is replication. When students work offline, their progress information is stored on their hard disk. When they work online, their progress is continuously updated and stored on the CBTCampus server. Students can use the Services Center to replicate and thereby update their progress stored on CBTCampus offline, with their progress stored on CBTCampus online. Also in the Services Center, students can download courses to their hard disk or to floppy disks, if this functionality has been given by the administrator. For example, they can change their personal details, including name and password; switch off toolbars and graphics; save the Center they used last, so their next CBTCampus session will open with that Center; change their cache size; and choose to view courses by curriculum.

The Messaging Center

In the Messaging Center, students can read information from the notice-board. The noticeboard is created by the administrator, so it is custom-made to suit the needs of the organization. It is HTML-based for easy navigation, and it can contain links to one or more Web sites. For example, by clicking the CBT Systems Info button, students can connect to the CBT Systems corporate Web site, where they can obtain course and product information. In the future, there will be other features, including e-mail, connection to an organization's own electronic noticeboard, and news-group and chat facilities.

CBTCampus Administration

CBTCampus Administration can be accessed only by a training administra-tor, which could be an HR staff member, a department manager or the training administrator. This tool allows the administrator to carry out a broad range of tasks, including:

- managing multiple CBTCampus servers;
- loading courses;
- batch registering large numbers of students;
- registering new students individually;
- removing obsolete student details;
- setting minimum pass levels;
- adding and removing course details from the system;
- setting students' passwords, as well as the administrator's own password;
- arranging students into study groups;
- granting individual students and study groups access to certain courses;
- creating custom curricula;
- granting individual students and study groups access to certain curric-ula;
- enabling or disabling features of the student environment;
- customizing the interface text of the student environment;
- running reports on students' progress;
- creating information to be displayed on the noticeboard in the Messag-ing Center;
- replicating student progress;
- converting existing CBT Systems WINTRACS and PCM data; and
- viewing and processing student course requests.

The administration and delivery system is an enterprise-wide tool that allows the administration of courses on both Web server and LAN servers. The benefit to the administrator is that he or she can manage the entire world-wide courseware library from a single site.

CBTCampus administration offline

Students may sometimes want to use CBTCampus in locations where they can't access the network, such as at home, at a remote office or when travelling. When students work offline, no information can be obtained from CBTCampus directly. They can, however, still use some of the features of CBTCampus, provided they download the course(s) they want to work with before they go offline. In the offline environment, students can take a course that is installed on their hard disk, or take course tests from courses that are installed on their hard disk. Upon completion of the courses, students can use the Services Center to replicate their progress stored offline with their progress stored on CBTCampus online.

CBTCampus configuration

You can configure CBTCampus differently to meet the needs of your organization. Here are five examples in which CBTCampus can be configured:

- Web configuration;
- LAN configuration;
- Web and LAN configuration;
- online and offline configuration;
- multiple CBTCampus servers configuration.

System requirements

To run CBTCampus, you need the following components: a server on which to install the CBTCampus server application; and a LAN server and/or a Web server to store the courseware.

Contact details

Web: www.cbtsys.com

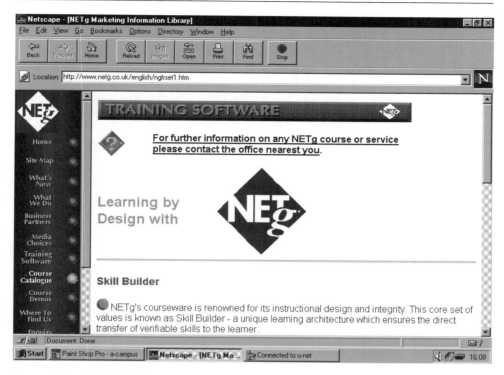

Figure 4.10   NETg SkillVantage Manager and Library

NETg SkillVantage Manager and Library

As one of the pioneers of multimedia training solutions employing the highest standard of instructional design, NETg (see Figure 4.10) is now among those few companies leading the field in harnessing the power of intranets and extranets to deliver its library of interactive courseware to customers. Corporate intranets offer the Internet's rich infrastructure for communicating, sharing information, distributing digital content and producing interactive applications in a cost-effective manner. Intranets offer the same accessibility to information, ease of use and platform independence. The only difference is that intranets are protected, and can only be accessed by authorized personnel within your organization.

NETg course delivery formats

NETg delivers instructional content via intranets in three major formats: Course Download, Learning Object Download and Active Content.

Course Download format

The Course Download format enables the learner to work offline, loading the whole course on to their PC over the intranet. The course arrives on the PC as a single, compressed, self-extracting, self-installing file. Once the file is downloaded on the PC, the user executes the file and the course installs itself. Local execution frees-up telephone lines, ensures the learner receives uninterrupted, high-level course performance (without the distraction of slow page displays and poor response time), and provides access to the course at any time, be it at home or while travelling.

Other advantages of this format are that learners have immediate access to courses as they become available; handling and administration of physical boxes and media are eliminated; and the learner can download the courseware from your intranet at their convenience. The Content Player plug-in supports all the user interactions and simulations necessary for effective instruction without requiring the learner to have a 32-bit operating system such as Windows 95 installed. The Course Download format is the easiest way for computer-based training vendors to utilize intranet technology. For those organizations where everyone has access to high-bandwidth connections, Full Course Download can be an effective solution. NETg's entire Skill Builder library is currently available in this Course Download format.

Learning Object Download format

While the Course Download format provides effective learning solutions within high bandwidth, stable intranet environments, the Learning Object Download format aims to counter the problems of providing interactive training within lower bandwidth, erratic network environments. Even companies with high-speed networks often have a percentage of remote or mobile employees who access the network through slower, less reliable connections. This deployment option is unique to NETg, offering training over the intranet which incorporates extensive use of simulations, user interactions and robust testing and tracking.

The Learning Object Download format divides a course into a collection of learning objects. Each learning object consists of a topic as defined in the course map for the course. Learners can load some or all of a course's learning objects to their PC. In this way, students can select those portions of a course they need, when they need them, and conserve bandwidth, which ensures quick and efficient downloading. This format offers all the benefits of the Course Download format, with the added advantages of minimizing disk space utilization and download times. This means the difference between a PC being tied up for a few minutes, as opposed to, at worst, 1.5–2 hours. Learning Object Download format offers the ability to begin learning as soon as the first requested topic has downloaded. This allows users to start learning in as little as two minutes, as further requested topics download in the background, even within lower bandwidth connections, such as 28.8 modems.

Recovery from download disruptions is also minimized. If you lose your connection in the last five minutes of loading a full course, you have to start again from scratch. With object loading, all previously loaded objects remain secure and, at worst, the learner experiences a minute or two of repeat activity. Another important benefit associated with the Learning Object Download format is the truly effective use of time it offers the learner. NETg courseware comes complete with Precision Learning technology. Precision Learning offers the learner a unique optional pre-assessment. The results of this assessment identify precisely those course objects that need to be learned, in the form of a Precision Learning Track. This eliminates time that would have been wasted going over old ground. Precision Learning allows the learners to customize the course to suit their specific needs. The course player (which only needs to be loaded once for all courses) is capable of determining and identifying for the user the course's learning objects which are loaded on a PC.

Learning Object Download format will run on Windows 3.1, Windows 95, Windows NT 3.5× and NT 4.0. No upgrade of hardware or software is required.

Active Content format

The Active Content format is computer platform independent, so you can access courses from Mac, UNIX, Windows 95 and Windows NT workstations. NETg's Active Content format training uses standard Internet formats and is playable by standard Web browsers without the need of a proprietary player. This saves disk space on the student's PC and provides a consistent interface between the training and other Web-based applications. The Active Content format requires high bandwidth for fast response time. Future technology developments will improve the bandwidth-hungry nature of this format. However, if your intended training audience does not have access to high-speed connections, NETg's Learning Object Download format is a more suitable deployment option. Active Content Download also does not cater for the need to work offline.

Learner management

For successful WBT, there is a need for systems to contain robust student management capabilities for managing student access to courseware, and for reporting student activity and results. This information is vital to ensuring and proving that business objectives are being accomplished with a technology-delivered learning programme. NETg has capitalized on the features offered within intranets, extranets and the Internet to provide quality interactive instruction, skills assessment and learning plan management applications to suit your organization. Their approach supports clients' particular course usage, reporting considerations and desired level of administrative control. NETg's education management software, Skill-Vantage Manager, means that utilizing multiple deployment options doesn't have to mean more administration or loss of control capabilities.

Web SkillVantage Library

Web SkillVantage Library offers access to a repository of interactive Skill Builder instruction and skill assessment, managed by software that works with your Web server. This software dynamically generates Web pages to simplify Web site management, as courses are added and removed from your server. Using a Web browser such as Netscape Navigator or Microsoft Internet Explorer, learners can:

- navigate through a catalogue of installed learning resources from NETg;
- view course descriptions;
- view course maps of Units, Lessons and Topics;
- download complete courses;
- select and download learning objects;
- play active content-based courses; and
- record assessment results.

Currently, the Web SkillVantage Library manages NETg Skill Builder courses. Future developments will support the integration of courses from other suppliers and with other learning information management systems.

Web SkillVantage Manager

Web SkillVantage Manager shares the same interface as the Web, using a standard Web browser. It simplifies the administration involved in maintaining courseware libraries and learner information management systems, providing clients with learning plan development and tracking software. Wherever a learner chooses to take training, SkillVantage Manager will ensure his/her training records are updated centrally.

SkillVantage Manager is an open system, supporting the use of third-party courseware in addition to NETg's extensive library. Learners can:

- create and edit their own user account;
- create and update individual learning plans from a Web SkillVantage Library and/or pre-defined curricula;
- track progress on their individual learning plan;
- record, maintain and view reports or assessments;
- view reports on course usage;
- launch interactive learning and Precision Learning assessment software;
- download courses from their individual learning plan;
- view course maps from their individual learning plan;
- select and download learning objects from their individual learning plan; and
- play active content-based courses from their individual learning plan.

Administrators can:

- create and edit user accounts;
- create and update curricula in a Web SkillVantage Library;
- assign learning plans and curricula to users and groups of users;
- view reports on course usage; and
- incorporate configuration information for non-NETg provided courses.

Contact details

Web: www.netg.com

Symposium

Centra Software's Symposium is billed as the first enterprise solution for live group training, self-paced learning and comprehensive knowledge management via the Web (see Figure 4.11). Designed to meet the needs of corporate training organizations, Symposium enables timely delivery of mission-critical information using an intranet and a multimedia PC. Symposium provides a structured online environment combining live, instructor-led training with just-in-time, self-paced learning and asynchronous communication in one integrated browser-based interface.

Accessed through popular Web browsers, Symposium's online delivery environment simulates a live classroom experience with functions for synchronized viewing of multimedia content, real-time audio, text chat and shared whiteboard. The Body Language facility lets participants raise their hands, respond yes or no, and provide instant feedback to the group on the pace and comprehension of the material being presented. All interactions are represented in Symposium's graphical Class List, including names of

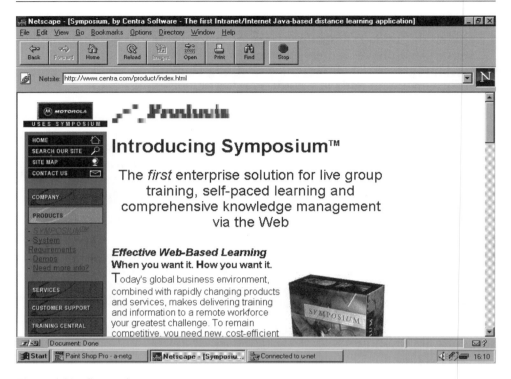

Figure 4.11   Symposium

participants in the online session. Symposium extends this live, online learning experience with capabilities for breakout sessions, role-plays, labs, group-enabled CBT and Web Safaris, allowing instructors to guide participants to relevant content on the Web during group discussions.

With Symposium the learning continues even after the live course ends. It includes capabilities for self-paced CBT, moderated and free-form threaded discussion groups and offline access to instructors, subject experts, chat logs, previous lessons and other participants. Centra's Symposium Course Builder makes developing and delivering your online course fast and easy. Simply import your new or existing multimedia training material – presentation slides, CBT, video and HTML – into the course sequencer. Use Centra's Choreography feature to customize the structure and control of the online session to meet your learning objectives.

Remote Registration and course administration features allow participants to browse course offerings and materials in advance. Instructors and course developers can use Symposium's registrar function to assign access rights and manage the distribution of materials prior to the online session.

A built-in Quiz Designer provides skills assessment and tracking capabilities.

System requirements

Symposium consists of a Web-based server and browser application for
instructor and participants. The product is hardware independent, requiring no special purpose hardware. Centra supports industry-standard
Windows platforms; other platforms are currently being tested. Each Symposium server supports up to 50 simultaneous users. These users can be
engaged in a live class, viewing material in self-paced mode or participating
in asynchronous learning modules. To deliver a high-performance, highly
interactive real-time learning environment, Symposium has the following
requirements.

Instructor and participant

- Hardware: Pentium 90 MHz (or better); Windows 95 or NT; 16 MB
  RAM; 800 × 600 × 256 colour display; speakers, microphone; 30 MB
  free disk space plus sufficient space for all course content.
- Web software: Netscape Navigator; Netscape Communicator; Microsoft
  Internet Explorer.

Symposium server

- Hardware: Pentium 200 MHz; Windows NT 4.0 Server, 64 MB RAM;
  350 MB free disk space plus sufficient space for all course content.
- Web software: Netscape Enterprise Server; Netscape FastTrack Server;
  Microsoft Internet Information Server.

Contact details

Web: www.centra.com

LOIS, Learning Organization Information System

One of the best-known systems is KnowledgeSoft's LOIS – Learning Organization Information System (see Figure 4.12). LOIS is 'knowledge management' software which lets you co-ordinate the learning process, as well as
monitor, measure and modify the skills and abilities of your organization to

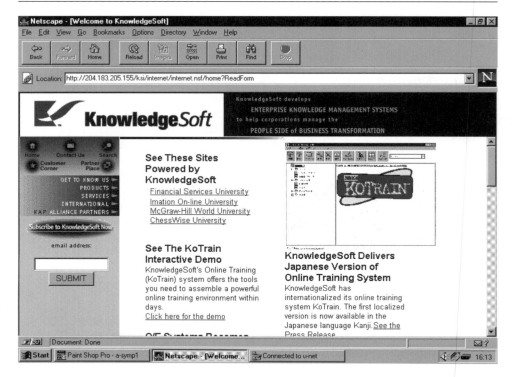

Figure 4.12   Learning Organization Information System (LOIS)

develop knowledge as a corporate asset. LOIS Version 3.0 is browser-based to allow any user on any desktop to access an array of information – course schedules, outlines, career plans and transcripts – using a Web browser. It comprises three main modules: Competency Management System, Training Management System and the Assessment System.

Competency Management System

The Competency Management System of LOIS identifies the difference between the skills you need to achieve business objectives and the skills you have. It helps you to plan effectively your training programme to avoid learning activities that don't fit your business model and waste your training investment. Features of the Competency Management System include:

- **Job Skills Database:** classified by organization, departments, job profiles or individual job roles.

- **Identifying Skills Gaps:** skills gaps are identified based on those which your company specifies for each job profile.
- **Curriculum Maps:** the module generates performance-based curricula of various learning events which are designed to eliminate skills gaps.
- **Career Plans:** managers and associates can work together to do periodic career planning using a web browser to determine what skills are required to move to a new job profile.
- **Reporting:** reports that can be generated by the Competency Management System for budget forecasting, career planning and skill charting include:
  - Organization Career Gap Analysis
  - Individual Skill Gap Analysis
  - Learner Profiles by Department
  - Periodic Training Plans
  - Budgets Required to Achieve Career Development Goals
  - Individual Career Development Plans
  - Curriculum Reports.
- **Budget Forecasts:** as a result of the career planning process, the Competency Management System generates budget forecasts to illustrate the financial investment required by each department to achieve its training objectives.
- **Updating Learner Profiles:** assessment modules integrate with the Competency Management System to update each learner's profile as new skills are achieved.
- **Skills Queries:** specific skills can be identified when special work teams are being assembled.
- **Historical Data:** this module captures the historic data you need to negotiate volume discounts if you purchase training from external sources, offering an easily measurable Return On Investment (ROI).
- **Certifications:** the Competency Management System tracks certification and re-certification programmes, providing a solid process for meeting ISO 9000 requirements and other TQM measurements.

Training Management System

LOIS embraces the idea that not all learning happens in the classroom. Learning may happen through a variety of learning events. This module offers a logistics planner and a content manager for complex learning programmes.

- **Electronic Course Catalog**. It all begins with an electronic catalogue of learning events: your 'content well'. The following list identifies some activities described as learning events:

- public seminars
- CBT
- books and periodicals
- video tapes
- instructor-led training
- conferences
- university degree programmes
- on-the-job training
- self-paced training
- certificate programmes
- journal and trade articles
- company-specific training activities.

With all company-sanctioned activities maintained in your learning events database, a LOIS administrator can schedule a variety of learning events based on course popularity and demand. The content, as an electronic course catalogue, can be viewed online or printed.

- **Registration Over The Web**. Learners can search the electronic catalog and pre-register for any events over the intranet or Internet.
- **Automatic Confirmations**. LOIS generates an automatic confirmation report when a student is enrolled which can be faxed or e-mailed to the attendee, a supervisor or both. A map to the training location is also available.
- **Wait Lists and Enrolment Data**. Waiting lists are maintained for classes that are full to highlight a need for more offerings of popular courses. It encourages intelligent scheduling based on demand.
- **Enrolment Prompts**. The module also prompts administrators with 'minimum required' and 'maximum allowed' signals to cancel low enrolment classes and redistribute resources or to avoid overbooking.
- **Departmental Bill-Backs and Invoicing**. LOIS generates departmental bill-back reports so that course fees can be charged to the appropriate work areas and it integrates with popular accounting software for invoicing external customers.
- **Instructor Database**. A database of instructor qualifications allows a LOIS administrator to make appropriate instructor assignments when building the schedule of events.
- **Search Capabilities**. Administrators can search courses by class name, by scheduled dates and by company. They can search the learner database by name, telephone number and other company identification tags.
- **Learner Transcripts**. The Training Management System maintains transcripts on each learner. A learner profile is updated each time an associate enrols in a learning event. Transcripts are updated each time a person successfully completes a learning event.
- **Class Enrolment Reports**. Prior to an instructor-led course, LOIS generates an attendance record to show the instructor who should be in the class.

- **Course Completion Certificates**. After class, LOIS automatically generates a course completion certificate for each student who has successfully completed the course.

Assessment System

Imagine having the capacity to administer a skills assessment to your entire workforce by putting it on your intranet and sending an e-mail asking them to complete it. The staff completes the assessment using a Web browser and submits answers which automatically update the LOIS database. Features include:

- **Create Tests and Surveys**. Your administrators, managers and senior staff have the ability to create tests and surveys online. These assessments can be completed by segmented groups of your workforce or by everyone.
- **Objective and Subjective Measurements**. This module offers both objective and subjective measurement options. Objective measurements are tests or observations which determine someone's actual ability to perform specific activities. Subjective measurements capture a person's own perception of his or her skill level.
- **Kirkpatrick's Level 1 Assessments**. The Kirkpatrick Level 1 to Level 4 Assessments provide valuable feedback on many variables related to your training activities. The results of Level 1 assessments can: provide recommendations for course modifications; point out facility-related distractions to learning; generate constructive feedback on instructor abilities; and identify course materials that need upgrades.
- **Pre- and Post-Course Level 2 Assessments**. Kirkpatrick's Level 2 Assessments relate to pre- and post-course tests which can be administered before and after each learning event to ensure that learning has occurred.
- **Constructing Level 3 and Level 4 Assessments**. The Kirkpatrick Level 3 and Level 4 Assessments are more complex and are discussed in the KnowledgeSoft methodology.
- **Refresher Hints**. This module also identifies areas where a learner's knowledge is weak and areas where it is strong following post-course assessments and prompts the user with study hints.
- **On-line Surveys**. You have the unique ability to create instant surveys for the workforce, customers or vendors. Surveys also can be administered to customers through kiosk machines in company lobbies or other locations. Survey data is collected in a database for future analysis.
- **Certification Assessments**. Certification assessments can be maintained and administered in the Skills Assessment System to ensure a secure and manageable certification process.

The Assessment System provides these key management reports:

- Pass–fail rates by various categories
- Learner reaction reports
- Specific survey results
- Certification achievements
- Statistical analysis on post-course tests
- Standard deviation scores.

LOIS Foundation

The base of each of the three modules is the LOIS Foundation. This provides the database engine and back-end logic behind the integration of all LOIS modules. It is the core component of the LOIS system and provides the database schema for this new Web-based training management system.

LOIS Virtual University

LOIS Virtual University (LVU) is an extension of the LOIS suite which has been enhanced for online learning. You can create your own Corporate University with your own courses, your own instructors, your own course materials and campus store merchandise. The LVU system can be customized with your logos and ad banners.

System requirements

- Server side: Netscape Enterprise Server 2.0; Netscape LiveWire 1.0; Oracle 7.1 or higher.
- Operating system: Windows NT; UNIX.
- Client side: Netscape Navigator 2.0 or higher; Internet Explorer 3.0 or higher.

Contact details

Web: www.knowledgesoft.com

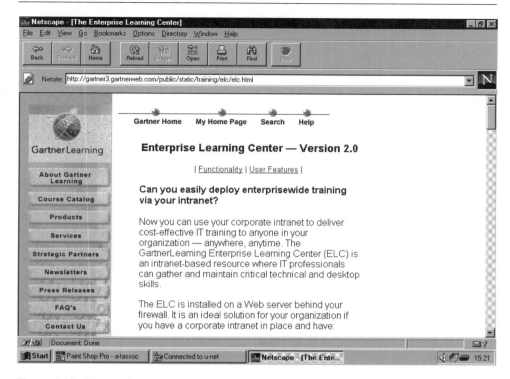

Figure 4.13   Enterprise Learning Centre

Enterprise Learning Centre

Gartner Group Learning, the IT training unit of Gartner Group Inc., has recently launched the Enterprise Learning Centre (ELC), an intranet-based resource for IT professionals and end-users to gain and maintain critical IT technical and desktop skills (see Figure 4.13). The ELC enables enterprises to deliver training directly to the desktop while eliminating Internet security, bandwidth and data confidentiality concerns. Additionally, the ELC provides tools for skills management, course and organization administration, and performance support through robust testing, tracking, reporting, course catalogue, organization management and full-text search functions.

The ELC offers skills management resources for IT professionals and end-users on a wide variety of subjects, including Lotus Notes, Microsoft Office 97, Oracle, Sybase, Informix, client/server, Unix, Java and SAP R/3. The ELC is installed on a Web server behind a client's firewall. Like Gartner's Internet Learning Centre, the ELC offers distinguishable features such as no downloading or waiting, no special configuration or memory requirements, as well as increased functionality and ease of enterprise-wide installations without requiring access to, or reliance on, the Internet. The ELC offers tracking, administrative tools and testing. Additional features include:

- Reporting. Allows administrators to monitor course usage, evaluate user progress, track costs and measure return on investment by generating reports at the user, organization and department levels.
- Searching. Users can conduct full-text searches across all courses within the ELC library. Students can then link to specific screens of instruction that match their needs. This provides performance, support and true 'just enough', just-in-time learning.
- Personal Home Page. Generated when students enrol in their first course, this feature creates a 'personal catalogue' of courses in which the student is enrolled. The Personal Home Page contains links to the course menu, course test and course bookmark.
- Bookmarking. Allows a user to mark a specific page or location within a course to enable later reference to that page, thus providing greater flexibility in accessing only the training that is needed and when it is most convenient.

System requirements

Installation of an ELC requires an Internet browser, Microsoft Windows NT 4.0 server, an intranet and a Pentium based PC server. Additionally, Gartner Group Learning will provide Microsoft SQL Server 6.5 and Verity Information Search Server 97 upon request.

Contact details

Web: gartner3.gartnerweb.com/public/static/training/elc/elc.htm

Librarian

Asymetrix Learning Systems has just launched Librarian (see Figure 4.14), an enterprise-wide learning system, designed to consolidate and streamline learning and training. It serves as a centralized management system for all courseware, including online learning courses, traditional CBT titles, customized training and traditional classroom training. Asymetrix Librarian runs on a UNIX or Windows NT-based Web server with user access through a Java-enabled browser. Located at the heart of an enterprise-wide learning system, Librarian is a powerful and flexible management system

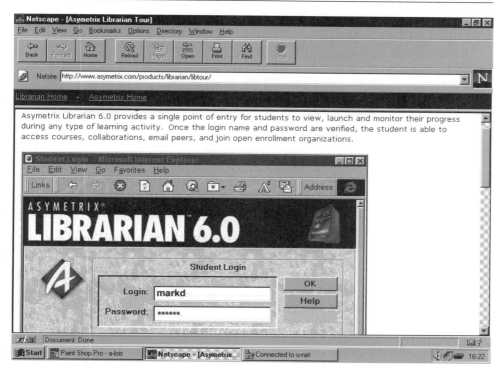

Figure 4.14   Asymetrix Librarian

which works not only with Asymetrix created courses, but also with third-party courseware.

Asymetrix Librarian is a client/server application which allows management, tracking and assessment of course materials using the Internet as a content delivery mechanism. The Librarian has been implemented on both the UNIX (Solaris) and Windows NT platforms using any Web server (HTTP 1.x, CGI 1.x) to deliver applications and course material. Data can be stored in an ODBC (2.x) compliant database management server. Clients use any Java enabled Web browser (Netscape, Internet Explorer) on any platform to access the Librarian. The client side of Librarian is implemented in the Java programming language for ease of portability and ease of client access.

The Librarian manages users and course material in the database, allowing users to take course material that has been assigned to them or open enrolment courses. The Librarian also tracks students' activity, recording scores, question answers, time taken, and so on, and providing that data to instructors in a number of reporting styles. The Librarian also has built-in e-mail facilities to allow mail to be generated at the students' completion of a course to be sent to the students' instructor and/or the students themselves.

The Librarian is based on the Asymetrix ToolBook Course Management System, but enhanced to take maximum advantage of the Internet as a medium. Librarian includes the ability to manage HTML and Java-based courses created with ToolBook II Instructor in addition to OLX-based courses such as native ToolBook files running through Asymetrix Neuron (Netscape Plug-in or ActiveX control in Microsoft Internet Explorer). Librarian incorporates all of the facilities required by learners, administrators, tutors and management:

- Learners need to be able to preview, register and enrol, access content, collaborate with tutors and review their own performance.
- Tutors want to deploy content, collaborate with learners and track class performance.
- Administrators need to be able to create and administer learning organizations, content and curricula.
- Managers need to track and measure individual, organization and programme performance.

Asymetrix Librarian provides:

- Flexibility of hierarchical organization structure; it allows online learning managers to organize users and content in whatever hierarchical structure they wish, including the mirroring of their own corporate organization.
- Flexibility of administrative roles and permissions; it provides precision granularity in assigning administrative roles and permissions. This allows online learning managers to provide departments, branch offices, workgroups and individuals with the flexibility and autonomy they need without compromising system security.
- Ability to manage third-party, legacy and offline modules; it can be used to manage third-party courseware, HTML documents, as well as offline resources such as video tapes or classroom presentations and seminars.
- Robust reporting provides powerful reporting features which enable online learning managers to determine the progress of individuals and groups, as well as the ability to obtain precision reports on a training module's effectiveness.
- Scalability through Librarian's client/server architecture being designed to scale with the growth of an organization. It can be deployed across multiple servers.

Contact details

Web: www.asymetrix.com

Chapter 5

What's currently available?
Online curriculum delivery sites

IT research firm IDC believes that adoption of Web-based training via both the Internet and corporate intranets will explode during 1998–99. Currently, some fine IT training Web sites are up and running, but much work needs to be done for the development of full-service Web sites with varied, desirable features.

Web site classifications

There are two main classifications of WBT sites: a facilitated, multi-supplier campus-style site and a single-supplier course-delivery site. The campus-style site offers features such as tutorial sessions with instructors, chatrooms to meet classmates, pre- and post-testing and more. It is a distribution centre for a variety of third-party training providers to offer their content and services. The start-up costs for the campus-style Web site are fronted by the owner of the main campus, and third-party providers pay administrative fees to offer their content on the site. Conversely, course-delivery sites offer courses and courseware from a single provider. Some course-delivery sites offer pre- and post-assessment courseware and other forms of curriculum customization.

Web-based training pricing

Pricing varies by Internet site versus intranet site. Typically intranet pricing is determined by a licence fee, normally based on the number of users, the number of titles and the duration of the contract. Internet pricing is generally on an *ad hoc* course-by-course basis; some sites offer an unlimited access annual subscription. IDC found individual course pricing to be as low as $4 and as high as $800. Because pricing is still being determined by most Web-based training providers, an average or high benchmark is not yet available. Most of the sites listed here charge a fee for the student to take a particular course, although some charge an annual subscription; but this does provide the student with unlimited access to the complete portfolio of courses on offer.

Subjects

This section outlines some examples of the numerous sites that offer training courses online over the Web. The majority of them offer courses in IT subjects (both IT applications and IT professional), but there are some that offer management and business subjects; there is even one called Enjoying Winel, as well as some that specialize in home educational courses for parents and schoolchildren.

This chapter does not outline every site offering online training today, but it does include the most well known. There is a more comprehensive listing of sites in the Appendix. Although the majority of the courses can be taken online, some training programmes can be licensed to run on the company intranet or LAN. To access these sites, you will generally need the following hardware and software:

- Pentium PC/Macintosh with at least 8MB RAM.
- Internet access, including at least a 28.8 modem.
- Netscape Navigator 3+ or Microsoft Internet Explorer 3+.

Where additional hardware or software is required, it will be outlined under the appropriate site. Additionally, some sites require you to have installed a special software program which gives you the ability to play video and/or audio files. This program is called a Plug-In and can usually be downloaded from the site if you do not already have it installed on your computer. Once again, any necessary Plug-Ins will be mentioned under the appropriate site.

Under each site I have also supplied contact information in order for you to contact the site. Please note that Web-based training is a rapidly expanding field and the typical courses outlined will probably have been added to by the time that you read this book. Finally, the descriptions of the particular sites and the facilities provided have been supplied by the sites themselves. The sites outlined in this section are:

- Microsoft Online Institute (www.microsoft.com/train_cert/html/online.htm)
- Peritas Online (www.peritas.com)
- Oracle OLA Online (ola.oracle.com)
- Gartner Group Learning (www.gglearning.com)
- Online College Oxford (olco.ocx.com)
- Logical Operations' LearnItOnline (www.learnitonline.com)

- Global Knowledge Network Mentys (www.globalknowledge.com)
- IMG WebUniversity (www.imguniversity.com)
- NIIT NetVarsity (www.niitnetvarsity.com)
- Street Technologies' Learning University (www.learninguniversity.com)
- CyberState University (www.cyberstateu.com)
- Wave Technologies' Online University (www.wavetech.com)
- DigitalThink (www.digitalthink.com)
- scholars.com (www.scholars.com)
- Training Associates (www.trainingassociates.com)
- ZD Net University (www.zdu.com)
- The Open University (www.open.ac.uk)
- CalCampus (www.calcampus.com)
- UCLA Home Education Network (www.then.com)
- Ask International (www.askintl.com)
- BT CampusWorld (www.campus.bt.com)
- NovaNET (www.nn.com)

MOLI, Microsoft Online Institute

Many of the WBT operations that are active today in the corporate market have evolved out of Microsoft's pioneering site MOLI, the Microsoft Online Institute (see Figure 5.1). During the last few months of 1997, Microsoft implemented some major changes to the way the site is accessed. Let us recap on the MOLI story.

Research carried out by Microsoft showed that of those students who were unsuccessful when taking the Sylvan Prometric accreditation exams in the USA, 80 per cent of them had never actually attended a formal, classroom-based course. In light of that fact, Microsoft began looking at ways to take the training to the individual students, rather than bringing the students to the training. They came up with the Microsoft Online Institute, a virtual campus sitting within the newly launched Microsoft Systems Network, MSN. Launched in August 1995 as part of the Windows 95 launch, MOLI offered training using distance learning material but which was supported by qualified tutors from Microsoft Authorized Technical Education Centres (ATECs). MOLI was accessible only on the Microsoft Systems Network.

MOLI was essentially a hosting site: a server holding courses delivered by established training providers, mainly from North America, but with the UK represented by Peritas. Considered a success by Microsoft, the highest number of students trained by any single ATEC during the pilot was 52 (taking the Windows NT 3.51 course from Peritas). In 1996, Microsoft decided to widen the audience and to migrate from MSN to the Web. Again, Microsoft carried out a pilot programme, with six training providers offering training programmes. The pilot went live in October 1996.

Figure 5.1   Microsoft Online Institute (MOLI)

MOLI was written by Microsoft to run on its own proprietary servers. This raised a number of issues for the participating training providers and students. Any problems associated with access to the site, no matter how trivial, had to be referred back to Microsoft's MOLI support team, not the ATECs, resulting in some delays for students. To alleviate the situation, Microsoft took the decision in September 1997 to move out of the 'Server Provider' role and hand over the service to their ATECs. Microsoft still market the MOLI service through their own Web site (www.microsoft.com/train_cert/html/online.htm). There you will find a comprehensive list of Microsoft courses available on subjects such as:

- Access
- ActiveX
- Visual FoxPro
- FrontPage
- Internet Information Server
- Visual InterDev
- Foundation Class Library
- Networking

- Systems Management Server
- SQL Server
- TCP/IP
- Visual Basic
- Visual J++
- Windows 95
- Windows 3.x/DOS
- Windows NT Server & Workstation.

Next to each course is the name of the Microsoft ATEC which supplies the course; by clicking the appropriate course, you are automatically sent to the appropriate course provider's site. Providers include ARIS/Oxford, Scholars, SEC, Training Associates and Atlas.

Contact details

Web: www.microsoft.com/train_cert/html/online.htm

Peritas Online

In developing and launching Peritas Online in 1995, one of the UK's largest IT training companies, Peritas, sought to bring the same values from the classroom to the Internet. Peritas Online provides the usual company information and news stories. Importantly though, Peritas Online has been designed to support students during their training (see Figure 5.2).

Choosing a course

Prospective students can view all the information necessary to make an informed decision about a course's suitability by looking at the relevant part of the site. This will provide information such as price, prerequisites, what to expect, availability of course exams, and so on. Having read all the material available the prospective student calls up a product interest form and books the course. The completed form is e-mailed to the online support team, and, if appropriate, credit card details are taken or an invoice raised.

Should a prospective student require more information about a course or about the workings of Peritas Online, they are at liberty to return the product interest form and request additional information. Additionally, there is a public access area available where prospective students can go to experience the way 'chat' sessions work in the online classrooms.

Once payment has been received the student is sent specifically designed

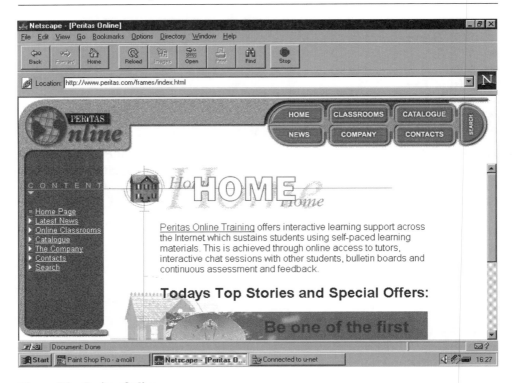

Figure 5.2   Peritas Online

distance learning materials and is advised when their tutor will be available and how assignments and exercises should be completed during the course. Training materials have mostly been either Peritas' own materials or Microsoft Press. However, at the time of writing a 'proof of concept' is being run to integrate interactive multimedia from NETg with the Peritas Online infrastructure. At their own pace, students then work through the course, conversing with their tutor and fellow students as appropriate.

The student joins a particular classroom depending on which course they are on, and is provided with a password which ensures that only authorized students can gain access to a particular classroom. Students are encouraged to use the classroom as often as necessary, with support being available eight hours each day. Students who experience problems outside of supported hours can access the classroom to review the Frequently Asked Questions section (FAQs). Should the FAQs fail to provide the necessary answer, the student can e-mail Peritas' online support who will answer, during the next period of online support.

Each week the tutor will e-mail assignments for the students to complete and e-mail back for marking. Once received, the tutor will assess the students' knowledge and respond with advice, guidance, suggestions and assistance as required. Contact between online students and course tutor provides motivational support to complete the course and instils a level of discipline for the individual. Customer feedback has shown this to be a very effective method of learning, particularly for those who want to learn at their own pace, without being tied to the speed of a classroom course, which often progresses at the speed of the slowest student.

Courses

As a shop window, Peritas Online provides details of several hundred classroom-based Peritas courses. Peritas Online itself currently has 31 online courses available in the following areas:

- Online Networking
- Online Soft Skills
- Online UNIX
- Online PC Applications
- Online PC Technical (MCSE/MCSD).

Course durations vary from two to six weeks.

Prices

Peritas Online courses range from £75 to £420. Prices exclude VAT and any exam vouchers. A number of Peritas' corporate customers have opted for a 'private' version of Peritas Online, called a Client Zone. A Client Zone provides all the facilities of Peritas Online, while adding specific additional courses and corporate communication facilities. An example of a Client Zone produced for Thames Valley Enterprise can be seen at www.peritas.con/tve. A description of the project may also be found in Chapter 6.

Contact details

Web: www.peritas.com

Oracle OLA Online

Oracle's online service OLA (see Figure 5.3) is a flexible and cost-effective training option which provides access to interactive, multimedia education through the Internet. With more than 400 training titles in the OLA

Figure 5.3   Oracle OLA Online

Library, you or your staff can receive the comprehensive training needed to keep up with a quickly changing marketplace. You can use the OLA online service to learn everything you want to know about IT. OLA makes IT training easily accessible, easy to use and cost-effective. Through partnerships with major vendors of media-based training, OLA lets you choose from the best course materials available, in either an interactive/online format or a downloadable/offline format.

The OLA online service offers a scalable education solution. The extensive course offerings are available on the service now. There is no need to implement any kind of application, and no need to develop any courseware. The administrative processes required to give your staff access are simple and straightforward.

Oracle Education is closely partnered with major vendors of media-based training to provide the widest choice of 'best-of-breed' course materials. Choosing titles from the OLA Library enables you to find the most cost-effective solution for your training needs. OLA online service features:

- personalized registered course listing;
- course and curriculum tracking;
- student forum;
- competency feedback via skills testing in selected content; and
- choice in educational solution.

The OLA range of options

OLA offers you a range of options for structuring your curriculum and reaching your training objectives:

- **Subject Libraries** offer a comprehensive, pre-packaged set of courses. They are designed to cover many aspects of a certain subject area, such as UNIX or Oracle application development. Subject Libraries are available for pre-defined sets of students and are easy to implement in your organization because they are each based on homogeneous content (one vendor, one training method, one delivery format). Subject Libraries can be used as building blocks to create a complete IT training solution. This gives the advantage of one-stop-shopping, while preserving freedom of choice among vendors and training methods.
- **Training Paths** offer a comprehensive series of courses which prepare employees for specific roles, such as Oracle DBA or Application Developer.
- **Certification Paths** offer a comprehensive series of courses which prepare a student to take assessment courses leading to formal certification as an Oracle Certified Professional.
- **Single courses** offer a pre-defined series of topics covering a certain subject. The courses follow instructional design standards, which are based on accepted theories of adult learning. The courses use a proven, effective approach involving objectives, theory, practice and summary. The courses are designed for IT professionals and have a typical duration of four to eight hours. Courses for end-users have a typical duration of four hours or less.

Courses available

OLA was developed for IT specialists, line managers and computer users who require convenient training on IT, and for IT and training managers looking to optimize their training budgets. OLA has more than 400 courses available, with more being added continuously (see Figure 5.4). Content is developed by Oracle and the leading computer-based training vendors, and covers a wide variety of Oracle-related and non-Oracle-related topics. Subjects covered include Oracle technology, database-related subjects, UNIX,

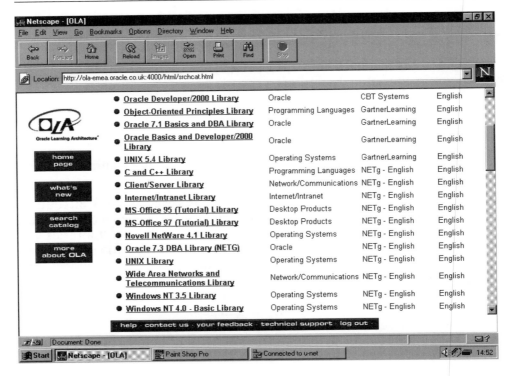

Figure 5.4   OLA courses available

client/server architecture and programming, application development tools, networking and desktop products. The most effective courses from the most experienced vendors on the most in-demand topics are available on OLA. You gain access to over 400 courses covering a wide range of IT topics, including:

- Oracle: DBA, Tools, SQL, PL/SQL
- Operating Systems: UNIX, Windows NT and Windows 95
- Novell
- Desktop Applications: MS Office, Lotus Notes
- Internet/intranet: HTML, Java.

New courses are continually being added to the OLA Library.

Multiple delivery formats

OLA courses are available in two delivery formats: online (real-time) and offline (download) courses. The format that works best for you depends on your needs and personal preferences. Online courses are easy to use since all titles are available and directly accessible and are platform independent: you can use a PC, Macintosh, workstation or Network Computer with an Internet connection to access OLA courses. Offline courses are downloaded to the student's desktop computer and are executed on that platform. These courses require some hard disk space and a Windows environment. Offline courses offer a significantly shorter connection time, which may save costs when connection time is expensive, and improved speed and performance, and higher levels of multimedia and interaction, because offline courseware is executed on the user's machine rather than on the remote server.

Alliances with leading training providers

Oracle's alliances with the best media-based training vendors bring best-of-breed training programmes to OLA. Current content alliance partners include:

- Relational Courseware (RCI)
- NETg
- CBT Systems
- PTS Learning Systems
- NIIT.

Prices

Individual-user, site or corporate licences are available for OLA.

System requirements

- PC, Macintosh, workstation or Network Computer with an Internet connection.
- A current Web browser, such as Netscape Navigator 3.0 or Microsoft Internet Explorer 3.0 or higher.
- Plug-ins required for select content.

Contact details

Web: ola.oracle.com

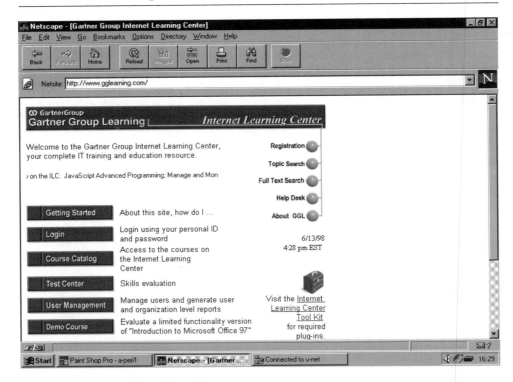

Figure 5.5   Gartner Group Learning

Gartner Group Learning

GartnerLearning's Internet Learning Centre (ILC) is a dynamic Web community where IT professionals and end-users come to learn and maintain critical IT and related skills (see Figure 5.5). Made up of real-time courses which feature questions, quizzes, interactive examples and simulated practice exercises, the Internet Learning Centre will allow you to maximize your organization's investment in technology and people. Some of the features of the ILC are:

- access to over 140 IT-related courses
- 'active' access to courses
- tracking and administrative tools
- pre- and post-test assessment
- advanced full-text search
- enterprise-wide administration
- organizational level reporting

- online student discussion forums
- online payment option for course access.

The range of courses currently available covers the latest networking tools, database management software, operating systems, desktop systems, client/server, mainframe and system development tools. The number of courses is increasing at the rate of approximately 15 per month. The ILC provides:

- Full support of value-added functionality such as tracking and administrative tools, skills analysis, continuing education programmes, customized course delivery and pre- and post-test assessment.
- Advanced full-text search within a topic and across all topics in the comprehensive Internet Learning Centre course library.
- Enterprise-wide administration and management to enable organization-level reporting of progress and test scores by individual and by course.
- Discussion forums to allow students to participate and pose questions on key training issues, interact with other users and instructors and converse with training administrators.

The GartnerLearning Internet Learning Centre is designed to exploit fully the publishing and electronic commerce capabilities of the Internet. This training delivery platform allows an immediate distribution of courses and the ability to continually update; it can reach client organizations worldwide.

GartnerLearning claims to be the first among major IT education vendors with courses on the Web. The ILC can be inspected at the Gartner Learning Web site: www.gglearning.com. There is always one full function course available for inspection at no charge.

Courses

Courses currently available cover Microsoft, Lotus, Novell, Oracle, SAP R/3, C++ Programming, Client/Server, Database Design, Informix, Object-Oriented Analysis and Design, Powerbuilder, Sybase, UNIX and Internet-related technologies including Java and JavaScript.

Prices

Prices for access to the Internet Learning Centre vary by the number of titles required and the number of people requiring access. Individual titles may be accessed by individuals at a cost of $99 for end-user and $199 for IT professionals per year. The minimum configuration corporate annual access licences start at $20 per person per course per year.

System requirements

The environment for access to the Internet Learning Centre is recommended to be no less than 28.8 modem. The ideal solution is a high bandwidth, dedicated line to the Web (i.e. 56K, T1, T3) which will serve to speed up the viewing of pages and images. It is optimized for Netscape Navigator 3.0 or above, and Microsoft Internet Explorer 3.0 or above. In addition, the ILC is greatly enhanced with the Shockwave plug-in which is freely downloadable from the Macromedia Web site (www.macromedia.com).

Contact details

Web: www.gglearning.com

Online College Oxford

Online College Oxford (OLCO) (see Figure 5.6) is the online training service from ARIS/Oxford, which has been providing IT training since 1983. ARIS/Oxford is a Microsoft ATEC and Solution Provider Partner and founding sponsor of the Institute of IT Training in the UK. As a Microsoft approved online training provider, ARIS/Oxford is able to offer an innovative, affordable route to certification.

OLCO is geared towards busy IT professionals who want to be trained to Microsoft Certified Professional (MCP) level, but who cannot attend classroom training, either because they cannot be spared from their desks, or because geography prevents them. Training is available via OLCO towards the industry standards of Microsoft Certified Systems Engineer (MCSE) and Microsoft Certified Solution Developer (MCSD).

How does it work?

At the core of each course is a self-study kit which students work through, fully supported by an online tutor. At the end of each section, a test is taken, using OLCO's own testing mechanism, delivered electronically and simulating the MCP exams. This shows the areas of understanding and highlights areas where more work is needed; the tutor then suggests work to help in these areas. Finally, students are fully trained to take the MCP exam.

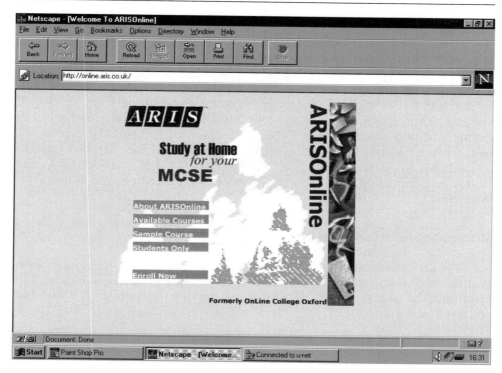

Figure 5.6   Online College Oxford

What's included?

Once students sign up for a course and are admitted to Online College, they are assigned a tutor and sent their self-study materials. The tutor is available via e-mail and through pre-arranged chat sessions to help with installation issues and any issues arising from the course itself. A 1-hour classroom chat session, open to all students currently reading each course, will be available at least every week (usually for up to three months, but this may often be extended). Additionally, up to two hours of one-to-one tutorial chat sessions will be available in total. For each course, the OLCO student will receive:

- self-study kit from Microsoft Press
- rapid, unlimited e-mail support from online tutors
- access to ARIS/Oxford Course Commentaries
- extensive testing with full e-mail feedback from tutors
- Q&A chat sessions.

Courses

Microsoft Certified Systems Engineer

MCSEs are qualified to set up and support Microsoft system software, networks and BackOffice products: the very heart of modern enterprise IT systems. The requirements to achieve MCSE status are passing four core exams and two electives (see Table 5.1). Internet Information Server 4.0 will soon be available as an elective exam for MCSE. Online training towards MCSE is also offered in the Windows NT 3.51 channel, with core exams in Supporting Windows 95, Networking Essentials and Supporting Windows 3.51.

Microsoft Certified Solution Developer

MCSDs are qualified to create real computing solutions, designing, integrating and tailoring applications to meet today's business needs. The requirements to achieve MCSD status are passing two core exams and two electives (see Table 5.2).

Contact details

Web: olco.ocx.com

Table 5.1   *MCSE courses and exams*

Course	Duration	Price	Exam
Networking Essentials	8 weeks	£349	70–58 Networking Essentials
Supporting Windows NT 4.0	16 weeks	£649	70–67 Implementing & Supporting Windows NT Server 4.0
			70–73 Implementing & Supporting Windows NT Workstation 4.0
Supporting Windows NT Server 4.0 in the Enterprise	8 weeks*	£349*	70–68 Implementing & Supporting NT 4.0 Server in the Enterprise
Hands on SQL Server 6.5	11 weeks	£349	70–26 System Administration for SQL Server 6.5
			70–27 Implementing a Database Design on SQL Server 6.5
Internetworking TCP/IP on Windows NT 4.0	8 weeks	£349	70–59 Internetworking TCP/IP on Windows NT 4.0

Final duration and price for courses with * will be confirmed when the course materials are released by Microsoft Press.

Table 5.2 *MCSD courses and exams*

Course	Duration	Price	Exam
Windows Architecture	8 weeks*	£349*	70–160 Windows Architecture I
			70–161 Windows Architecture II
Hands on SQL Server	11 weeks	£349	70–27 Implementing a Database
			Design on SQL Server
Programming with Visual Basic 5.0	11 weeks*	£349*	70–165 Developing Applications with Visual Basic 5.0

LearnItOnline

LearnItOnline is a subscription-based service from Ziff-Davis Education (formerly Logical Operations) which gives you access to ZDNet's library of online computer training courses (see Figure 5.7). The self-study courses are powered by LearnFlow plug-in technology, which delivers a realistic inter-active simulation of the software environment on your desktop, as if you are

Figure 5.7 LearnItOnline

running the actual software. LearnFlow is a proprietary technology that LearnItOnline uses to deliver audio-enhanced, simulated software training.

You can try out a tutorial free of charge by logging on to the LearnItOnline Home Page and click on Free Trial. Complete the form and when you receive your password by e-mail, return to the LearnItOnline Home Page and Login. If you like what you see, you can purchase a one-year subscription, which includes unlimited access to the library. LearnItOnline offers a way for you to streamline your time and choose only the tutorials you require. When you take their Skills Assessment for a particular course, LearnItOnline will recommend a Personal Training Plan for you based on your response. LearnItOnline will also keep track of the tutorials already taken. When you want to take the Skills Assessment again to see how far you have progressed, LearnItOnline will update your profile.

Courses

LearnItOnline's initial course offering includes tutorials covering Microsoft Office 95, Windows 95, Netscape Navigator, Internet Explorer and Office 97. Courses coming soon include Outlook 97, Word 97 Level 2 and Powerpoint 97 Advanced.

Prices

Once you have experienced the free trial, you can subscribe to LearnItOnline by going to the Home Page and clicking on Subscribe. The cost of a Charter Membership for an annual subscription is currently $29.95. This introductory price gives you unlimited access to their growing library of courses. When you subscribe to LearnItOnline, you will be asked to provide a valid credit card as well as other necessary information in order to process your payment. All transactions are encrypted and secure and you will receive an e-mail to confirm your payment.

System requirements

The requirements for using any LearnItOnline tutorial include:
- Windows 95 or 3.1
- Internet access
- Netscape Navigator 2.02 or higher or Microsoft Internet Explorer 3.01
- LearnFlow plug-in (downloadable from the LearnItOnline site).

Contact details

Web: www.learnitonline.com

Mentys

The Mentys Learning Network is Global Knowledge Network's network-based training service (see Figure 5.8). Mentys delivers competency-based, interactive training via a custom installation on a corporate intranet, or via the Internet/Web. This leading-edge delivery option provides a custom learning path and 'just-in-time' training for maximum convenience to students and managers alike.

Mentys' competency-led assessment tool – The Competence Key – evaluates an individual's knowledge and skills based against a given job profile. This helps to focus the training curriculum only on an individual's knowledge and skill gaps, saving organizations considerable time and money. Originally developed in conjunction with Canada's Software Human

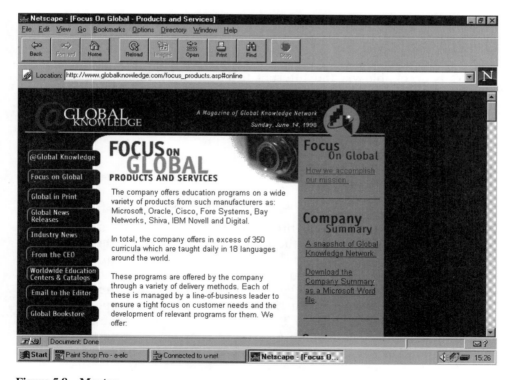

Figure 5.8   Mentys

Resource Council, Mentys is available through the Internet or corporate intranets.

Using Mentys on your corporate intranet

The Mentys Learning Network can be custom-installed on your corporate network, for access via your intranet. By installing the Enterprise Learning Server on your intranet, you can utilize all the communication capabilities supported by your network, including audio, video and multimedia. This method allows you to manage your company's training better. You can allocate courses to your employees, monitor their progress and generate reports in any style or format.

To meet your organization's specific needs, Global Knowledge Network can also provide customized solutions tailored to specific requirements. They can, for example, adapt the Competence Key to your own corporate structure, job profiles and training needs. Additionally, they can link learning solutions in the database to your training department, directly to external training providers or to your company's subject matter experts and mentors.

Using Mentys via the Internet

Mentys is accessible via the Internet to allow individuals to update their knowledge and skills. At the same time, the Competence Key feature enables individuals to carry out their own skills assessment, allowing them to monitor their own progress.

Mentys: the features

The Mentys system comprises the following features:

- **The Competence Key.** A brief and focused self-assessment is done using an online tool called the Competence Key. With the help of this tool, users can compare their current capabilities against skills their organization requires. From this competency assessment, a personalized development plan is generated which outlines the appropriate training and development curriculum to meet the user's specific needs.
- **The Learning Warehouse.** The development plan generated by the Competence Key consists of a series of courses, or professional development resources. The public Internet version of Mentys offers a large selection of technical IT courses, including C++, Visual Basic, Java, Windows 95 and NT, Client/Server Concepts, TCP/IP Architecture,

Microsoft SQL Server, Office Exchange and Database Design. For corporate intranet installation, Global can build a customized Learning Warehouse for customers which incorporates automated 'pointers' to learning resources available to client employees. These include instructor-led courses, computer-based training, reference materials, professional journals, seminars, workshops and internal subject-matter experts within the client company.

- **Electronic Conferencing.** The electronic communications forum allows for exchanges between subscribers of Global Knowledge Network's Internet services. This online interaction enables students to share ideas that benefit all subscribers.
- **Online Tutoring.** This module provides electronic access to specialized training consultants and instructors for help with various aspects of course content.

The Ministry of Education of the Government of Singapore is a major user of Mentys. In August 1996 they announced the implementation of a nation-wide knowledge delivery infrastructure known as Mentys Singapore which will equip the Singapore workforce with the skills and knowledge to meet the challenges of the 21st century.

Courses

The courses are all in the IT professional and end-user area and are broken down into four main categories: Client/Server, End User, Networking/ and Back Office. There are also two free demonstrations, but you will need to register with Mentys before using the free courses.

Prices

Prices range from $38 (Introduction to Windows 95) to $260 (Using C++ Advanced Features).

System requirements

For the Enterprise Learning Server, which can be custom-installed on your corporate network for access via your corporate intranet, you will need:

- Pentium PC
- Windows NT Server 4.0
- Microsoft SQL Server 6.5.

For individual users on the Web, you will need:

- PC (486 or higher)
- Windows 95 or 3.x
- Internet access using a standard 28.8 modem
- Internet Explorer or Netscape Web browser.

Contact details

Web: www.globalknowledge.com

IMG University Online

Since July 1995, the Information Management Group (IMG) has been delivering online training via the Microsoft Online Institute (MOLI) and is one of the few MOLI providers to provide content online, in a browser-accessible HTML format. In addition, they have supplemented their online courseware with value-added services, such as:

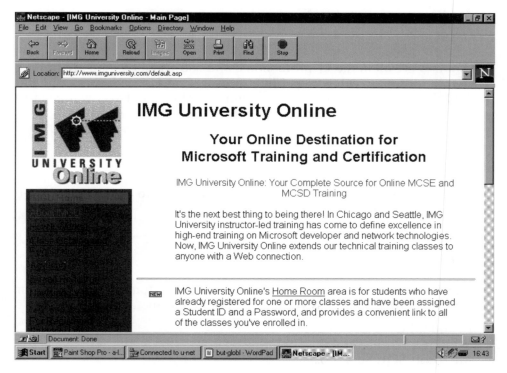

Figure 5.9   IMG University Online

- scheduled chats
- discussion groups
- weekly instructor e-mails with supplemental information
- e-mail between students and the instructor, or each other
- FAQ documents.

In Spring 1997, IMG began moving their MOLI classrooms to their online learning environment, IMG University Online (see Figure 5.9). Since then, IMG has been providing a comprehensive public and private instructor-led training to a wide range of corporate and individual clients. IMG is a Microsoft Authorized Technical Education Centre (ATEC) and uses Microsoft Official Curriculum to skill students in Microsoft developer, network and Internet technologies, and to prepare them for Microsoft certification. IMG also develops, instructs and licenses its own high-end developer courseware under the IMG University brand.

IMG University online classes are 'open enrolment,' that is, you can enrol at any time and don't need to worry about class start and stop dates. Classes are a combination of self-study material and instructor-guided activities. They consist of five main components which combine to give you a complete online learning environment.

Online classes

Technical content

One of the primary advantages of IMG University Online classes is that all of the content is online and easily accessible to anybody with a Web browser. They allow you to download and work with the material at your leisure, but the full textual content of every class is always provided online. This allows IMG to keep the content fresh and current. An IMG University Online class consists of:

- objectives-based technical content,
- step-by-step exercises,
- screen simulations of key learning points,
- clearly defined lab exercises which reinforce learning objectives, and
- review questions.

In addition, if you would like hard copy course materials, you can purchase them for an additional $30.

Moderated chats

Online content is ideal for self-study, but a complete learning experience should be much more than that. The self-study materials are complemented with regularly scheduled chats, each of which is moderated by the instructor for the classroom. All of the instructors are technical professionals and have extensive real-world experience applying the tools they're teaching, so you get much more than theoretical knowledge. IMG firmly believe that the ideal online learning experience is a mix of synchronous and asynchronous learning activities. Chats are an excellent way of providing the former, and can build a strong sense of cohesiveness which many online environments lack. Every class has at least two scheduled chats per week, and the instructor archives each chat's contents, so that if you miss one, you can still benefit from the discussion at your leisure.

Threaded discussions

Threaded discussions are a great way of adding value to an online classroom experience. These are near-synchronous activities, in which a student or the instructor can post questions or comments, and other participants can respond, creating threads on related subject matter. The discussion threads are moderated by the instructor, but much of the value comes from students' participation. IMG has found that the value of the online classroom environment is significantly enhanced as discussion threads are built throughout a class.

Self-assessment tests

Serious self-assessment testing capability is a critically important part of an online classroom, since it provides an objective measure of a student's mastery of key learning objectives. However, since self-assessment testing is difficult and requires relatively complex programs to administer, many online learning environments give it short shrift or leave it out altogether. IMG University Online classes feature entirely Web-based self-assessment tests which students take through the flexible IMG WebTest application. These tests can be taken in practice or graded mode, and soon you'll be able to take a pre-test for a class if you want the system to help you create your own customized syllabus which focuses on areas you need the most help with.

Instructor e-mail

Whatever other components a learning environment has, sometimes there's no substitute for simply asking a question of an expert. That's why all IMG University Online classes feature instructor e-mail on class topics with a guaranteed one-business day response time.

Courses

Courses offered are Microsoft Certified Professional, Internet, Access, Visual Basic, CJ++ and BackOffice.

Prices

Course prices range from $350 to $995.

Contact details

Web: www.imguniversity.com

NIIT NetVarsity

NIIT NetVarsity (see Figure 5.10) was established in July 1996 as a site offering Internet-based training, and providing free services to a few thousand students for more than a year. At the core of NetVarsity is a unit of learning called a Skillette, a small segment which imparts a skill in a single learning session which typically lasts for 30 to 40 minutes. Even though people usually enrol for a whole course, NetVarsity gives them the option to enrol either for a whole course or just a specific Skillette. Pre-sequenced Skillettes constitute a module and pre-sequenced modules constitute a course. At a later date, they plan to put some of their programmes on Net-Varsity so that pre-sequenced courses make up a learning programme.

Learning at the NetVarsity comes with services like query services, newsgroups and tutorials through the chat facility. NetVarsity encourages learners who have a problem to:

- First try to solve it by themselves. NetVarsity provides FAQs which come with the content.
- Then try to solve it with the help of peers. NetVarsity provides relevant threads on newsgroups which can be used. New threads can also be added.
- Then try to solve it with the help of the faculty or an expert. NetVarsity provides support through query services and expert tutorials through chat.

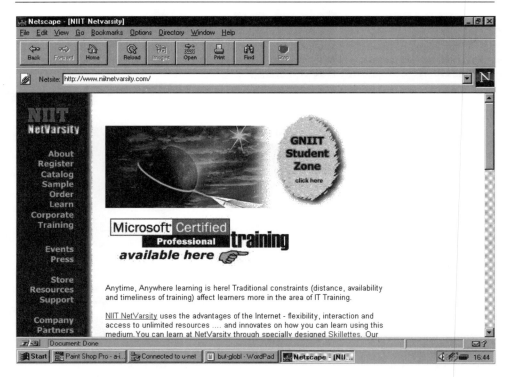

Figure 5.10   NIIT NetVarsity

Courses

NetVarsity's course offerings include:

- Java Programming
- HTML Programming
- Accessing the Web for Searching and Communicating
- Web Publishing Using Front Page
- Sizing and Installing Netscape Enterprise Server 3.0
- Sizing and Installing Internet Information Server 3.0
- Livening up your web site using Java Applets
- Livening up your web site using JavaScript
- Livening up your web site using JScript.

Prices

Registration is free at NIIT NetVarsity. All it needs is an online form to be completed and submitted. The registration process gives a learner a valid login and password.

Contact details

Web: www.niitnetvarsity.com

Street Technologies' Learning University

Street Technologies' Learning University courses are self-paced and feature fully synchronized audio, video and full screen animated simulations (see Figure 5.11). This state-of-the-art training requires a one-time download of Street's player/plug-in: a software program which extends the capabilities of your browser, enabling you to play interactive multimedia. Once you have the player/plug-in installed, no further downloading is required.

Courses are available in several different subscription lengths to suit individual needs. You can enrol in a single course or multiple courses, subscribe for a week, a month or six months and get access 24 hours a day, 7 days a week. Your subscription begins at the time you register and enter your credit card information, or the day your payment is received, and ter-

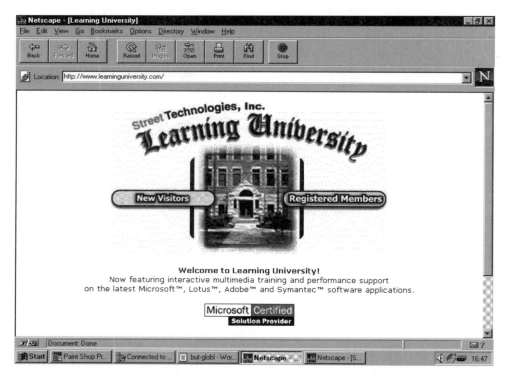

Figure 5.11   Street Technologies' Learning University

minates automatically at the end of the selected time period. Your sub-scription length is calculated by consecutive days. For example, a 1 week subscription which begins on a Saturday, ends seven days later on the following Saturday. This is the case regardless of how often you have accessed the course(s).

The length of each course varies according to many outside factors, including Internet traffic and modem connection rate, which will contribute to the speed at which a course will play. On average each level of the course is between 30 and 45 minutes if played from beginning to end. In other words, Word 95 has three levels, Introduction is 30–45 minutes, Inter-mediate is 30–45 minutes and Advanced is 30–45 minutes. A particular topic within a course may be played individually; individual topics vary in length and can be anywhere between 30 seconds to 3 minutes.

Courses

The Learning University currently offers the following courses:

- **Office 95:** Learning Access 95, Learning Excel 95, Learning PowerPoint 95, Learning Schedule+ 95, Learning Word 95, Learning Office 95 Suite.
- **Office 97:** Learning Access 97, Learning Excel 97, Learning Excel 97 – Special Topics, Learning Outlook 97, Learning PowerPoint 97, Learn-ing Word 97 Learning Word 97 – Special Topics, Learning Office 97 Suite.
- **Windows NT 4.0:** Learning Windows NT 4.0 – Administration, Learn-ing Windows NT 4.0 – Installation, Learning Windows NT 4.0 – Mes-saging, Learning Windows NT 4.0 – Security, Learning Windows NT 4.0 – User, Learning Windows NT 4.0 Suite.
- **Desktop applications:** Learning Publisher 97, Learning Corel WordPer-fect 8.
- **Programming and Development:** Learning Visual C++, Learning FrontPage 97, Learning Photoshop 4.0.
- **Internet training:** Communicating with the Internet, Learning Internet Explorer 4.0, Learning Netscape Communicator 4.0.
- **Other:** Learning Windows 95, Learning ACT! 3.0, Learning Lotus Notes 4.0.

Prices

Typical course prices range from $9.95 to $29.95 depending on the length of the course. For example, the price for Access 95 is $9.95 (one week), $19.95 (one month) or $29.95 (six months).

System requirements

- Microsoft Windows 95 or Windows NT.
- Web browser (Netscape Navigator 3.0+ or 4.0+ or Internet Explorer 3.0+ or 4.0+ or AOL 3.0 for Windows 95).
- 486 16 MB RAM (Pentium recommended).
- 28.8 modem or faster.
- Audio device, installed and configured.

Contact details

Web: www.learninguniversity.com

CyberState University

CyberState University (see Figure 5.12) claims to be the first organization to develop and deliver complete certification training via the Internet. The company was founded on the belief that online training, using the Synergy Learning system, is superior to most traditional educational choices and makes certification training substantially more effective and affordable. CyberState University has been delivering online training since March 1994 and has helped hundreds of students obtain their Novell CNE/CNA and Microsoft MCSE certifications.

Key attributes of CyberState University's certification training include:

- up to 60 per cent less expensive than other certification alternatives;
- 100 per cent certification rate for students who have completed the course study time paced to average five hours per week;
- guaranteed support resources throughout the entire training programme;
- programme length adjustable to individual requirements and learning styles;
- completion of all the certification exams is incorporated into the programme schedule;
- remote administrative access to a real network Practice Lab for hands-on experience with the network management utilities needed to pass the performance-based exams;
- unlimited use of campus facilities, classroom and the network Practice Lab;
- study any time with 24 hour internet access to campus; and
- study anywhere, from home, office and even while travelling.

Figure 5.12   CyberState University

Studying at CyberState

Students log into a 'virtual classroom' on a weekly basis to obtain their lessons. Each lesson includes review sessions from the previous week's assignments and homework for the coming week. Homework can include reading assignments, watching video tape segments, completing exercises in the online network practice lab and taking practice exams. A new lesson is posted into the classroom each week for students to work on during that week. All the previous weeks' lessons are also kept in the classroom, which allows students to review material and catch up if they get behind. The weekly lesson plan format provides a structured learning environment and gives students a reasonable amount of material to learn and apply each week. The weekly pacing helps motivate students to keep up with the pro-gramme and gives managers an easy way to track an employee's progress.

Programmes are designed as asynchronous teaching environments and average about five hours of training per week. This gives students the ability to decide where and when they want to learn, without having to accommodate a traditional schedule of classes. Asynchronous training also allows students to work around peak workloads, projects or vacations without missing vital training. If a student falls more than a few weeks behind, they may start to feel overwhelmed. If this occurs, students have the option to be moved to a different classroom that has fewer weeks of lessons in it. This relieves the student's pressure in feeling behind and restores motivation. Classroom moves can be requested via e-mail to CyberState University's Office of Student Affairs.

A programme's duration can be shortened or extended based on the individual's learning style or organizational requirements. For example, the Online CNE Program was designed to be a 27 week programme and could be shortened to 27 days (5 hours per day), or extended for as long as needed to complete the programme. The Online MCSE Programme was designed to be completed in 35 weeks.

Support from CyberState University's instructors is set up like an online tutor to help students if they get stuck. At any time, students may e-mail a question to 'Professor Wire', CSU's virtual instructor, and get a response back within 24 hours. Using campus chat, students are able to interact with each other, and even arrange world-wide study sessions. Students can also access an online Bulletin Board and Message System, which provides useful information from both students and instructors on a range of subjects from real-world troubleshooting scenarios to exam tips.

Taking the certification exams at a local testing centre is incorporated into the programme's schedule. For example, in the Online MCSE Programme, students will study for eight weeks and then be told to go and take their NT 4.0 Workstation Exam at their local testing centre. They will then study for a few more weeks and take their Networking Essentials exam. This process of training for the next exam continues throughout the entire programme. Thus, at the end of the 35 weeks, students will have completed their training and have obtained their MCSE certification.

Passing the certification exams is the best indicator that the student has successfully acquired the needed skills from the training programme. CyberState University's 100 per cent certification rate for students that have completed the programme underscores its commitment to helping students and organizations acquire the desired certifications and skills.

Synergy Learning System

To deliver high-quality, cost-effective training on the Internet, CyberState University developed a new method of teaching called the Synergy Learning System. This system was specifically designed to reduce the student's total study time by accelerating retention and improving recall of the course material. The Synergy Learning System accomplishes these goals by combining multiple teaching media into a structured learning environment. These media then incorporate auditory, visual and kinaesthetic sensory inputs into the educational process. A student then uses one of these inputs as their primary method of learning while the additional inputs are used as reinforcement. The result is quicker absorption and easier recall of the course material.

The teaching media utilized in the course include:

- books by leading industry authors;
- videotapes which focus on 'how to do it';
- online lectures to direct study efforts;
- online review sessions to reinforce key concepts;
- online assignments in a live network Practice Lab to anchor course material;
- multimedia skills assessment to focus on critical study areas;
- multimedia testing to measure proficiency with the course material;
- online interaction with students via 'chat forums'; and
- online support from instructors via CyberState University's e-mail system.

It is the interactive combination of these complementary teaching media which makes up the Synergy Learning System. By accelerating retention and improving recall, this innovative approach to online certification training effectively reduces the total number of study hours needed to prepare for the certification exams.

Courses

Courses at CyberState University are broken down into two main sections: Novell Intranetware/NetWare Certification (CNE/CNA) and Microsoft NT4 Certification (MCSE).

Prices

Prices are $2395 (CNE), $595 (CNA) and $3495 (MCSE).

Contact details

Web: www.cyberstateu.com

Wave Technologies' Online University

Building on many years of Web-based training experience, Wave Technologies' Online University was established in 1997. Wave Technologies is dedicated to assisting IT professionals master technology and prepare for certification. While training more than 40 000 professionals each year, Wave has discovered two key characteristics of successful training programmes: they are targeted to an individual's needs and they have specific goals. Wave's Online University integrates these characteristics into the training experience.

To begin using Wave's Online University, you first need to login (see Figure 5.13). If you have been given a Login ID during a Wave instructor-led class, simply enter that Login ID along with your last name in the appropriate boxes on the Wave Online University homepage. Then click the Submit Login button. Wave needs your e-mail address in order to keep in touch as you progress through the Online University. If Wave does not have a record of your e-mail address, when you click on the Submit Login button, you will enter an area where you can Update Your Personal

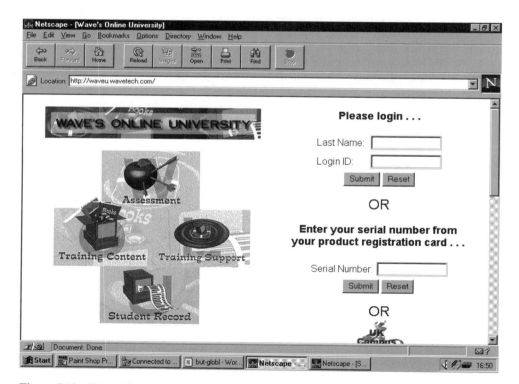

Figure 5.13   Wave Technologies' Online University

Records. Here you will be able to enter your e-mail address. Once you have done so and submitted the form, you will enter the Online University.

If you have purchased a Wave Self-Study Kit recently, you should have received a card with a 24-character code printed on it. This Serial Number may also be entered in a box on the Wave Online University homepage. This number will give temporary access until your Login ID is issued.

The Wave Online University masthead serves as your primary navigational tool. It contains links to all of the major departments, and the Wave Online University graphic will take you back to the home page of the university.

Student record

Once you have logged in to Wave Online University, you will be taken to your Student Record page. This page serves both as your transcript and as a means for gaining access to different 'campus' activities. In the upper left corner of your Student Record is your Login ID and the name of your faculty adviser. Your adviser will occasionally send you information related to your course work. If you have a question or would just like to make a comment about a course, you may send an e-mail message to your adviser by clicking on his/her name. On the upper right side is a link to instructions.

The heart of the Student Record page is the information that relates directly to your own course work. This information is updated daily and goes back one full year. So, if you took an instructor-led class 11 months ago, or bought a self-study kit last week, the information on these courses is there for you to review. Each course is accompanied by an assessment button which allows you to comment on the classes you have taken.

Instructor-led training

When you enrol in one of Wave's instructor-led courses, you can link to your instructor's biography and yearbook photo. This will give you an introduction to the person with whom you will be taking your course. Also, Wave's instructors want to know more about incoming students in order to be able to tailor their classes better to particular needs and goals. So each instructor has provided questions intended to gather information about the people enrolled in a future course. If you click on the assessment button for a course that has not yet taken place, you will be taken through a few questions which will help hone the class to fit your needs more closely.

Self-study training

The self-study area of the student record provides you with an opportunity to view the courses you have purchased, and it will soon allow you to arrange for occasional reminders to help you get through courses in a timely fashion.

Assessment

Wave Technologies' online assessment is an innovative system designed to help you get the most from your training experience. You simply answer a series of questions which concentrate on your IT experience, skills levels and professional objectives. The questions are course-specific and are presented in a multiple choice, multiple select and short answer format. The whole process takes less than 15 minutes to complete. Group results – not individual responses – will be presented to your Wave instructor so that he or she can tailor the class to your needs more effectively.

Courses

Wave covers the full range of the Microsoft, Novell and A+ certification programmes:

- Microsoft MCSE: Win 95 Admin, NT4 Workstation, NT4 Server, NT4 Enterprise, Networking Essentials, TCP/IP, SQL Server Admin, MS IIS, MS Exchange.
- Microsoft MCSD: Windows Architecture 1 & 2, SQL Server Implementation, Visual Basic 4 & 5, Visual C++, MS IIS, MS Exchange.
- Novell: IntranetWare 4.× Admin & Advanced Admin, Building Intranets with IntranetWare, Design & Implementation of IntranetWare, Data Communications Technologies, TCP/IP.
- PC Service & Support (A+): Current exams. New exams will be available in June 1998.

Prices

Each course module is £495 and is delivered and monitored through the Wave Online University, with a full certification guarantee: Wave will support the student until they pass the exam.

Contact details

Web: www.wavetech.com

DigitalThink

The DigitalThink site (see Figure 5.14) comprises two areas: the Orientation area and the Course area. In the Orientation area you can:

- read descriptions of the current and upcoming courses, learn about the instructors and register for courses;
- preview course syllabuses and become acquainted with the course before you make the decision to purchase it;
- learn about the tools available on the site to help you learn online;
- contact the people who manage the site; and
- take a free trial course, Smart Searching: The Power of Simple Searches.

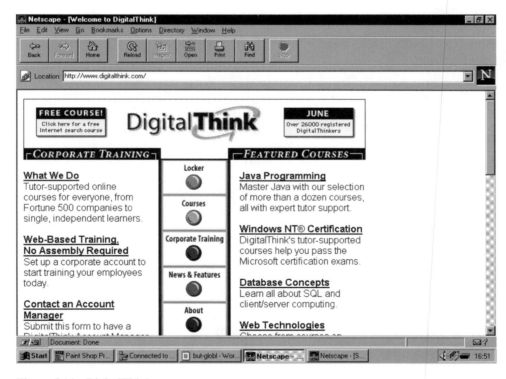

Figure 5.14   DigitalThink

The Course area is where you take your courses and interact with other students, instructors and tutors. The area is open to registered students only. Here, you will find:

- your personal locker page, with links to your classes, instructors, tutors and online classmates;
- course lessons, complete with colour graphics, hypertext and audio;
- interactive quizzes;
- hands-on exercises;
- course-specific discussion boards;
- live, instructor-led chat sessions;
- help, via e-mail.

How it works

An example of a DigitalThink course page is shown in Figure 5.15. As you proceed through your course, new lessons, hands-on exercises, interactive quizzes and other materials will appear on the screen. The DigitalThink

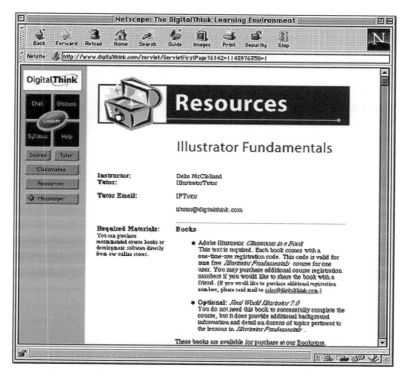

Figure 5.15   DigitalThink course page

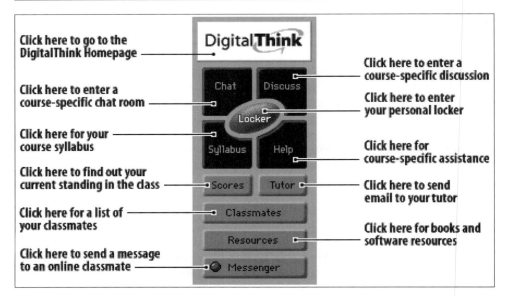

Figure 5.16   DigitalThink toolbar

toolbar provides you with one click access to the features you will use while taking the course. The toolbar will be your guide everywhere you go in the Course area (see Figure 5.16). The toolbar comprises the following options:

- Chat: this will take you to a specific chatroom.
- Discuss: click to enter a course-specific discussion.
- Locker: enter your personal locker page.
- Syllabus: obtain the syllabus of your course.
- Help: ask for course-specific assistance.
- Scores: find out your current standing in the class.
- Tutor: send e-mail to your tutor.
- Classmates: find a list of your online classmates.
- Resources: find out what books and software resources are available for your course.
- Messenger: send a message to an online classmate.

Courses

DigitalThink provides a series of IT-based courses which include C & C++ Programming, Certification (Java and NT), Design & Publishing (Illustrator, Photoshop, Pagemaker), Internet Literacy, Java Programming, Perl Programming and an interesting course on Enjoying Wine.

Prices

Course prices are around $300.

Contact details

Web: www.digitalthink.com

scholars.com

scholars.com (see Figure 5.17), a CBT Systems company, specializes exclusively in providing online Microsoft and Novell certification training, focusing on delivering high-quality courses by integrating technology with proven learning methodologies. It provides the flexibility of self-paced study using Microsoft and Novell approved courseware together with the benefits of expert active mentoring from Microsoft and Novell certified

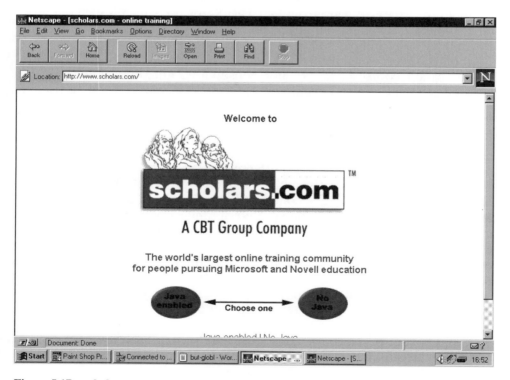

Figure 5.17   scholars.com

learning advisers (instructors) who are online twelve hours a day including weekends, ready to help you as you need it. The learning advisers are not only Microsoft or Novell certified in the courses you are taking, they also have extensive real-life experience in implementing Microsoft/Novell technologies.

scholars.com is an approved training provider for the Microsoft Online Institute (MOLI) and offer Microsoft and Novell certification training courses to prepare students to take the appropriate certification exam. Rather than taking a five-day intensive instructor-led course, through online training you learn the same concepts but at a slower pace over a longer period of time. This methodology allows the knowledge to slowly 'sink in' yet gives the reassurance that if you need clarification or help you can get assistance from teams of learning advisers who are online every day.

But scholars.com do more than just provide advisers ready to help you as you need it, they also send out daily questions and simulated helpdesk scenarios, informational e-mail, online lab exercises, exam preparation questions, and so on. In short, they do everything possible to make sure that you are prepared to pass your certification exam. By taking your online training and reviewing with the official Microsoft and Novell Personal Exam Prep (PEP) software from Self Test Software, which is included in all of the courses, scholars.com guarantee that if you don't pass your exam on the first try, they will pay for you to re-take your exam.

scholars.com is exclusively dedicated to online training; they do not offer instructor-led courses and are not consultants, and this philosophy has allowed scholars.com to become one of the world's largest online training companies.

With this method of learning, you essentially learn offline using the approved multimedia courseware CDs, and go online to get help from learning advisers as you need it. This online training approach allows students to work on courses while not being connected to the Internet (saving online connection costs), plus you are able to use the CDs as ideal reference tools once the course is completed. You progress through the course at your own pace over a specified period of time (usually 12 weeks).

When you take an online course with scholars.com, you receive Microsoft Approved courseware and active mentoring from the learning advisers. This approach allows you to learn offline by using the courseware and to go online to get help. Active mentoring not only means that you are able to get help from your learning advisers through e-mail, chats and newsgroups, but you will also received daily personalized questions (corresponding to where you are in the course), helpdesk scenarios, online lab exercises, exam preparation questions, and so on. You will also receive your own private Scholars Web Mailbox so that you can read your e-mail from any Web browser, from any location.

By becoming part of the Scholars Community, you are able to benefit from the experiences not only of your learning advisers, but also of the other students taking courses from scholars.com. Also included in the Microsoft courses are extensive supplemental materials for each course such as STS Microsoft exam preparation software, which contains realistic simulations of Microsoft's exams with valuable references, so you know what to expect and where to focus your study. For their Novell courses they include a two-user version of Novell NetWare 4.11 (IntranetWare) along with STS's Big Red exam preparation software. To ensure quick access, the scholars.com Web site is connected to the Internet using a T1 line, one of the fastest types of Internet connection possible.

Courses

scholars.com run 12 Microsoft-based courses and 13 Novell-based courses. The Microsoft courses include Windows NT 4.0, NT Server and Work-station, Windows 95, Internet Information Server, SQL Server and Exchange Server. The Novell courses include IntranetWare, NetWare, Web Server Management and Web Authoring and Publishing. The courses provided are from CBT Systems and Microsoft Press. All have been reviewed and approved by Microsoft and Novell.

Prices

The cost of a scholars.com course is currently $695.

Contact details

Web: www.scholars.com

Training Associates online learning

Training Associates, Inc. (see Figure 5.18) is an Arizona-based corporation. Started in 1996, they have offered Microsoft certified training to over 1000 students to date. In addition, they have created a number of paper-based and CD-ROM-based training courses for both Microsoft and MS Press. Training Associates are a Microsoft Solution Provider and Microsoft Authorized Technical Education Center. Their staff of online instructors are all Microsoft Certified Trainers with classroom experience.

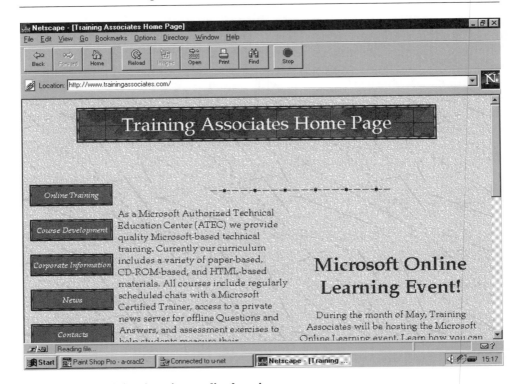

Figure 5.18   Training Associates online learning

How does online training work?

As the student progresses through the material, they will have access to the Training Associates Web site. Here, students will find a secure classroom area including a course Lesson Plan, additional labs/reading material and their exclusive online assessment exercises. In addition to the materials found on the Web site, students will have access to regularly scheduled chat sessions.

Online support: assessment exercises

Since these courses are self-paced, students often need a better tool to assess whether they have learned the topics they have been reading about. In addition to the chat sessions, Training Associates offers a self-paced answer. Through their Web site, students can log in and walk through a series of free-form questions. These online assessment exercises are mapped to the material the student has just covered. Therefore, if a student needs to review a particular section, they will know this while they are taking the class, not at the end when they may fail an exam. This is also an excellent tool for instructors to evaluate the progress of, and make suggestions to, students who are studying off-hours.

Online support: chat sessions

The one aspect of traditional classroom training that is lacking in distance learning is the trainer. No longer can an experienced trainer gain visual clues from a student's facial expression or body language. However, as the Internet begins to support more advanced technology, such as videoconferencing and data sharing, the potential for more interaction will be realized. Currently, Training Associates maintain their own Internet 'chat' server. This server is based on the IRC (Internet Relay Chat) protocol. Students will receive (or can download) a free chat program which allows them to connect their computer to Training Associates' servers. Using this chat client, students can have a live, interactive session with a Microsoft certified instructor. The chats are not a requirement to complete the course; students can utilize as many or as few as they wish to get specific answers to questions, or to get a more detailed discussion from the instructor.

Instructors

Training Associates uses only Microsoft Certified Trainers to conduct the courses. Experienced with real-world knowledge, the trainers also conduct live training. This provides online students a high level of quality assurance when help is needed. To support their trainers, Training Associates also employs Learning Advisors, who are well versed in the technology they support and are all working towards becoming Microsoft Certified Trainers. The typical Learning Advisor will facilitate chat sessions, review e-mail and support content development.

Courses

The range of courses offered focuses on Microsoft products: Introduction to Programming Using Access 95/VBA; Fundamentals of Visual Basic 4.0; Mastering Microsoft Visual Basic 4.0; Fundamentals of Microsoft Access 95; Mastering Microsoft Access 95; Networking Essentials; Introduction to Programming Using Access 97; FrontPage97 End User Certification; Mastering Visual Basic 5 Fundamentals; Introduction to Programming Using

Visual Basic 5; Mastering Visual Basic 5; Windows Architecture for Developers.

Prices

Prices are around $325.

Contact details

Web: www.trainingassociates.com

ZDNet University

ZDNet University is an online learning community which offers classes in computer and Internet-related topics. For a monthly subscription of £4.95, you receive full access to the ZDU campus. As a subscriber to ZDU, you can:

- take as many classes as you want;
- meet other members in Class Cafés and Graduate Lounges;
- chat live with members and instructors; and
- receive special offers from the Campus Store.

Apart from the monthly subscription fee, there are no additional fees to pay for taking classes at ZDU. You will be charged the monthly subscription whether you take a class or not.

Taking a class

ZDU classrooms are moderated message boards which work in a similar way to newsgroups. Each week, the instructor posts lessons and assignments, and you can connect to ZDU and read them any time you wish. Members can also ask questions, make comments or help others in the class by posting their own messages. Teaching assistants and other staff moderate the classroom so that you see only messages that are relevant to the topic. Most classes last either four or eight weeks, and most classes require a textbook, which you can purchase from the Campus Store. You can be a full student in a class, or you can audit the class, which means you can read the messages but not post your own. You can also earn Continuing Education Units and get credit for classes.

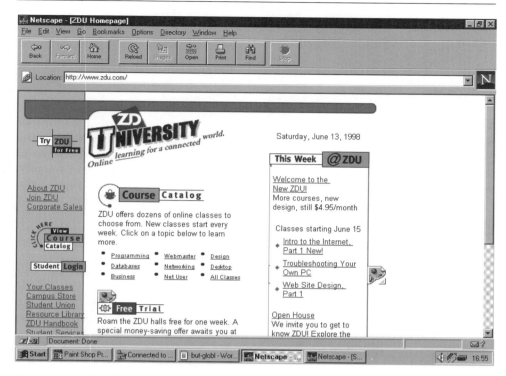

Figure 5.19　ZDNet University

Cafés and Lounges

When you take a class at ZDU, you also gain access to the special Class Café, where you can get to know other ZDU members in your class. This message board is the perfect place for meeting people and having casual discussions. After you've completed a class, the classroom closes, but you are granted access to the Graduate Lounge that's related to the class. Here, you can continue discussions that began earlier, meet other people who share your interests and share the latest problems, solutions and news with your peers. Only those who have completed a ZDU class in your topic can enter the Graduate Lounge.

Student Union

Live chat is a great way to meet other ZDU members, whether it's in the classrooms for a study group or in the ZDU Pub for casual conversation.

The Student Union is the home of chat on ZDU, and it's also where you'll find several ongoing clubs you can join, such as the Chess Club and the HTML Diner.

Campus Store

Visit the Campus Store for the easiest way to buy your course textbooks. Books can be ordered online at a discount through BarnesandNoble.com. Some books are offered in electronic format, so you can choose to download the book. You will also find special offers for ZDU members on software. A typical course textbook costs $32.

Resource Library

Members also get access to the Resource Library, which contains everything from free CGI scripts to helpful how-to guides for using services like FTP.

Help Desk

Finally, the Help Desk is the place to go for answers to any support question about ZDU, or for e-mailing ZDU with a question or comment.

Courses

ZDU courses are available on a first-come-first-served basis. Many classes are offered monthly. If a course is full, you can register for the next one running and you will be notified by e-mail when the next class is about to open. One nice feature of ZDU is that you can 'listen in' to a course while not actually being an official delegate. ZDU call this 'Auditing' a course. When you audit a course, you can only read messages in a classroom. Generally it is advisable to audit a course if you are not sure of your commitment to the class, if you cannot decide whether it is at the right level, or if you do not have all the required materials (e.g. you do not want to purchase the required textbook until you are sure that the course is right for you). At the end of the course, you can obtain a ZDU certificate of completion by downloading it from the Web site.

ZDU has a wide range of courses in the IT and Internet field. There are eight main categories:

- Programming: Java, Visual Basic, C++, Visual C++, CGI.
- Databases: Microsoft Access, SQL, Powerbuilder.

- Networking: Windows NT, Web Servers, UNIX.
- Business: Marketing, Advertising, Web Management.
- Webmaster: HTML, JavaScript, Dynamic HTML, Push Channels.
- Design: Photoshop, Graphics, Web Layout.
- Net User: Netscape Communicator, Searching the Net.
- Desktop: Upgrading and Repairing, Office Applications.

Prices

For $4.95 a month, you become a full member of ZDU, and get access to the entire campus. Your monthly subscription allows you to take as many classes as you want. You can join in all the live chats, use the Resource Library and Help Desk, order books and get special offers through the Campus Store, and more. ZDU accepts credit cards as payment. Your credit card is automatically charged each month. You can provide your credit card information via secure Web forms or via fax. Note that ZDU is a monthly subscription service. That means you'll be charged every month even if you're not currently attending a class.

System requirements

To access ZDU, you will need the following hardware and software installed and configured: (i) Internet connection with at least 28.8 bps modem; and (ii) a Web browser which supports JavaScript or ActiveX technology. Suitable browsers include Netscape Navigator 3.02 or higher, Netscape Communicator 4.04 or Microsoft Internet Explorer 3.02 or higher.

Contact details

Web: www.zdu.com

The Open University

The Open University (OU) has, since its inception in the 1960s, pioneered the use of innovative study aids and distance learning techniques. It has not been slow to recognize the implications and possibilities of the Internet for the way people can access course material and utilize interactive teaching aids.

The delivery of the majority of OU courses is traditionally paper based,

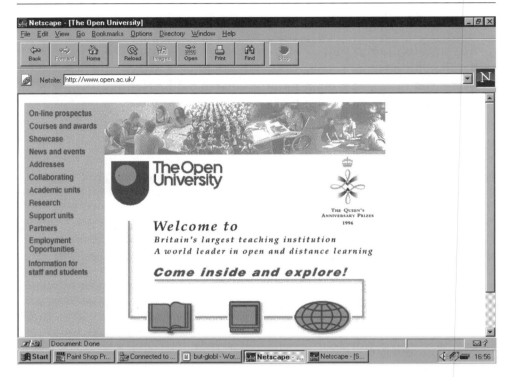

Figure 5.20   The Open University

but in early 1997 the OU successfully completed its first ever course conducted over the Internet, User Interface Design and Development. The OU (see Figure 5.20) has now become the UK's first academic institution to introduce a postgraduate course in software development for the Internet itself (course M874). Both of these courses have been developed by the Computing for Commerce and Industry (CCI) programme, part of the Faculty of Mathematics and Computing.

Although used by the academic world for the last two decades, the Internet has only in the last two or three years been accessible to the general public, which forms the majority of the OU's student base. Falling costs of technology and telecommunications services, and the development of user-friendly Internet interfaces such as the Web, have created this explosion in use. Most Internet users now access the Web from home or the workplace, rather than a conventional place of study, making it an ideal tool for distance learning.

The Internet offers massive potential for distance learning. Users can swap and exchange information with tutors and peers in real time. They can search for and access a vast array of information from around the world and integrate it easily into their projects and reports. This type of Internet use is relatively commonplace, but what sets the OU's initiative apart is the provision of dedicated and structured material which can be accessed by students. The advantage of this concept is that course material can be kept much more up-to-date than would be possible with paper- or even disk-based resources.

Students can also engage in interactive learning sessions, working through coursework on their own or in conjunction with their tutor or other people on their course. They can receive instant feedback on their work and interact with each other in ways that can be difficult on traditional OU courses. One of the principal reasons for developing Internet-based tuition was to offer communications procedures for students, in the UK and overseas, who are geographically remote/or who have physical disabilities. And, of course, the Internet is the natural place to learn about the Internet.

The OU's first-ever course conducted over the Internet was a postgraduate module from the CCI programme (MZX867) on the design and development of computer user interfaces. It marked a major innovation in large-scale supported distance learning and was completed successfully earlier this year. Plain-text Internet e-mail was used to enable delivery of a number of course components, including a Web-based automatic course registration form. During the course an electronic assignment handling procedure was used to manage student submissions, marking and monitoring. Examinations were carried out using encrypted papers downloaded via the Web at strictly supervised examination centres. The course also employed Internet conferencing and access to a variety of pertinent Web resources.

The OU identified a number of benefits from the new style of course, including faster feedback for students, increased tutor collaboration and communication and improved administrative efficiency. 'This electronic means of delivery reflects the changes in society and business by practically applying new technology to teaching . . . The potential now exists for global access' (Blaine Price, Faculty of Maths and Computing, personal communication). The introduction of a course in the Java programming language makes the OU the first academic institution in the UK to offer a course on Internet Software Development. The Software Development for Networked Applications Using Java (course M874) also marks a major innovation in method of delivery. Instead of paper-based study guides, M874 students will use Web documents which take them through the 5-module course, set exercises, and connect them to other sites containing relevant material.

Another major innovation in M874 is the capacity it offers for self-assessment. Answers to set questions will be monitored and logged at a central site which students can access to compare their progress against their fellows. 'Java has experienced explosive growth over the last year, and virtually every major computer and software manufacturer including

IBM, Microsoft, Novell, Oracle and Fujitsu – has adopted it as a core Internet technology. . . Java is arguably the programming language of the future, and will make languages such as C++ redundant. We believe the OU is at the forefront in deploying Java in the academic environment' (Professor D. Ince, Department of Computer Science, personal communication).

M874 is one of the first master's-level courses to use Java and forms part of the OU's Computing for Commerce and Industry MSc programme. It teaches students with existing experience of object programming to develop software for use on the Internet and in Web documents. 'Practical work permeates the whole of M874 . . . By the time a student completes the course he or she will have developed several pieces of software which either facilitate computer communication or implement some executable function within a Web document' (Professor D. Ince, Department of Computer Science, personal communication).

Contact details

Web: www.open.ac.uk

UCLA Home Education Network

The Home Education Network (THEN) and UCLA Extension (see Figure 5.21) have joined in a unique collaboration to offer a series of business courses available to anyone with a computer and a modem. The classes are ideal for busy professionals who want to enhance their skills but have a difficult time fitting continuing education into their schedules.

All of the courses are conducted online. To date, THEN has enabled students from the USA and eight other countries to benefit from the resources of UCLA Extension. THEN has acquired the world-wide exclusive electronic and online rights to courses offered through UCLA Extension, the USA's largest single-campus continuing higher education programme.

You can access your coursework at any time. Once your course begins, you should log-on once a day to access any new e-mail notes. Class 'discussions', assignments, lectures and tutorials are all conducted via e-mail notes. You will also have the opportunity to visit the online 'student lounge' where fellow UCLA Extension students from all around the world meet, share experiences and socialize.

On average, you can expect to spend 10–15 hours a week on coursework, including accessing lectures, participating in class discussions, completing and submitting assignments and reading supplementary texts. The curriculum and assignments are accessed through special secured networked soft-

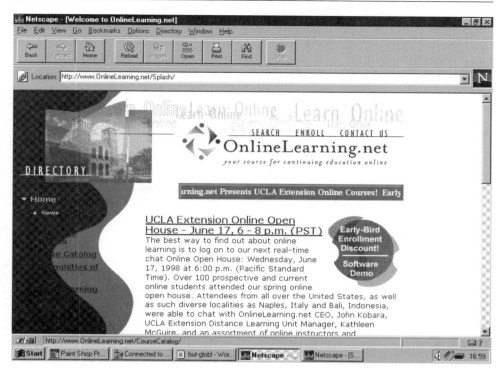

Figure 5.21   UCLA Home Education Network

ware. You read and reply to notes offline, then briefly connect to the host computer to exchange notes and files with others.

Most online courses follow a workshop format, with feedback from the instructor to supplement the dialogue taking place with fellow students. You receive a similar amount of class/instructor contact time as students in 'on-the-ground' courses. Online classes are no larger than 20 students and are usually smaller, allowing you to get to know your instructor and fellow students personally. Online instructors are industry experts, community leaders and working professionals with extensive hands-on experience. They are experienced educators who find the new medium a dynamic and interactive educational environment. You receive individualized attention and all the benefits of a small class size.

Courses

THEN's Winter 1998 schedule includes the widest variety of business courses that UCLA Extension has ever offered online, including:

- Computer Skills Training (Business Computer Programming, Configuring and Supporting PC Hardware, and Introduction to Visual Basic for Windows).
- Management (Elements of Human Resource Management, Management and Supervision).
- Hotel and Food Service Management (Food and Beverage Management, Hotel Front-Office Management).
- Writing (Business Writing and Technical Writing).

There are additional course offerings in the fields of design, public relations and advertising, fundraising and human resources. And there is a certificate programme aimed at the small business owner – the Award in General Business Studies – which includes courses in accounting, finance, marketing and advertising and sales promotion. Business people can also prepare for graduate coursework such as the MBA, or explore options for a career change.

Prices

Course prices range from $450 to $500.

System requirements

Access to an IBM compatible or Macintosh system, modem and phone line. Although Internet access is optional, it may be required for some courses:

- IBM compatible 486/33 or better, including all Pentium PCs; Windows 3.1 operating system or higher (Windows 95); 8 MB of RAM (16 MB preferred); 20 MB of free hard drive space (50 MB preferred). Modem: 14 400 bps (28.8 bps preferred).
- Macintosh or Macintosh compatible with a 68020 processor or better, including all Power PC machines; Mac Operating System 6.05 or higher (System 7 or higher preferred); 8 MB of RAM (16 MB preferred); 20 MB of free hard drive space (50 MB preferred). Modem: 14.4 bps (28.8 bps preferred)

Contact details

Web: www.then.com

CALCampus

CALCampus (see Figure 5.22) is a private, international online learning centre, which offers courses solely through the Internet. Enrolment is open to all individuals anywhere in the world. CALCampus is totally Internet-based and has been teaching courses online since 1986.

CALCampus offers individual courses and certificate programmes for job skills enhancement, continuing adult education, personal and professional development, support for home schooling on the secondary level and support for high school and post secondary study. They also offer a High School Diploma programme and an Associate Degree programme; these special instructional programmes are available through administrative co-operation with other institutions. CALCampus issues a hard copy certificate for individual course or certificate programme completion. Diplomas and degrees are conferred by the co-operating institution for the particular programme completed.

Courses are presented as Directed Independent Study and are available to anyone who has access to the Internet. Directed Independent Study courses are designed so that students receive lessons from their teachers

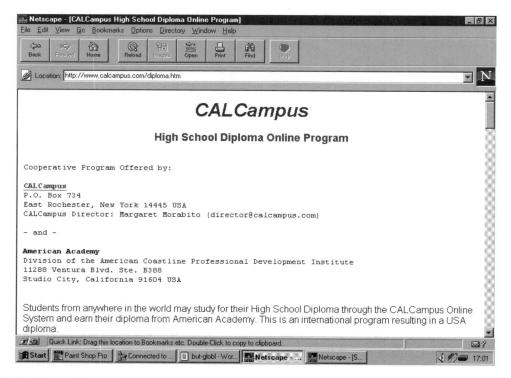

Figure 5.22   CALCampus

through the Internet to study offline. Course materials come in the form of all-in-one disk texts which are run on a computer, text lessons which are downloaded and printed or in some cases a hard copy textbook. Students are required to do homework assignments and quizzes which are e-mailed to their instructors for evaluation. Instructors and students have the option for online meetings on the 'online campus'. Certain courses are presented in a live online classroom format. CALCampus courses are designed for completion within a 12-week term. Students may begin their Directed Independent Study courses soon after they register.

Courses

Courses are offered in business, computer programming, computer applications and technology, English, mathematics, science, social science, foreign language, general studies and test-preparation. English courses are offered for non-native speakers. CALCampus offers individual courses and certificate programmes for job skills enhancement, continuing adult education, personal and professional development, support for home schooling on the secondary level and support for high school and post secondary study. They also offer a High School Diploma programme and an Associate Degree programme; these special instructional programmes are available through administrative co-operation with other institutions.

Prices

Course prices range from $50 to $95.

Contact details

Web: www.calcampus.com

BT CampusWorld HomeCampus

The Internet is a powerful learning environment, with the potential to transform education in the home. Recent research has shown that children valued the information that they discovered on the Internet more highly than material that came from other sources. And it is likely that children will have far greater access to the Internet in the home than through sharing a scarce resource in school.

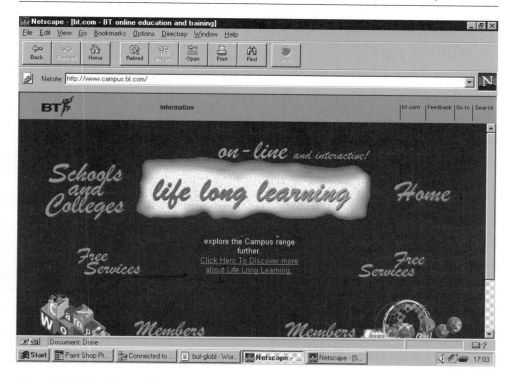

Figure 5.23   BT CampusWorld, HomeCampus

BT's HomeCampus (see Figure 5.23) uses the online world to exploit the potential for extended learning. BT is uniquely placed to lead these developments as one of the major telecommunications companies in the world.

Every teacher knows that a good learning environment in the home is a key factor. The Internet has already blurred the distinction between home and school, although many recognize that while the Internet contains much that is valuable, it lacks focus and its uses can be aimless and unproductive. HomeCampus provides specially created content, focused precisely on UK education. It has evolved from the success of CampusWorld, BT's schools Internet product. CampusWorld has been taken up by over 2500 schools and colleges in the UK and is pre-eminent in providing content that is tailored to the school, to the statutory curricula in the UK and to the concerns of teachers. HomeCampus takes the concept a stage further, bringing similar content, advice and interaction to the home.

HomeCampus is genuinely new. It is a content only subscription service whose sole concern is to provide an online learning environment for the home. Regardless of who supplies your access to the Internet, if you can use the Web you can join. It is a dynamic, living service, with new content being added all the time. The developing site is aimed at parents with children of any age, from pre-school to primary and secondary and beyond. It is for parents who intend to take an active part in learning and who wish to promote the learning development of their children. The service is dynamic, constantly changing, keeps you informed of innovations and at the same time is developing an educational archive which will be a national asset.

What's on the site?

The site includes information and resources to help you and your family in the lifelong learning process: from curriculum documents and OFSTED reports to online conferences and guidance on revision. The site comprises four main sections:

- **Schools and Curricula:** resources to help you find curriculum information, school reports and league tables.
- **Educational Information:** links to government and educational information sites.
- **Teaching and Learning:** help on developing learning and revision skills, and using IT in a learning environment.
- **Subject Information:** carefully selected and vetted resources to help your family in their school and college work.

Prices

The monthly subscription is £4.99 (inc. VAT); £49.90 (inc. VAT) for an annual subscription.

System requirements

You need a frames-capable browser to view HomeCampus, and it looks best with Netscape 3 or Internet Explorer 3, and with an access speed of 28.8 k or above. You need a Shockwave plug-in to view the Random Access area, but you can see everything without going there.

Contact details

Web: www.campus.bt.com

ASK International Internet Camp for Training & Development Professionals

California-based Internet and multimedia training and development firm ASK International have brought back the excitement of the Summer Camp for participants in its newly launched online distance learning workshop, The Internet Camp for Training & Development Professionals (see Figure 5.24). Although they cannot smell the pine trees or get bitten by mosquitoes, Internet 'campers' are promised an unforgettable experience with this 20–25 hour online distance learning experience.

The course is designed to teach training and development and HRD professionals basic Internet skills and how to maximize use of the Internet specifically in their jobs. They will learn everything from basic Internet concepts and buzzwords through to actually developing their own personal Web pages. They will also interact with others – exchanging e-mail, participating in chat sessions and trading 'campfire stories' – in a casual online discussion forum. Specifically students will learn how to:

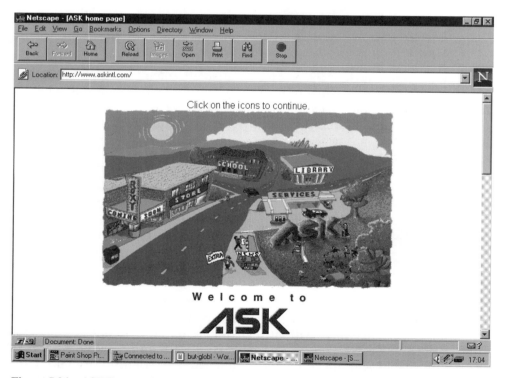

Figure 5.24   ASK International Internet Camp

- get connected, use e-mail, and transfer files;
- browse the Web for information;
- search training, HT and education databases;
- link into valuable training and HRD sites;
- join and participate in chat and newsgroups;
- find unique training and HR opportunities and techniques; and
- author their own Web page.

At their own desktop, participants link in and pass through five online modules (or camp sites):

- Orientation
- Tools & Skills
- Exploration
- Making Friends
- Setting Up a Campsite.

According to the President of ASK, Dr Eric Parks, 'the key to distance learning online is an experience that incorporates a sense of community. That's what makes the camp special. The basic concept of the site . . . is to emphasize that learning can be fun' (Dr E. Parks, personal communication).

Price

The price of the course is $295 (multi-course/attendee discounts available). You can also take a preview tour of the Camp to help you decide whether to register for the course. Course participants receive a Camp Handbook, a CD-ROM tutorial, an audio cassette series and full access to the site for hands-on exercises.

Contact details

Web: www.askintl.com

NovaNET

NovaNET (see Figure 5.25) is an online computer-based education and communications network with instructional material in more than 150 subject areas. NovaNET currently delivers more than 2.5 million hours of instruction each year to adult and young adult students throughout the United States. NovaNET combines the power of an Integrated Learning

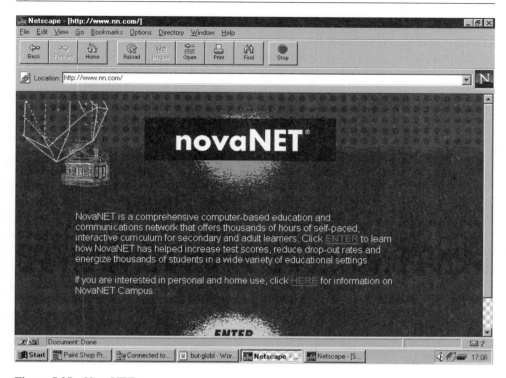

Figure 5.25   NovaNET

System with the flexibility of a wide-area network, producing one of the most comprehensive educational resources available today. Continuously upgraded and enhanced, NovaNET is the culmination of 30 years of research and is used by a growing community of more than 100 000 learners and educators in the USA.

Your link to learning

NovaNET harnesses modern computer technology to empower educators, enhance student learning and increase productivity. NovaNET is a service whose subscribers generally establish one or more computer labs, each of which is connected to NovaNET via a single data circuit. Once connected, subscribers may access the full library of NovaNET lessons and tests. NovaNET automatically stores all student data for instructor review. Instructors also can develop customized courses and communicate using NovaNET's Internet-compatible e-mail.

NovaNET is compatible with industry-standard DOS, Windows and

Macintosh computers and does not require a large investment in specialized hardware. NovaNET can also be distributed through existing local or wide-area networks to bring state-of-the-art educational software to every computer in a facility. Because NovaNET is self-paced, interactive and easy to use, learners spend less time achieving the same level of mastery as those in traditional classroom programmes. NovaNET offers:

- the world's largest library of interactive curriculum materials;
- powerful student management and record-keeping tools, Internet-compatible electronic mail, notes files and online conferencing;
- testing, assessment and test construction and delivery software;
- the ability to develop customized curricula; and
- membership in an innovative, technology-enriched community of educators.

Who can NovaNET help?

NovaNET has delivered convincing results with adult and young adult learners in diverse instructional settings. With courseware accommodating levels ranging from pre-skills through to post-secondary, NovaNET is used in schools, colleges and universities, corporations and community-based organizations.

How it works

The Schoolhouse is the heart of Campus. Here you'll find over 1200 lessons ranging from elementary addition to calculus; from spelling to job searching. NovaNET Campus' lessons have been used by over one million students. These lessons are now available via the Internet.

Student management

NovaNET Campus brings these lessons to your home, together with easy-to-use student management features:

- Lessons are organized into logical scope-and-sequence so that beginning students can progress through Campus 'courses'.
- Pre- and post-tests are included, which provide instant results and allow teachers, parents and students to monitor progress.
- Teachers can assign and restrict access to lessons and activities, to structure the student's learning. Alternatively, students can be allowed to select Campus lessons at will to encourage exploratory learning.

Subject areas

Campus lessons range from third grade through to high school level, and include many academic subjects. The lessons are useful for supplementing schoolwork, or to assist in home-schooling. The subjects include the following:

- English
- Social Studies
- Mathematics
- Science
- Career and Technical
- Keyboarding
- Library
- Games
- Assessment and Preparatory Testing.

Prices

Access to over 1200 lessons on NovaNET Campus is free of charge.

Contact details

Web: www.nn.com

Chapter 6
WBT in use

Old-style CBT had a number of drawbacks: it isolated students from one another and the lecturer; it was slow and cumbersome to use; and it offered no facility for tracking students' progress or keeping courseware up to date. In fast-paced industries such as information technology and medicine, for example, CBT often became out of date almost as soon as it was issued, and sometimes even before, wasting a great deal of time and money. However, that was before the Internet – and its corporate cousin, the intranet – opened up a whole new world of possibilities.

Today a new wave of Internet-based products is making it possible for companies and educators to deliver far more sophisticated and useful education programmes. The best of these new systems are like virtual colleges. Not only do they let people work at their own pace from wherever they are and allow organizations to add their own knowledge to ready-made materials, they also act as course administrator and tutor – registering users, assessing their abilities pre- and post-course – even going so far as to build skills profiles of all the people using the system.

In this chapter we shall look at how four organizations in the UK have harnessed WBT to improve the effectiveness of their education and training operations. The organizations featured here are:

- Civil Service College/Ford Motor Company
- Glaxo Wellcome
- Thames Valley Enterprise
- Derwentside College of Further Education.

The Civil Service College

According to industry analysts IDC, the market for computer-based learning is growing at about 31 per cent each year. One of the companies hoping to get out in front of this growth market is Futuremedia, based in Arundel.

In February 1998, Futuremedia launched what it calls 'the first complete Internet-based service for managing world-wide education'. The new system, dubbed Solstra, has been jointly developed by Futuremedia and telecoms giant BT, and is the result of substantial research and pilot tests.

One such test took place in the summer of 1997 at the Civil Service College (CSC) in Sunningdale, Berkshire. The college provides training primarily for UK government employees and private industry but has recently developed a burgeoning overseas market. The majority of their courses are instructor-led, using the traditional chalk and talk method. Testing Solstra was their first step into the new medium.

A regular CSC course, Selling to Government, was adapted for the trial using a combination of text, graphics, scanned photographs and digitized audio for presentation over the Internet. The students linked up to Solstra via the Web and used a Netscape browser to navigate the site. A question-naire administered after the course revealed that 100 per cent of the students reported that they 'liked the way the content was divided into small modules that could be accessed without downloading'. And nine out of ten said they 'would be interested in doing other courses this way'.

> We normally teach that course face-to-face . . . but I think this type of training is going to become more and more common, because our customers are getting farther and farther away. We are doing a great deal of work with customers in Eastern Europe and Africa – places where people have to be transported [to the classroom] – which is so expensive. So we could have a very widely dispersed group of students who could still chat and work together in a virtual classroom via the Internet. It also allows us to do a mix and match face-to-face training and some distance learning. This is technology that people are going to use (D. Hargrave, Senior Lecturer, CSC).

However, these new systems are by no means a replacement for face-to-face training. They are not going to eliminate a lecturer, nor the require-ment to have everyone together in a classroom.

> What they are particularly well suited for . . . is the kind of situation where everyone can't get together or when the teacher wants to expand the classroom beyond the four walls. Then, an Internet-based system can help companies reach a much bigger audience without a time delay, and keep track of all students' progress through their coursework (M. Johansson, Director, Futuremedia).

Ford Motor Company

This is precisely what sparked Ford Motor Company's interest. Ford already has a global intranet reaching plants throughout the world. No stranger to the pitfalls of corporate education programmes, Ford has also been using CD-ROM, CBT and interactive video training since 1986. 'There's an audience that requires training who can't leave their work place for a two- or three-day training course, and may not even be able to allocate time in a learning centre for a couple of hours. But they could access small chunks of manageable learning at their desktops' (Susan Metté, a learning development specialist working as a consultant to Ford).

Ford, in Dagenham, Essex, carried out a pilot trial of its QS-9000 awareness course during December 1997. Like the Civil Service College programme, Ford already offers this course in a classroom setting. There were two purposes to the trial. The first was to get feedback from the customers who will use the Solstra system. In other words, what do they think of this new training method, the effectiveness of the delivery method, and the fact that they can now access it through the company intranet? The second was to trial the computer-based course itself. About 1000 Ford employees who have already taken the half-day, classroom course were asked to take it again online to enable Ford to evaluate how the intranet-based version compares with the classroom training.

The Ford system comprises four main elements:

- An adviser who delivers only those lessons needed.
- A reference library which offers books, disks and contacts to telephone for further information.
- A 'tools' section for producing projects.
- The training programme itself.

One unique aspect of the system is how a student can dip-in and dip-out of the different course sections. Participants can go straight into the Tools section, and if they discover they don't really understand how to use it, they can go directly back into the training, or into the reference and back again.

> That's a kind of flexibility I haven't seen on the market before . . . If you go to a classroom training session, you're inevitably taught elements that you already know as well as gaining the new information you require. With Solstra, you can focus on what you don't know, and you can do it whenever you want (P. Pestell, Ford Motor Company).

But what is really revolutionary is the way the trial system administers itself.

It is not enough just to supply material to those who need training. I have to know whether they have accessed this information, or whether I need to chase them. It is extremely important that I keep their records up-to-date. We try to ensure training requests made by our managers are met within an agreed time frame. Before now there was no way a commercial package could monitor and record people's progress. I had to rely on them to report back to me that they had completed a course so that I could input the data into my own records. Now their training can be kept up to date automatically, freeing up managers' time and reducing administration dramatically (P. Pestell, Ford Motor Company).

Like most companies, Ford develops its own training courses. For this reason, a course authoring tool has been included in Solstra to allow companies to create their own training, though it is also expected to run most existing packages.

For the first time, you can really make learning and knowledge available and exciting . . . On the one hand, an organisation can push out materials to the individual. On the other, the individuals can raise their hands and say, 'these are things that I'm really good at; these are things that I want to do; these are things that I'm an expert in' and to make the information available as needed throughout the company. This will allow companies to find people who have a specific expertise and an interest in doing something new (M. Johansson, Director, Futuremedia).

Today – in the era of the virtual team – this could be the kind of competitive advantage businesses won't want to miss.

Contact details

Mick Durham at BT
E-mail: DURHAMN@gresham.agw.bt.com
Tel: 0171-356 3603
Mats Johansson, Futuremedia
Tel: 01243 555000

Glaxo Wellcome: IT training over the intranet

The growth in the use of corporate intranets has resulted in major cost savings when deploying software throughout an organization. Training in particular is significantly more cost-effective when it is delivered in this way. Glaxo Wellcome is a pioneer in using and deploying training software to its IT professionals throughout the organization via its corporate intranet.

Glaxo Wellcome is one of the leading pharmaceutical companies in the world, manufacturing many market leading drugs. Since the merger of Glaxo and Wellcome in 1995, IT training has been organized through external classroom-based vendors as and when it seemed necessary. There was no real internal training path for IT professionals. By late 1995 Glaxo Wellcome, a fully merged organization operating on the leading edge of technology and development, put plans into place for restructuring its IT infrastructure. The migration to Windows NT 4.0 as an operating environment, which was known as the InfoEdge programme, demanded the mass re-skilling of many IT staff, both in the UK and the USA.

As with any new technology or technology migration, the importance of sufficient training should never be underestimated. However, until the advent of CBT, this was considered to be one of the costly sides to implementing new technologies.

> We needed to ensure that the roll-out of Windows NT was as seamless as possible. Historically, we had used Windows 3.x and Windows for Workgroups. Windows NT provides more functionality and flexibility for remote access over our global network, gaining some semblance of desktop common log-on. Training is a major part of its success. We wanted it to be cost-effective, flexible and easy for our entire population of IT staff to access.
>
> Our experience of CBT to date was that it was basic text and graphics, without the course content. We were therefore pleasantly surprised when we picked up a CD-ROM from CBT Systems and carried out a trial on it. After extensive evaluation, we realised CBT would be an affordable way to provide individual training to all of our IT staff. We initially considered deploying CBT onto over 250 workstations in the UK and 250 workstations in the US, but we really wanted something we could implement instantly (T. Smithies, Glaxo Wellcome).

The intranet seemed like the obvious choice. At Glaxo Wellcome, the intranet is widely used by most of the organization. Access to it is controlled and most workgroups are Web-enabled. The intranet is used to distribute a range of company information such as divisional and project information, annual reports and departmental reports. In addition, it is used by workgroups to communicate and by internal newsgroups to discuss issues such as strategic initiatives. Glaxo Wellcome could now extend its use by deploying company-wide IT training.

> At the time, CBT Systems were developing CBTWeb, a new product that would for the first time enable us to deliver IT training for Windows NT over our intranet . . . CBTWeb would allow us to extend the reach of our training to all employees wherever they are in the enterprise. What's more it would mean that we could deliver the training immediately without the implementation time-scale normally associated with the deliverance of training, nor the administration overheads (T. Smithies, Glaxo Wellcome).

Late in 1996, Glaxo Wellcome reviewed CBTWeb and the full Microsoft curriculum for Windows NT 4.0. It also received WinTRACS, CBT Systems' comprehensive administration and management system which would enable Glaxo Wellcome to monitor the usage of the training software over its intranet.

> Once the interactive training software was set up on the intranet, IT professionals could access the course they wanted from an easy-to-use menu. For management of the training, we use the WinTRACS software, which allows enrolment details for each course to be logged by the training administrator. Pre-defined menus ensured that only students registered for the training courses are allowed access to the courses that they have registered for (T. Smithies, Glaxo Wellcome).

Once registered, a student can access the intranet, using any Web browser and access the NT 4.0 training courses Web page. This takes the student directly into the CBT Systems Training homepage menu and requests his/her name and system ID before allowing them to download the course. The course downloads quickly, taking only a few minutes. It automatically decompresses and installs a Windows 3.1 icon or Windows 95 shortcut, instantly recognizing the operating system being used by the student. Once downloaded, the course can be accessed and completed at the student's discretion.

  Glaxo is also looking at the recently announced CBTWeb LivePlay, which adds real-time interactivity to CBTWeb, enabling students to run training software live over its intranet. With CBTWeb LivePlay, courses located on Glaxo's Web Server can be accessed over the intranet and taken live in real time, without having to be downloaded to a hard disk. Once a course module is complete, the student uploads his/her results to Win-

TRACs using FTP (File Transfer Protocol) within the NT server to a special directory set up on the intranet.

> Using CBTWeb to deploy the training courses over the company intranet has meant that we have already achieved time and cost savings by significantly reducing the company administration . . . Students have access to full course descriptions and details of course availability, and can review recommended training paths to help them identify courses that meet their training needs. This means that for the first time at Glaxo Wellcome there is a training path for IT staff to develop real skills and take industry certification if they require. (T. Smithies, Glaxo Wellcome).

WinTRACS enables Glaxo Wellcome to monitor course usage. It produces full audit reports so that the company can manage the effectiveness of training programmes. Because WinTRACS receives the course results back from the student, it can track their progress and flag any problem areas and respond to them directly in person.

> We now have a direct control over the training paths of our employees as well as being able to train more people for the same budget . . . Because the students can refer back to the course any time that is convenient to them, it makes far better use of their time. It's also useful if later on you want to refer back to a particular course instruction and take some refresher training . . . The Windows NT 4.0 courses themselves are very good . . . Each course is interactive, ensuring that the student receives skills transfer by asking questions. Graphics are used throughout the courses to aid skills transfer where appropriate. We are very impressed by the course content and quality of the learning . . . The use of good quality training software that can be deployed in a cost effective way throughout any organisation can only mean that our IT staff are truly skilled in the technologies that the organisation is using (T. Smithies, Glaxo Wellcome).

Each CBT Systems course is developed in conjunction with Microsoft and other vendors to ensure the right quality of course content that will lead students on the path to certification where appropriate. The Microsoft Windows NT courses being used at Glaxo Wellcome will prepare students for the Microsoft 70–7 and 70–5 examinations. Glaxo Wellcome have achieved quality training for over 250 IT professionals in the UK and US which is both cost-effective and flexible, allowing these IT professionals to access the intranet from their workstation wherever or whenever they want to, particularly if they are working remotely.

Contact details

Angela Kyte at CBT Systems
E-mail: ukcbt@cbtsys.com
Tel: 0181-283 1800

Thames Valley Enterprise

In August 1996, Thames Valley Enterprise (TVE) and UK trainers Peritas offered 50 unemployed people free courses, each for 300 hours of training, delivered by the Internet through the Peritas Online service. The offer was open to anyone who had been out of work for at least six months, even if not registered as unemployed. Preference was given to those in the Thames Valley area, although the courses were open to anyone in Europe.

The project was designed to help those looking for work to improve their skills and confidence and make more informed choices about employment and training needs, reintegrating them into the job market. The objective was 80 per cent of all participants to achieve a relevant qualification and 90 per cent to progress to employment, further education or training. The project could then be used as a blueprint for schemes in other areas of the country.

Peritas Online gives access to training to anyone with a PC and an Internet link, anywhere in the world. It provides for those for whom classroom training is not a viable option, perhaps because of cost, mobility, geography or time. The TVE project enabled participants to choose from the full range of Peritas courses, including technical training, office applications such as Microsoft Office and personal skills training such as time management. As well as gaining access to expert tuition from their PC, participants can take advantage of the online forums and user groups which provide contact points for advice, and information on local and national job vacancies.

Eight months after the start of the scheme, 56 unemployed individuals had undertaken training with 74 Microsoft-approved qualifications being achieved. 'These individuals have gained valuable skills and expertise that undoubtedly leave them better prepared for the increasingly competitive job market place' (J. Thompson, Thames Valley Enterprise). The personal statements of the two following candidates made during interviews with the author demonstrate some of the benefits they have experienced from training through Peritas Online.

Colin Ewart (46, mature student) was in his final year of an Information Technology degree at Portsmouth University. He was keen to use the summer recess of 1996 to work on developing his PC skills in order to improve his working practices and personal efficiency. Ewart began training in June 1996 and has since completed courses on Word for Windows 6, Excel for Windows and Access 2 for Windows, and is currently working through the Networking Essentials course. Ewart was not an IT novice when his training began, being spreadsheet and word processing proficient, but he understood that there was a lot more he could learn about the applications, rating his knowledge level at about 20 per cent. 'The training opened my eyes to the levels I could achieve and enabled me to improve my personal productivity.'

Ewart received his courseware and course brochure through the post but, from that stage onwards, all communication with his tutor took place electronically via e-mail, including the submission and return of assignments. 'My tutor was very supportive and always responded quickly to my queries via e-mail.' Studying through Peritas Online enabled him to work at home at a time and pace of his own choosing. Although the PC applications Ewart studied online were not directly related to his IT university degree course, he says that training online has improved his personal productivity to such an extent that he completed his university dissertation in about half the time it would have taken without the training.

Although now concentrating on studying for his finals, Ewart intends to complete the Access 2 for Windows course and go on to get a top-level degree pass. 'I believe the combination of the theoretical and technical knowledge gained at university and the practical computing skills developed through the Thames Valley Enterprise Project make me more employable. I feel confident that these skills will help me to find rewarding work in an increasingly competitive job market.'

Haydn Evans (47, former building contracts manager) became unemployed from his job in the building industry, an area hit badly by the recession of the late 1980s. Having long had an interest in computers he was keen to move in this direction in his search for work. He understood the competitive nature of the industry and recognized his need to retrain in order to find employment. Evans read about the free training places on an e-mail bulletin board which is used by the unemployed as a focal point for discussion and job hunting tips. He had already undertaken a number of training courses: six months after becoming unemployed he began the Government's 'Training For Work' scheme through which he learnt the 'C' computer programming language and began voluntary teaching at a local college.

Evans saw Microsoft training as the key to breaking into the computing industry. Peritas Online enabled him to gain professional skills training at home and at times that worked around his work at the college. He has completed the Word 7 and Access 7 courses and explained that he found the training slotted easily into his daily routine and felt the manuals were clearly written and user friendly. He readily admits that the training has made a difference to his life. 'This new form of training has enabled me to build up my CV by completing recognized professional training courses.

This gave me confidence in my job search, knowing I had some real preparation for my new chosen career path.'

Evans is now working for a computer company that specializes in a new programming methodology, '4GL Magic language'. He works alongside others with programming qualifications, diplomas and university degrees. His background may not be a traditional one and he now faces the difficult task of consolidating his knowledge and position, but the online training he undertook has given him a way into this highly competitive industry. He recognizes that the hard work is only just beginning but happily comments, 'It has helped me to retrain for a new career. Next to winning the lottery, being offered my current job after two years of unemployment was the best thing that could have happened.'

Phase 2 of this project ran from April to June 1997, and places for a further 25 students are available under Phase 3.

Contact details

Stephanie Tanser at Peritas
E-mail: stanser@peritas.com
Tel: 01753-604125

Derwentside FE College reaches out

Derwentside Further Education (FE) College in the former steel town of Consett in County Durham has achieved remarkable success over the past year in signing up over 600 students for electronically delivered Rural Vocational Training across a wide rural area of Northumberland and Durham (see Box 6.1). IT may play a key role in delivering education in the future and the funding which keeps further education colleges viable.

There is little doubt that incorporation has brought many changes to the way FE colleges operate and finance the courses they offer. Probably one of the greatest changes has been the breakdown of geographical barriers. Just because a potential student might live nearby doesn't now necessarily mean that the college of choice will automatically be the closest one. Where FE colleges once had their own distinct patch and a virtual monopoly on students within it, new communications technologies are enabling those fleet of foot down the superhighway to grab students for new courses, and the FEFC funding that goes with them. For some it is a major new opportunity, while for others it is a distinct threat. Who will win out?

In November 1996, County Durham's Derwentside College of FE, located in the middle of Consett, launched a programme to provide basic

Box 6.1   Derwentside College's Rural Vocational Training Programme

Study material

The study material for the course is in the form of a computer-based training programme (CBT). Students either download the four CBTs by e-mail as they need them or they are installed by their tutor at induction. The programs are self-running and simulate the relevant application on screen, prompting the student to respond using the keyboard and mouse in order to learn certain tasks. This information is later used by the student to complete the assignments.

Student assignments

The assignments, which students undertake after studying each CBT, are written in RSA examination format and are transmitted by e-mail to each student as required. On completion of the assignment the student returns it electronically to his or her tutor who marks it on screen and returns it with comments again by e-mail.

E-mail learning

Electronic mail (e-mail) is used as the prime means of communication between student and tutor. CBTs and assignments are transmitted by e-mail and students may communicate with their tutors on any other issues either by e-mail or telephone. In practice, students quickly adapt to using electronic mail and make greater use of it than just for study purposes. Over 80 per cent of students found e-mail a satisfactory method of distance learning.

The courses

The basic nature of RSA CLAIT level 1 is reflected in the ability level of students taking the course. Many are raw beginners and consequently their reason for taking the course may be as broad as wanting to learn about computers. The initial course offers up to 30 hours of basic computer training covering Windows applications in e-mail, word processing, database and spreadsheet management. In a survey of those who had taken the course almost half said that they wanted to learn a specific application and a significant proportion indicated an interest in accounting and business skills courses delivered in this way.

The students

The majority of students felt that their employment prospects were enhanced. Almost everyone felt that their confidence in using computers had increased. In broad terms, both their promotional and employment prospects are improved in the long term.

Finance
The RSA CLAIT training programme is significantly subsidized to attract students in the early phase and to ensure that it is financially viable. Funding is received from the European Community from the ERDF and Single Regeneration Budget (SRB), and supported by the Rural Development Commission and Northumberland TEC. Students pay £50 and receive a rebate of £32.50 when they successfully complete the course. A fee of £17.50 is retained to cover administration and the RSA examination fee. The refunded element serves as an incentive to students to complete their studies and to some extent reinforces the fact that software and a modem is being made available to them on loan for the duration of the course.

The future
Participants in RVT have identified future areas of training to enhance their specific areas of business activity. Most of the participants had their first introduction to one aspect of the Internet by using e-mail on this course. The value of e-mail in the business environment is evident. The greater value of the Internet as a business tool for communications, marketing, intelligence, information and, of course, training is quickly reaching the kind of SMEs participating in the Rural Vocational Training programme.

computer training to local small business and the self-employed under the Rural Vocational Training (RVT) programme. The programme was designed to deliver training to RSA CLAIT I and II standards via e-mail links. Derwentside provided a tutor to help install a modem (if necessary) and provide assistance by telephone. Otherwise the students downloaded courses and test assignments on to their own computers and communicated with their tutors and each other by e-mail.

The programme had to attract 100 students from a defined Objective 5b rural area to gain European funding. In this part of the UK, small businesses (SMEs in Eurospeak) are really small, most with just a handful of employees for whom the luxury of even taking a few hours off work for training was a major obstacle. The distances involved and travelling times to Derwentside also effectively precluded part-time evening and weekend courses.

But from the same town which gave the world Phileas Fogg crisps and snacks, in just under a year, Derwentside now has an enrolment of more than 600 students for its RVT course, has established a number of outreach centres beyond its traditional catchment area, and plans to extend the programme to more advanced RSA standards and use videoconferencing to enhance the electronic course delivery. Students have been enrolled across a wide area of Northumberland and County Durham, and many are in areas that are much closer geographically to other FE colleges. Some had never even heard of Derwentside before the programme.

So, how did they do it and do their neighbours in further education look at them as a threat or wish to emulate their success? Will courses delivered by new information technology pose a threat to traditional teaching jobs?

> 'The real threat is probably in doing nothing, in standing still . . . If you don't explore these technologies, someone else will. That's our philosophy.' In a way this epitomizes the spirit of a town that died and then was reborn. Consett lost its reason for being when the steel industry that supported it closed down in the 1980s. It has taken the town nearly 20 years to get back on its feet and it doesn't want to slip back; the waste land of the old steel mill may have recovered, but many of the people are just now beginning to emerge economically. There was an in-built need for new skills and training, much of which depended on Derwentside's survival and success.
>
> We didn't really think that we were that ahead of many other colleges, but we've since found out that most are just looking at the technology and how to use it, starting pilot programmes to find out if it will work . . . It certainly hasn't been that easy to get where we are today with over 600 students on one electronically delivered course. There are probably no short cuts. It requires an enormous amount of commitment from the top and throughout the organisation . . .
>
> Rather than being a threat to traditional, in-class teaching, electronic delivery absolutely requires the assurance of a real presence. It's the tutors that make the courses work, the rest is just mechanics, replacing the ride in the car or bus to the college . . . Training the tutors to an excellent standard was one of the single most important facets. They must first understand the concept and be committed to using it. They also had to be on call virtually all the time, seven days a week, because the courses are designed to be taken at the student's convenience, not ours (C. Miller, Derwentside College).

Another key factor was the establishment of college outreach centres, in effect bringing Derwentside and its resources to the smaller communities, being closer to the people and the growing numbers of students taking courses. One such centre is in Haltwhistle, Northumberland. It's a long way up the South Tyne valley and over 30 miles from Consett. On Haltwhistle's main street a small door leads the way to architect Gerry Hagon's practice and here, in a tiny room which is the front office, Gill Hall is Derwentside College. There's no doubt that Gill's calm demeanour and well placed advice could remove the fear from the most confirmed technophobe. The steady chatter of students inputting on keyboards attests to the fact that this is a busy centre for learning new skills for a wide variety of people: the local newsagent, a policeman, farmers and their wives, a postman; more than 100 people in total from what is a relatively small, dispersed rural community. Gill provides the on-site help which makes it all work, tutor and outreach centre manager rolled into one. A live presence, but one which is also linked to the college and the company which helped set up the system, TNL in Hexham, by videoconferencing links.

'There's no doubt that with just electronic links, you lose the immediacy of reaction and feedback that comes with live teaching' (C. Miller, Derwentside College). A survey of students has revealed that while they usually take readily to using e-mail and consider its use as a newly acquired skill in its own right, the live presence of a tutor greatly enhances learning. Derwentside has also established outreach centres in Hexham, roughly halfway between Haltwhistle and Consett, and at Stanhope and Lanchester in County Durham. The Durham outreach centres, while a bit closer, are still in relatively remote places where public transport services are few and far between; Lanchester has almost 200 students on the RVT programme, while the Durham Dales Centre in Stanhope has 50. Over 200 students take the courses directly from home or at their workplace.

Has all this activity created any reaction from others in the local educational community? Hexham's Queen Elizabeth High School, with its own role in providing further education to protect, has expressed some reservations about Derwentside setting up a local extension in Hexham. 'The great concern must be that colleges from outside the area such as Derwentside, will wish to be involved in activities where they see an opportunity for profit but will not be prepared to become involved in the socially necessary but non-lucrative aspects of community education', stated Sandy Mearns, Chairman of the Community Education Sub-Committee, in a letter to the local newspaper.

In an age of competition everywhere, is this true? 'We would much rather approach this with co-operation rather than confrontation . . . but we've got to face the fact that new communications technologies mean that competition can come from anywhere in the world. The only way to compete in the marketplace is to provide excellent courses that are well run' (C. Miller, Derwentside College). A survey among students taking the RVT course showed over 80 per cent of respondents found e-mail a satisfactory method of distance learning. Only one-third said they were actively looking for a course of this type, and only half said they would have considered other courses if the RVT programme had not been available. This would seem to suggest that electronic delivery has created an entirely new market for FE colleges, rather than attracting potential students away from traditionally delivered courses at other colleges.

With distance learning by electronic communication, getting the technology to work smoothly is also a large part of the equation. To do this Derwentside turned to TNL, an IT company based in Hexham, which had hands-on experience in using IT to run its own operations. There were some teething problems, but these were ironed out with experience and they've now moved on to the next stage of development, supplementing the text communication with videoconferencing, linking the outreach centres to the college. 'This allows us to bring the element of human interaction between the tutor and the student as well as being able to share an electronic desktop to actually work together . . . It's more active video working than just the passive role implied by videoconferencing' (P. Rodger, TNL).

TNL was also responsible for marketing the programme and managing the team of tutors. Apart from getting the technology to work, the competence and motivation of the tutors is absolutely critical. 'They find the concept of teaching remotely exciting and we put in place a system of stage-based payments as an incentive to high completion rates for the courses' (P. Rodger, TNL). After a year's experience, TNL have now derived a fully-costed model which works out at roughly £115 per student; while the RVT programme was designed for small business and self-employed people, this will be applied to individual students under the Remote Independent Learning Programme (RILP).

The future?

> From its first conception it took Derwentside almost three years to achieve success with the RVT programme . . . But the communications technology has improved drastically in that time and we are quite well up on the learning curve of using it. There will always be a role for live teaching, but the teaching profession shouldn't see remote electronic delivery methods as a threat. It will involve a change in their thinking and culture, but a positive change at that. Learning must be the basis of success, not the technology employed (C. Miller, Derwentside College).

Derwentside's Centre in Management Studies has already launched a project to use the system to teach basic management skills using e-mail, videoworking and the Internet. The virtual is becoming more real every day.

Contact details

Barry Roxburgh, TNL Hexham
E-mail: barry_roxburgh@tnl.co.uk
Tel: 01434-681987

Chapter 7

Evaluating and justifying WBT for your organization

In this chapter we concentrate on how to evaluate and justify WBT for your organization. In particular, we shall explore the necessary steps in evaluating whether WBT is right for your organization, how to run a pilot trial programme to quantify the benefits and how to justify WBT to senior management.

WBT: the end of the classroom?

I am often asked whether the proliferation in the use of technology-based training, and the increasing use of online learning, means the days of the classroom are numbered. One of the foremost commentators on training, and online training in particular, Elliott Masie, believes that it is one of the great myths of learning technology: 'No, it actually grows in importance by changing and adapting to the new needs of learners . . . Sure, we would all like to find ways to decrease our travel and accommodation budgets, and there are clear pathways towards alternative delivery. But the classroom is not going away'. Masie has produced a list of reasons why people want to go to instructor-led classes:

- They want to get away from the distractions of the workplace so they can focus on learning.
- They want to verbalize as part of the learning process.
- They want to work with technology or systems that are not available at work.
- They want to interact with a teacher, subject matter expert or instructor.
- They are comfortable with the classroom environment.
- They love to hear instructors' stories.
- They want their manager to value the effort they put into the learning process.

These are all legitimate and powerful forces. Even the most interactive WBT will not eliminate these drivers. And the Masie Center has discovered the most interesting trend – online learning actually increases demand for classroom instruction. The more you get your workforce excited about learning, the more they want to learn – including visits to classrooms.

Masie argues that we have to accept these drivers, then think about how the classroom can be repositioned in our organizations:

- **Make classes shorter**. Three hours may be closer to learners' needs than five days.
- **Blend your modalities**. Use online learning for information delivery and blend it with short sessions which focus on verbalization, remediation and interaction.
- **Blur the distinctions**. Use the classroom as a facilitated lab, providing an alternative to the workplace as a learning location. Several hours of a class could be delivered via an intranet, right to the classroom.
- **Add interaction to online learning**. Conference calls, threaded online discussions and visits to the workplace by subject matter experts add interaction to technology-delivered learning.
- **Ask 'why?'**. Ask your learners the real reasons for preferring classroom instruction. This may point out weakness in your online learning strategy.
- **Market with equivalence**. Make sure that you spend as much on marketing online learning as traditional learning.
- **Build value perception**. Work with senior management and with your staff to build respect and value for learning that occurs outside the classroom.
- **Change your language**. Lead a dialogue about the performance improvements that will occur, rather than the modality of delivery.

So now let's start on the business of evaluating and justifying WBT and online learning in your organization. To make a start, you need to revisit the prime benefits of online learning.

Revisiting the benefits

The following are some of the points that you will first need to consider and then validate for accuracy within your own training set up. Once you have quantified that the statements are correct for your own situation, you can use them as the basis of your final report to management. Although we have covered the points before in the book, it is worth considering them again.

Firstly, the benefits of distance learning. These, of course, apply to all forms of CBT or multimedia training programmes, as well as online learning:

- **Lower cost of training**. With instructor-led training, a large percentage of the total cost is made up of instructor salaries, and travel and facility costs associated with bringing instructors and students together. These costs can often be eliminated when using distributed learning to deliver training, thereby reducing the total costs of a training programme. Studies have shown that training costs can be reduced by as much as 25–75 per cent over instructor-led training (*Multimedia Training Newsletter*, 1996).
- **Decreased learning time**. Distributed learning is interactive allowing learners to control their own learning experience. They are able to bypass training modules that are not relevant and concentrate on only those topics they need. This reduces the training time required. Recent studies have shown that learning time can be reduced by as much as 20–80 per cent compared to instructor-led training (*Multimedia Training Newsletter*, 1996).
- **Higher retention rate**. The ability of distributed learning to combine text, graphics, audio and video in an interactive environment enables the development of courses which simulate real-life scenarios and provide immediate feedback. Although more difficult to measure, it is believed that in many situations learners actually retain more using simulation models.

Now, let's outline the additional benefits brought by WBT. By combining the interactive and rich multimedia capabilities of CBT with the power of the Internet as the communications medium, significant new benefits can be achieved:

- **Lower development costs**. The Internet has introduced a common set of industry standards for developing applications, HTML and Java. What makes these so powerful is that they can run applications independent of the computer platform (computer type and operating system) on which they run. With WBT, it is not necessary to develop a different version of the course for each platform.
- **Lower distribution costs**. Once a course has been installed on a Web server, it becomes immediately available to everyone. When a course needs updating, it can be updated immediately by downloading it on the Web server. For CD-ROM courses, any updates require costly duplication expenditure for the producer and every user must install the new course on their desktop. With WBT, updated courses are available to everyone immediately.
- **Measuring effectiveness of training**. The Internet is the only medium, other than the telephone, that supports two-way communication. With distributed learning, we are able to take advantage of this two-way communication to track the performance of every student. Using this data, we can measure the overall effectiveness of the training programme and improve on it based on the results. Individual learners'

results can be used as part of the management or education process. In this way, distributed learning can actually be used to support formal certification and accredited degree programmes. With traditional CBT, it is often difficult to verify whether training has been received and the extent to which the information has been understood. As a result, it is difficult to measure the overall effectiveness of the training and the value of the investment.

Setting up and running your own pilot trial

To be aware of the value of WBT and online learning, you should take some of the many demonstration courses that are available. These courses are normally free of charge and will not upset the training budget. The choice of suppliers is up to you, but I would recommend taking some different courses, each utilizing different WBT elements. Experiencing good online chat facilities with your tutor and other students is extremely educational. A good way to start is to follow the steps outlined in Chapter 3.

Once you have taken a course module and feel more conversant with WBT, then you will need to carry out some pre- and post-course evaluations yourself to obtain some brief 'scientific' data which can be used later in both the Full Pilot Trial and your report to management. Points to address in your evaluation are listed below. They are by no means comprehensive but do cover all of the major areas. You may like to draw up your own Evaluation Sheet, which you can use to carry out some site comparisons. Additionally, these sheets will be necessary when you carry out your Full Pilot Trial later:

1. **Administration**
   - Were you able to connect to the service frequently?
   - Was it easy to navigate and was the interface user-friendly?
   - Did information download in an acceptable manner?
   - How long did each session take?
   - What were the times of day and which days did you log-on?
2. **Communication**
   - Was the communication between you and the instructor/other students good? What benefits did you achieve from the communication?
   - Did the instructor provide a good service to you?
   - Was the interaction between yourself and instructor important? Why?
   - Did you feel that the interactivity was about right, too little or too much? Why?
3. **Testing**
   - Were the tests helpful or a hindrance?
   - Did the tests encourage you?

- Was testing used enough, too much or too little?
- Was there pre-course testing?

4. Learning points
- Describe, in overall terms, how the WBT helped you to learn.
- Was the training clearly explained?
- Was the amount of information easily digested?
- Did the use of graphics, audio, animation and video help you to learn?

Once you have carried out your personal trials, write a detailed report summarizing all of your findings; include facts and figures, as they will be useful later. This report can remain private to you, to help you set up the Full Trial programme and later act as useful reference for your final report to management.

The next step is to choose just one of the courses, and give your work colleagues the project of taking the trial course. Make sure that they use the same evaluation sheets that you compiled previously. Take an interest in their course and monitor their progress; a highly motivated trialist will achieve better results. At the end of their course, ask them to compile a report on their findings. This will be invaluable in confirming your observations or highlighting any points you may have missed or perhaps not encountered. Ask them for a personal statement about the course, whether they found it beneficial, whether it could have been better in the classroom or on CD-ROM, and what they thought of the WBT experience overall.

Now that you have experienced WBT yourself and feel fairly familiar with its advantages and pitfalls, you need to concentrate on how you can justify WBT for your organization.

Justifying Web-based training

Let's now look at how you can go about identifying whether WBT is right for your company, and if so, how to go about setting up your own strategy to obtain management commitment for your WBT project.

Is WBT right for your company?

For every type of training project the total cost of training can be split between two categories: the up-front costs of developing the training and the ongoing costs of delivering the training. Generally speaking, distributed learning has higher development costs and lower delivery costs than instructor-led training. Distributed learning is most effective in situations where the savings in delivery offset the additional costs of development. This results in a lower cost of training and a higher return on investment.

Below is a list of issues, from Asymetrix Learning Systems, which will help you to decide whether WBT is right for your environment:

- **Geographic location**. Using classroom training to train students throughout a geographically dispersed organization may be prohibitively expensive owing to the significant travel and accommodation costs involved. If your company is geographically dispersed, with many people to train, distributed learning is often a much more efficient approach to training.
- **Size of audience**. There are significant logistical complexities involved in training larger audiences, including classroom facilities and the amount of time it takes to train large numbers. As a result, distributed learning will often be a more efficient method of reaching larger audiences, whereas instructor-led training may be more adequate for reaching smaller audiences.
- **Dynamic information**. When training is of a dynamic nature, such as fast-changing methods, procedures or products, it is important that learners are kept up-to-date with the latest changes. In these situations, it may be more efficient to deliver incremental training using distributed learning.
- **Timing of delivery**. When situations arise demanding rapid distribution of training, such as the release of new products, timing may be critical. In these situations, distributed learning is the most effective method.

In addition to the factors above, there are several additional issues which need to be considered when determining whether or not distributed learning is the right way to go for your organization:

- **Objective vs. subjective**. You need to consider the degree of objective versus subjective content. If the training is associated with more objective skills, such as how to complete a given task, then distributed learning may be all that is necessary. If, on the other hand, the training is associated with more subjective skills, such as ethics or leadership, then classroom or group work may also be required.
- **Level of expertise**. Another important consideration is the level of expertise that the training is expected to produce. If the learner needs to reach expert status, then some combination of classroom-based training and distributed learning would be required. If, however, the learner only needs to develop a level of general understanding, or learn how to carry out procedures, then distributed learning is often all the training that is required.

Cost savings analysis

This section will show how the benefits provided by distributed learning have a dramatic impact in lowering the total cost of a training programme. By lowering the costs, and in some cases improving the quality of the learning, distributed learning is able to raise the return on training investment significantly. The analysis, provided by Asymetrix Learning Systems, compares the cost of distributed learning with traditional instructor-led (ILT). We shall also compare distributed learning with conventional CBT delivered on CD-ROM.

Asymetrix's findings show that in a typical training scenario, CBT delivers a 3 per cent saving over ILT during the first year of implementation. By taking advantage of the Internet to deliver the training, a 23 per cent saving over ILT is achieved during the first year, a full 20 per cent higher than savings with CBT (see Figure 7.1). Cost savings become even more dramatic when we look at consecutive years following the initial investment in WBT. These savings are primarily due to a lower cost of training development.

In year 2, CBT delivers a 26 per cent saving over ILT, while WBT delivers a 43 per cent saving over ILT (see Figure 7.2). The benefits attributed to the Internet are, therefore, 17 per cent higher than those of CBT. In Asymetrix's hypothetical scenario, the reader can apply the costs which are

	Classroom Training (Year 1)	Computer-Based Training (Year 1)	Internet-Based Training (Year 1)
Development Cost	$160,000	$600,000	$500,000
Delivery Cost			
Wages of Trainees	$192,000	$115,200	$96,000
Opportunity Cost	$288,000	$172,800	$144,000
Travel Cost	$120,000	–	–
Trainer Wages	$150,000	$75,000	$75,000
Trainer Travel	$104,000	–	–
Distribution	$50,000	$64,000	–
Total	$1,064,000	$1,027,400	$815,000
Percentage Savings		3%	23%

Source: Asymetrix Corporation

Figure 7.1   Cost savings analysis: year 1

Cost Savings Analysis - Year 2

	Classroom Training (Year 2)	Computer-Based Training (Year 2)	Internet-Based Training (Year 2)
Development cost	$80,000	$300,000	$250,000
Delivery cost			
Wages of Trainers	$192,000	$115,600	$96,000
Opportunity Cost	$288,000	$172,800	$144,000
Travel Cost	$120,000	-	-
Trainer Wages	$150,000	$75,000	$75,000
Trainer Travel	$104,000	-	-
Distribution	$50,000	$64,000	-
Total	$984,000	$727,400	$565,000
Percentage Savings		26%	40%

Source: Asymetrix Corporation

Figure 7.2   Cost savings analysis: year 2

relative to their own situation to approximate the potential for savings within their own organization.

Obtaining management commitment

The transition from traditional training to web-based learning is still a new, quite radical, unfamiliar change for many of today's businesses. Not only can Web training embrace many different technologies and appearances, but costing can range anywhere from questionably low to unbelievably high. So how can you approach decision makers to build a case for initiating Web-based training now rather than a year or two later? Good salespeople often advise you to first find out what is important to the decision makers, then present your case to emphasize that perspective.

There are at least four different perspectives that you may need to think about to build a case for Web-based training. In an interview with the author, Wayne Schaaf, who helps businesses plan for, design and produce WBT and post-training job aids, outlined the scenario from the perspective of four different decision makers.

Competitive advantage

First, consider George Mossel. To George, 'competitive advantage' is always a main factor in making decisions. Businesses continue to become more globally competitive. Providing value-added services to his customers and giving employees access to current information and technology is a priority for George. This priority is a strategic element in his company's plan for short-term growth. To emphasize competitive advantage, you could approach decision makers such as George with the following points:

* Now is the time to offer your customers access to information that few, if any, of your competitors offer.
* Internet and intranet training will increasingly be used to deliver training over the years to come.
* Initiating Web-based learning now will offer potential press and media visibility for your business. Your company will be viewed as an innovative leader in customer service and learning technology.

Trends and statistics

Sandy Blacketer is a decision maker for a business very similar to George's. Like George, Sandy considers competitive advantage to be important, but needs to see documented trends and statistics to feel more comfortable with supporting Web-based learning. The American Society for Training and Development recently completed a survey and published their findings in their November 1997 magazine. From that extensive article, several trends are worth mentioning when approaching someone with the perspective Sandy holds to:

* The trend towards downsizing is straining the ability of companies to continue to deliver training using the traditional group presentation approach.
* Skill requirements will continue to increase and change more and more as technology continues to advance at a rapid pace.
* Close to 50 per cent of employees currently rely on computers to perform at least portions of their work.
* The use of the Internet and internal intranets will account for 35 per cent of all training within the next three years. By the year 2000, instructor-led training will decrease from 80 per cent at present, to 55 per cent of all training.

Evidence

Ron Kool can appreciate the above perspectives. However, he is more personally moved towards action by evidence that this technology will result in increased effectiveness for his business. Ron was immediately convinced of the value of Web-based learning when he considered its flexibility to present training anywhere his employees and customers are located, at any time, in small enough modules that can meet their immediate need for help or added information. The following arguments represent issues that are important to decision makers like Ron in supporting Web-based training:

- The larger and more geographically dispersed your company, the more likely it is that Web-based learning will save money. It will also minimize the time between the employees' need for training and the time they can receive it.
- When compared with classroom training, there is significantly less chance of embarrassing a learner who needs more detail or more time to understand what is being taught.
- Web-based learning provides a consistent, easy to learn and sometimes fun way to navigate through learning material at the learner's own pace.
- Properly designed, Web-based instruction provides small learning modules which will not overwhelm a learner.
- Aided by close-up illustrations, useful animations, text, colour and sometimes sound, learners often remain more alert when navigating through a short learning module on the Web. Compare that to a lengthy classroom session which may follow a normal working day.
- Training on the Web can be ongoing. This allows for constant improvements and overnight additions and corrections.
- In some cases, Web-based learning may serve as either an effective prerequisite or a follow-up to a class session which continues to be valued by, and offered to, learners at set times.

Bottom line cost/benefit analysis

For many decision makers, like Lori Facchini, only a bottom line cost/benefit analysis will provide the evidence they want before initiating Web-based learning. At present no easy fill-in formula exists to quickly assess this. Lori wants facts on the costs and an understanding of what savings will be gained by making such a major change in the way training is provided to her employees or customers. Costs can be broken down into at least four categories:

- **Web access costs**: one-time costs providing the computer hardware, Web-browser software, networking access to the learners; one time cost of purchasing and establishing a Web server or ongoing costs of leasing server space.

- **Design and project management costs**: one-time costs for collecting basic tutorial copy, optimizing course navigation, analysing essential vs. supplemental learning content, assessing the need and impact of inter-active media, motif selection and layout design, content asset and Web page tracking setup, and user/content-owner design input and approval.
- **Production costs**: Web page construction, creation and preparation of graphics, creation of animation, creation of Java applets, database cre-ation and linking (if required) and administrative shell creation or acquisition (if desired).
- **Ongoing support**: Webmaster monitoring and maintenance of the Web site, establishment of learner IDs (if desired) and revisions to keep material current.

Tangible savings need to be assessed against the current training or alterna-tive training costs. They include:

- No costs for creating, duplicating, inventorying and distributing hard-copy training material/updates.
- No printing or CD-ROM pressing costs.
- Reduced testing costs due to simplified technology, minimal cost updat-ing and multiple platform capability factors.
- No facility and reduced equipment and room setup costs and time.
- No travel-related and course-related participant costs.
- No (or reduced) facilitator/instructor costs.
- No unrecoverable costs due to last-minute participant cancellations.
- No manual grading and reporting of participant testing (if required).
- Depending on the training topic offered, the potential for reduced process errors, reduced scrap, more immediate customer service deliv-ery or a more immediate reduction in the potential for work-related injuries.

Depending on your corporate culture, securing costs and savings of alterna-tives can require some effort or reasonable estimating. A balanced assess-ment would include both quantification of the tangible costs and savings, as well as consideration of the many less tangible benefits outlined earlier.

Full-trial pilot WBT programme

Once you have gained management commitment to carry out a Full Pilot Trial, your work really starts in earnest. So far, you should have gained a considerable amount of experience of WBT, as well as justifications for applying it to your organization and some valuable pre-pilot trial data. But the real test is yet to come. You need to carry out a 'make-or-break' full-blown pilot trial using real trainees and compile a report to management with full justifications attached. Although I cannot guarantee success, if you run your pilot trial following the guidelines below, you will be well on the way.

Before you think about the Full Trial Pilot project, you must ensure that you are ready to proceed. The following checklist will be useful in validating your readiness. Check it now. Can you say 'yes' to all of these points?

I currently have:

- the knowledge and experience to explain the concept, advantages and disadvantages of WBT to all levels of personnel, from senior management to end-user;
- experience of taking WBT programmes;
- the necessary information to outline the cost/benefits, ROI and business benefits of a WBT programme;
- senior management and business unit management approval to conduct a full trial using a sample of current staff;
- adequate resources to run the pilot programme: people, hardware, software, resource centre (if necessary);
- budget approval to access Internet-based WBT site for participants;
- a clear plan on how to carry out pre- and post-course evaluations of the project.

Pre-project planning

As with all projects there is a multitude of things to plan before you can even consider running the project. But, the better and more thoughtfully you plan, covering every possible angle, the more successful your project will be. Time taken at the planning stage will be well spent and the pay-off enormous. The main areas to cover are discussed below; they are not exhaustive, or in any particular order, but by covering these essential points, your project will be guaranteed to get off to a good start.

Project co-ordination

Assuming you are the co-ordinator of the project, you will need to ensure that you will be available and on-call throughout the project. This may include out-of-work hours for participants taking a course module at home in the evening or at weekends. You will also need to be full of enthusiasm and constantly monitoring and taking an interest in each participant. Remember that each of the participants will have different educational backgrounds, concerns, fears and apprehensions. Talk to them and encourage them at all times. Make them feel important.

You will need to identify the course that you use as the pilot programme and arrange log-in passwords for each participant. You will probably also need to arrange payment with the course vendor prior to starting the project, so get that done early and give the online supplier an expected date of project commencement.

Management commitment

Prior to delivering the training programme, ensure that you have received the full commitment from your own manager and the appropriate business unit managers from whose staff you will select the participants. Ensure that the room that will be used for learning (Resource Centre, participant's own desktop, etc.) is reserved for learning for the length of the sessions required. Make sure participants will not be interrupted by their regular job responsibilities during the training. Why don't you encourage your manager to be a participant?

Learning environment

Consider carefully where you expect the learning to take place. Can you use an area of the Resource Centre (if you have one)? Will the area be available on demand for the project? If the participants will be using their own desk or office, ensure that a suitable notice is installed – 'Do not disturb, please. Learning in progress' – in a prominent position. If the participant intends to access the course at home, is there a similar interruption free area available at home?

Technology

This is one area which must be investigated; it is absolutely vital that reliable, dependable equipment is available. If the technology fails, so will your project. So check it out, or get it checked out, early in the planning stage. For each participant, ensure that you have the infrastructure you need: latest version Web browser with appropriate plug-in installed and configured, at least 20 MB free hard disk space, Internet connection, modem, e-mail and chat programs (if required). You may consider this to be an onerous task, but it is absolutely vital to ensure that the equipment does not get in the way of the learning process. Perhaps you can ask one of your friendly IT people to do it for you?

Participants

To be successful you will need full co-operation from the course participants. One of your greatest challenges will be helping them to understand the benefits to them of the project. Just because you may feel excited and enthusiastic about this new course delivery method, you should not assume that everyone will share your feelings automatically. To get everyone working together as one team, including your manager and the business unit managers, you must ensure that everyone is comfortable with the project and, additionally, looking forward to it. One way to do this is to interview would-be participants and ask them why they want to be part of the project. In this way, you will end up with a team focused on its success.

Start your participant selection process by inviting representatives from the various interested groups. Set up a cross-functional team made up of trainers, instructional designers, network staff and end-users (and a manager too, if possible). Provide focus and status for the instructors. Ensure that your instructors are made to feel part of the project, so build a strong sense of their identity and value. Identify in advance any concerns or needs related to the training process and technology and resolve them prior to delivering the first programme.

As the project gets closer, creating a good team spirit is important. So, why not hold a pre-event briefing a couple of weeks before the project goes live? Tell them what you have done to date and walk them through the project: What is the scope of the project? What are the objectives? What is expected of them? What tasks will you be requiring from them? At the pre-event briefing also show them the forms you will need them to complete and the logbook they will need to keep up to date on their daily learning activities. It is important to eliminate any fears, concerns or needs of participants at this stage. Find out what they are and get them fixed. Send them away happy and enthusiastic about the project ahead.

During the project

Once the project is under way, you cannot sit back and let your students simply get on with it. You need to be around, available and on-call to monitor, encourage and report on the progress of the project. It is wise to keep a daily log of events yourself, so that you can refer to them later when you carry out your post-project evaluation meetings. A brief weekly report outlining the progress of the project to your manager, and the appropriate business unit managers, will also help to keep them involved in the success of the project. Communication with them, so that they are fully aware of the progress, is vital to ensure that you keep their commitment and interest. So, as you can see, this period will be a busy one for the project co-ordinator.

Post-project evaluation

At the conclusion of the project, you will need to be ready for a whole range of work. Your aim to is evaluate the effectiveness of the project and report your findings back to your management. It is wise to hold a post-course de-briefing, firstly with the individual participants and secondly with the whole team:

- **Use a multi-level evaluation approach**. To evaluate effectively you will need to note the programme and its impact: student satisfaction, learning transfer, improved job performance, financial impact to the company.
- **Keep the technology transparent**. Discussions at the end of the pilot trial should focus on course content and outcomes achieved and not the technology.

Presenting evaluation findings

Armed with all the facts, figures and written reports from the participants, your task is now to compile the evaluation findings into a concise but factual report to management. I'm sure that you are familiar with writing reports to your management, so we will not go into that here. However, one important point to bear in mind. Your participants are your 'WBT champions'. They can be your ambassadors for WBT in your organization. So, involve them: hold a brief meeting to discuss your final report with them. This will keep them involved, it will make them feel valued and it will enable you to check and verify your information. Make them feel part of the WBT team, for they are the ones who will spread the gospel for you when you come to implement, hopefully, your first, full-blown WBT programme for your organization.

Once your report has been submitted to management, another important thing to do is to let everyone in the organization know how the project went. Ensure that everyone in your business unit is informed about the achievements you have made with your pilot trial. Get some quotes from your participants. Then spread the word to other business units through internal newsletters, word of mouth, company presentations and every other communication vehicle you can think of, including posters on staff noticeboards.

As I said at the beginning of the chapter, I cannot guarantee the successful outcome of your project; not even you can do that. However, by following these simple guidelines you will at least be assured that you gave it your best shot. Remember too that, although WBT can bring amazing results to some environments, WBT is not necessarily the best approach for every situation. So good luck!

References and contact details

Distributed Learning: The Opportunity for Training & Education, Asymetrix Learning Systems. Web: www.asymetrix.com

Multimedia & Internet Training Newsletter, 1996, Brandon Hall. Web: www.brandon-hall.com

Elliott Masie is president of the Masie Center, a New York-based technology and learning think-tank.
Web: www.masie.com

Wayne Schaaf helps businesses plan for, design and produce Web-based training and post-training job aids.
Web: www.ITcetera.com

Chapter 8

Training and learning: the way ahead

In this final chapter, we shall explore the trends in the training environment with a focus on the future implications of WBT. In order to do this we need firstly to look at the current state of play in the training market and discover how training budgets are being spent, what the obstacles are in meeting those training needs and what training delivery methods are being employed. Then we shall explore some of the perceived hurdles to online learning and WBT, and investigate some of the new technologies emerging in the field. Finally, we shall look at some predicted trends in training and outline how today's professional trainers can position themselves for training and learning of the future.

Training: the current state of play

Expenditure on training in both the UK and the USA is growing briskly; but lack of time for training continues to be the major obstacle, exacerbating management's ability to maintain optimal staff skills sets. As companies implement increasingly heterogeneous environments, the time to get trained in multiple disciplines is at a premium. This reported increase in training expenditure, however, cannot be attributed to the investment in training for incremental personnel, because staffing levels remain flat. Instead managers are investing more heavily in updating the skills of their existing staff. In the light of the growing skills shortages – apparent in both the UK and USA – the emphasis on increased spending for current employees makes sense. With technical expertise in such high demand on both sides of the Atlantic, some companies now require employees to sign contracts to stay with the company for a specified time as a condition of training. The fear is that employees will move on to another employer soon after being trained.

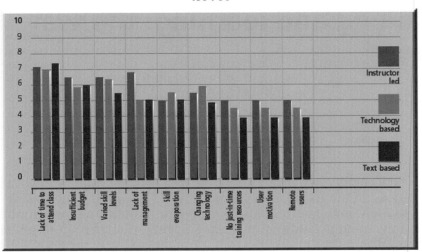

Figure 8.1   **Obstacles to meeting training needs**

Obstacles to meeting training needs

In International Data Corporation's (IDC) survey on the training market (1997), a lack of time to take training continues to be the main obstacle preventing managers from meeting the training needs of their staff (see Figure 8.1). However, this is closely followed by 'varied skill levels of employees' and 'insufficient training budgets'.

An interesting and significant change from IDC's previous surveys is the ranking of 'no just-in-time resources' and 'reaching remote users'. With the growing availability of self-study materials, including CBT and Web-based training, interactive video, online help/tutorials, and books and manuals, it is clear that the training industry is now starting to tackle the problem, making it easier for staff to learn at any time and anywhere (including from their home). Reaching remote users has clearly been helped by the advent of groupware and Web-based learning tools.

A lack of time for training will, no doubt, always be a significant challenge. The solution is that both management and staff need to view training as a necessary and priority element of their schedules.

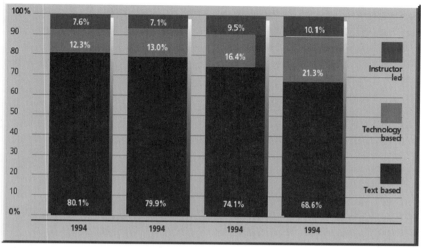

**IS Managers: Training delivery formats
1994-97**

Source: IDC

Figure 8.2   Training delivery formats

Training delivery

Although instructor-led training continues as the preferred delivery method, its dominance over technology-based training is declining (see Figure 8.2). The ease of use of learning tools, such as multimedia CD-ROM and WBT, is making training at the desktop a viable medium for many organizations. The recent arrival of the Internet and intranets for training delivery has expanded the technology-based training segment. In 1996 and 1997, these formats still represented only a comparatively small portion of technology-based training purchases (see Figure 8.3), but IDC expects these two media to emerge as significant growth areas over the next few years.

IDC predicts that managers will increase their purchases of WBT because it offers employees just-in-time continuous learning at the desktop, remote training and access to multiple resources. However, those managers are more likely to favour Internet-based training over intranet-based training, due to the higher maintenance and support costs that an intranet entails for the IS department. The advantages of the Internet and intranets include easy access, convenience and scheduling flexibility. On the other hand, according to IDC, at present there are serious obstacles to overcome for both the Internet and intranets to become viable and cost-effective:

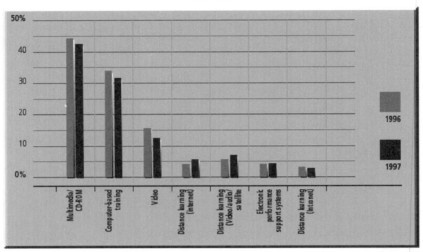

IS managers: Use of Technology-Based Training 1996-1997

Source: IDC

Figure 8.3   Use of technology-based training

- Inadequate number of employee connections and cost of gaining access.
- Lack of service provider.
- Insufficient hardware.
- Bandwidth and connection problems.

Additionally, IDC highlight the following key obstacles for intranet-based training:

- Development and maintenance costs for hardware and network, and running the training courses.
- The need for full-time management for managing the training.
- Lack of interactive learning courses.
- The inability to measure employee learning retention.

Although training purchasers see both advantages and disadvantages to using WBT, IDC found that they were 'excited by the potential' of the new medium.

It is clear from IDC's research that companies in the business of providing corporate training must take notice of their clients' strong opinions about what they want, not what they think they want. Now is the time for them to look at their areas of expertise and align them with their current and potential clients' needs. One of the strongest findings of the survey is that training companies must be able to offer technology-based training solutions. Purchasers of training want a variety of training delivery methods. Additionally, managers (especially IS managers) are concerned about the support and maintenance issues surrounding WBT via corporate intranets. Training suppliers with Web-based solutions should consider offering hosting services or partnering with an Internet Service Provider to facilitate this need.

WBT online learning market futures

Research findings

The Web-Based Training Information Center, which is an independent, non-profit making information resource on WBT run by Tim Kilby, carried out some excellent research during September 1996 through to June 1997. It polled site visitors on the following issues:

- Organizational training capabilities.
- Current implementations.
- Current plans for WBT.
- Current attitudes.

The results show participant interest in WBT and Web-based performance support systems for workplace training, and organizational interest in the financial, cultural and technical structures necessary to implement such systems. While respondents were self-selected, the high degree of participa-

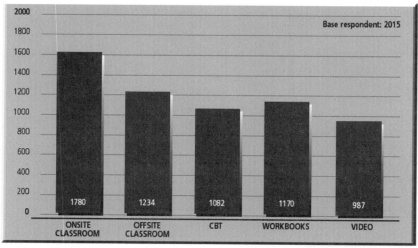

Source: Web-Based Training Information Center

Figure 8.4   Training delivery methods used

tion offers sufficient data from which to draw meaningful conclusions. For a full extract of the survey, visit Tim Kilby's excellent Web-Based Training Information Center site (www.webbasedtraining.com). The survey reveals that of the 2015 respondents, some 1402 have implemented or plan to implement WBT for their employees in the next 12 months. Currently (see Figure 8.4), those respondents trained their staff by:

- onsite classroom instruction (1639);
- offsite classroom instruction (1234);
- CBT (1082);
- workbooks (1170);
- video tapes (987).

The type of training most required was skills-based training (1607), followed by knowledge-based training (1321) and attitude-based training (529).

On the subject of the resources staff should have access to online, the following categories were most popular (see Figure 8.5):

- reference material (1780);
- newsletters (1277);

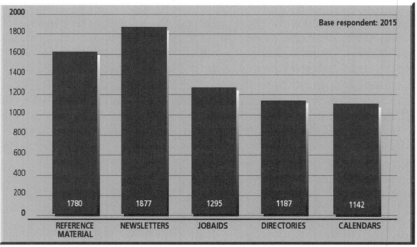

Source: Web-Based Training Information Center

Figure 8.5   Resources required online

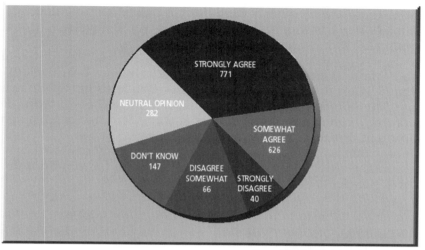

Is CBT/Online training cost-efficient?

STRONGLY AGREE
771

NEUTRAL OPINION
282

SOMEWHAT
AGREE
626

DON'T KNOW
147

DISAGREE
SOMEWHAT
66

STRONGLY
DISAGREE
40

Source: Web-Based Training Information Center

Figure 8.6   Cost efficiency of CBT/WBT

- job aids (1295);
- directories (1187);
- calendars (1142).

Others mentioned were forms (1110), project schedules (1035), position announcements (1006), bulletin boards (996), catalogues (868) and videos (654).

The cost-efficiency of WBT/online training (see Figure 8.6) was not in dispute, with 'Strongly agree' (771) and 'Somewhat agree' (626) by far the most popular responses to the question: 'All things being considered, CBT and online training are cost-efficient.'

Barriers to creating widespread online learning

You have bought the desktop computers, you have access to the Internet and/or company intranet with standard browsers. So just what is standing in the way of delivering learning to every employee at their desktop? Why can't you put all of your training online? There is, of course, no one simple answer. Elliott Masie, President of the online learning think-tank, the Masie Center, has outlined seven main hurdles which hinder the rapid, widespread acceptance of online learning.

Standards

Currently, there are no official standards for online learning development. The industry needs standards and an HTML-type equivalent for learning development, which is coming. Some of the major software publishers, such as Oracle, are focusing on a set of standards for training development and the Masie Center has launched the Online Learning Council (otlc@masie.com) to propose a first round of standards for online learning content development. The council includes Microsoft, Oracle, Lotus, Coopers & Lybrand, American Express and a wide range of training managers, content providers and technology companies. The goal is to help the growth of online learning in an 'open' environment, where a worker will be able to access multiple sources of learning content in the viewer or desktop of his or her choice.

Piloting and experimentation

There is currently little research on the components of the effectiveness of online learning. Organizations will be investing tens of millions in the development of intranet-based learning delivery. It is critical that corporate training departments take the time to pilot and evaluate the impact of these efforts.

New images and new metaphors

Trainers are viewing online learning as an extension of the classroom. Their framework is classes, instructors, lessons and modules. For business unit managers online learning should be more performance-oriented. They are interested in small 'chunks' of learning, support for single tasks, access to knowledge and expertise, rather than faculty and lesson plans. Trainers should listen carefully to the business unit mantra. The future of online learning will blur the distinctions between training programmes, knowledge databases and performance support.

New skills

We need to develop rapidly a new set of skills for managing and deploying online learning in our organizations. Training managers will need to understand a new set of characteristics of excellence when evaluating intranet-delivered training products. Developers and authors will need to create new models for sequencing and bridging elements within training programmes. Classroom trainers will need to integrate online learning into their class curriculum.

Technology

There are several aspects of intranet delivery which will need to mature in the next two years before we have the full capacity needed. It is predicted that although bandwidth is still an issue in many companies, audio and video delivery will get easier through streaming technology.

Business models

We need to develop new models for the pricing and chargeback for online learning.

Patience

Setting standards, conducting pilots and research, absorbing new models and metaphors, and gaining new skills all takes time. The push to wide-scale intranet delivery is a great thing. However, we have to give ourselves and the technology a bit of time to mature along the way. We cannot afford to deliver bad training online. We may not get a second chance.

Issues for WBT of the future

Let's explore some of the various issues that we shall face in deploying a distributed learning solution over the Internet.

Standards-based vs. proprietary content

Most software tools, including CBT authoring tools, do not produce applications that are based on Internet standards. As a result, Web browsers are unable to provide access to these non-standards-based applications. To get around this problem, many tools vendors have developed add-on software which extends Web browsers to run non-standards-based applications. These add-ons are called Plug-Ins (for Netscape Navigator browser) and ActiveX Controls (for Microsoft Internet Explorer).

Although there are advantages to being able to access existing applications without having to convert them to Internet standards, there are some disadvantages that need to be understood. One of the reasons why the Web has been so successful is its simplicity; the fact that you only need a Web browser to access the Web content, irrespective of the computer platform. Introducing the Plug-In requirement adds complexity, since it is up to the user to ensure that they have downloaded the required Plug-In and installed it for use by their browser so that they can view the particular content required. For example, to run a LearnItOnline course, before you can access the course, you need to have their proprietary LearnFlow Plug-In installed.

Additionally, Internet technology is evolving rapidly. By basing applications on Internet standards and not requiring the use of browser Plug-Ins, you are in a much better position to take advantage of the new Internet standards as they happen. For example, if a new Internet standard is developed for video, it would be much easier to integrate this with a standards-based application than one that requires the use of a Plug-In.

Network performance/bandwidth

Many of the Internet's current limitations are related to network capacity, often referred to as Bandwidth. Bandwidth is the rate at which information moves across the Internet. The reason why video and audio transmission is relatively slow over the Internet is that the bandwidth cannot cope with the large capacity required. On average information travelling over the Internet through a telephone line and a modem is around 4 kilobytes a second (equivalent of a short e-mail message). However, information accessed over a corporate intranet travels at 1.25 megabytes per second (equivalent to a few seconds of video). As a result, a combination of rich multimedia can be used.

Streaming media

The problem of bandwidth restriction over the Internet is currently being actioned and solutions are on the way in the near future. A new technology is already in use which alleviates – though not completely solving – the problem. This is called audio and video streaming. Streaming is a term that refers to the breaking down of a course, application or file into small pieces or 'chunks' followed by delivery of the beginning of the application so that it can be accessed by the user as the remainder is sent concurrently. From the user's perspective, their experience is the same as if the whole application was running from their desktop.

Video and audio streaming allows the distribution of full video, audio and animation sequences over the Internet immediately and simultaneously with no transmission delays or waiting time for the whole item to download. The specially compressed content is interleaved to ensure that it plays properly over the often unstable Internet. Street Technologies (www.streetinc.com) offers an excellent example of video and audio streaming over the Internet. Street's technology polls your PC to establish what bandwidth rate it can handle. The video plays only as fast as the client PC can 'pull' it. There are currently efforts under way to develop industry standards for streaming and it is expected that these will be appearing in the next 12 months or so.

Group interaction

There are many situations where group collaboration is important to the learning process. There is a wide range of existing and emerging technologies that support group interaction over the Internet. Some of the more well-known technologies are e-mail, chat technology, newsgroups and list servers.

Another invaluable technology for holding synchronous (taking place at the same time) discussions and conferences is videoconferencing. Previously, videoconferencing required dedicated conference rooms, special televisions, cameras and networks. Videoconferencing has been available from the desktop for a few years now, but in the not too distant future, videoconferencing technology will be another application which is accessible from the Web browser as the norm rather than the exception.

Security

Security is an important topic associated with the Internet and warrants some discussion here. In reality, the Internet is relatively safe. The amount of security required should be commensurate with the amount of risk involved. If corporate training involves sensitive corporate information, then a greater amount of security should be put in place. The following are the most important issues related to Internet security:

- **Access control**. There are many techniques for controlling who has access to a network. Corporate intranets are often protected through the use of firewalls: hardware and software that serves as a gateway between the internal intranet and the external Internet. Additionally, the process of authenticating users is another type of access control. By issuing users with passwords, access can be controlled.
- **Information confidentiality**. I am sure that most people are concerned about information privacy; for example, is it safe to give out credit card details over the Internet? My answer to them is: did you worry about that when you gave out your credit card details the last time you booked your theatre tickets over the telephone? Although that answer

is, of course, not really a reason to be concerned, it does put the problem into perspective. There are relatively safe methods in place to pass confidential information over the Internet. Encryption is the technology used to ensure that information passing through the Internet remains private. It does this by essentially scrambling the information so that only the sender and the receiver can make sense of it. Web browsers and Web servers are being developed with encryption capabilities built in.

Positioning yourself for the future*

Two major forces – global competition and rapid technological advances – have profoundly changed, and will continue to change, the nature and content of work. Sustainable competitive advantage is no longer based on technology or machinery. Corporate leaders are saying, 'People are our most important asset'. Even so, corporations on both sides of the Atlantic have undergone massive downsizing, restructuring and reorganization. At the same time, many organizations are creating high-performance work systems and transforming themselves into learning organizations. They're giving more responsibility to workers, who have been asked to do more with less, often for less. But it is not known whether such efforts will, in fact, be successful, especially in the light of the increasing pressure on workers.

These changes have made the tasks of training professionals and departments more important, and more difficult. They too are being downsized, but they're also being asked to become a core part of their organizations: a refreshing new role. The training function is expanding beyond managing employees to shaping strategic direction. Training has become a strategic investment, not just a cost to be budgeted for.

In surveys, training executives say aligning training with core business goals is a top priority. Yet many business leaders think that training professionals don't fully understand the mission and business of the companies they work in. It will be critical for HRD and training departments to close the gap between the recognized goals of alignment and the perceptions of senior management. The training/HRD profession also faces the challenges of how to:

● ensure successful customer satisfaction;
● move from training to performance improvement;
● keep up with the pace of re-engineering;
● manage and train current and new employees;

* Extract from a series of articles by Laurie J. Bassi, George Benson and Scott Cheney from the American Society for Training and Development (1996).

- attract qualified workers; and
- maximize training technology.

One strategy is to move training closer to people's jobs through just-in-time and just-what's-needed interventions. This approach addresses strategic business concerns and makes more efficient use of time and resources. Modular training in short, flexible courses focused on specific needs is already replacing traditional classes.

Though such developments may improve an organization's capacity to meet short-term training needs, they may not be consistent with long-term goals, such as promoting organizational learning and skill building. And they may not be the best way to attract the most desirable workers. Decreasing wages and reduced job security will make workers more interested in having flexible skills deemed essential by their organizations and the marketplace. In other words, the most cost-effective training strategies in the short run may not meet an organization's long-term needs. Training strategies that focus on narrow, specific needs can make it difficult to attract and retain the most qualified workers, who will expect their employers to provide opportunities to help ensure their ongoing employability.

The 'top ten' trends in training are described below. They aren't listed in order of importance. In fact, they're interrelated and reinforcing. They herald where the profession is going and show how you can direct your development accordingly. Please note that the figures quoted are for the US marketplace.

1. Skill requirements will continue to increase in response to rapid technological change

The demand for skills has been growing substantially during the past 20 years. Simply put, more sophisticated machinery and work processes require more sophisticated workers. The increase in the demand for skills has led to an increase in the need for training. Between 1981 and 1993, there was a 17 per cent increase in the number of employees who reported getting any type of skill-improvement training at work. During that same period, there has been a 45 per cent increase in the number of workers receiving formal training. As the demand for training in critical skills grows, training professionals will have to ensure that more workers receive such training, and cost-effectively.

2. The workforce will be significantly more educated and more diverse

Traditionally, the most educated workers receive the most training from employers. Women and minorities – as well as temporary, part-time and older workers – receive less training than prime-age male workers. If those patterns continue, they will cause conflicting forces in the workplace. The challenge for training professionals is clear: training practices must become more sophisticated and adaptable to meet the diverse learning needs of the new workforce.

3. Corporate restructuring will continue to reshape the business environment

The same forces creating a growing need for training are also making it difficult to provide training. Historically, Fortune 500 employers accounted for a bigger share of training because their workers had stable job prospects. Though job tenure hasn't declined overall, it has declined for males over the age of 40. Employment in Fortune 500 firms shrank as job creation shifted to small- and medium-sized firms, which traditionally have provided less formal training than large employers. In general, employees give large companies high marks for providing new job skills and low marks for their loyalty to employees. Interestingly, employees who rank their employers low on loyalty tend to be more receptive to learning new skills.

These indicators suggest that performance improvement specialists operate in complex work environments. Large firms no longer provide stable environments for training and small firms experiencing growth offered little training in the past. But now, the kind of companies that provided the least training in the past appear to be the most promising prospects for training in the future.

4. Corporate training departments will change dramatically in size and composition

Already, training departments have shrunk, and outsourcing has become prevalent. An implication of these changes is that a greater proportion of training professionals will operate as independent consultants outside of traditional organizational training departments. They will have to be responsible for their own development, and they will have to approach training with a more entrepreneurial view as the consultative role takes precedence.

5. Advances in technology will revolutionize the way training is delivered

Traditional classroom delivery of training still predominates, but the use of technology-based delivery will increase immensely. Advances in hardware, computer networking, multimedia software and videoconferencing have tremendous potential for multiple-site delivery and for bringing training closer to people's work sites. Within organizations, the increased use of technology is due to many forces: smaller training departments, shorter product cycle times, less employee travel to cut costs and time away from work for training, and the need to keep employees updated on changing skill requirements. But in order to use technology effectively, training professionals must know the appropriate situations and content for each learning platform.

A major implication of the shift towards technology-based training is the need for training professionals to work in tandem with technical experts to develop such systems. Training departments must partner with IT and IS departments. In many cases, the latter departments are leading the way in developing expert systems and electronic performance support systems, and in delivering training via computer networks.

Though the use of technology is gaining ground, evidence indicates that many companies are cautious about how, and how much, technology-based delivery should be part of training. Surveys of the member companies of ASTD's Benchmarking Forum show that many still don't use technologies for a significant part of training delivery. Although reliance on classroom training is decreasing, classroom sessions accounted for 70 per cent of all training in Forum companies in 1995. As the quality of technology continues to improve and technology-delivered training becomes more pervasive, technology-based delivery will become a tried-and-true approach.

EPSS and embedded support

In a 1994 survey on emerging technologies conducted by the International Society for Performance Improvement in Washington, DC, responding companies predicted that EPSS applications would become the most commonly introduced new technology. Although one-third of the training departments in the ASTD's Benchmarking Forum companies say that they already use EPSS for training delivery, it typically accounts for less than 10 per cent of all training time.

Computer-based training

Based on various surveys, computer-based training budgets are on the increase, especially for off-the-shelf courseware. Improvements in the quality of CBT packages and in the hardware capabilities of multimedia, animation and video have made trainers more confident in using such technology. Recent research has found that the use of CD-ROM as a delivery platform for CBT had increased and that the emergence of CD-ROM and LAN-based delivery systems indicates a trend towards centralized CBT delivery overall.

The Internet and intranets

For trainers and HRD professionals, the Internet has almost unlimited potential, especially for professional development. Newsgroups, listservs and the Web offer ways to exchange information and experiences with colleagues around the world. The Internet provides connection to a wealth of resources as training professionals continue to look outside their organizations for development opportunities. We are also beginning to see the application of the Internet and company intranets for multiple-site delivery of training and performance support. The Internet has tremendous advantages over current CBT technology in both cost and convenience. Using the Web, you can make course updates instantaneously, without recalling diskettes or reprinting CD-ROMs. Courses delivered via the Web are independent of platforms and operating systems, requiring only a modem and Internet access. Still, the Internet has a long way to go before it eventually becomes an integral part of every trainer's tool kit. Limited bandwidth capabilities and the sometimes snail's pace of downloading still make the delivery of video, sound and animation somewhat cumbersome.

Distance learning

'The new techniques and technologies of distance learning have the potential to revolutionize executive education'. (Alan F. White, senior associate dean with the Sloan School of Management of the Massachusetts Institute of Technology) MIT, Harvard, Dartmouth and the University of Michigan are among a growing number of universities whose business schools are making standard courses and customized instruction available to executives through the use of distance-learning technologies.

The use of distance-learning technology and short, customized training meets the needs of corporate executives, especially with reductions in training staff and budgets. For example, Westcott Communications – an education and training firm based in Carrollton, Texas – is working with eight businesses to provide high-tech executive education. The venture, the Executive Education Network, has nearly 100 corporate classrooms at such companies as Eastman Kodak, Walt Disney and Texas Instruments.

6. Training departments will find new ways to deliver services

Training and HRD departments have hardly been immune to the massive changes in both UK and US organizations. Such departments have been downsized, restructured, outsourced and asked to do more with less. At the same time, they're being pushed to move instruction closer to people's work sites in order to reduce costs and deliver training in more flexible environments. Training departments are being realigned along with strategic business units, reflecting the overall trend away from traditional, hierarchical bureaucratic structures.

This ongoing shift raises new challenges for training professionals, who are finding that they are increasingly responsible for purchasing training from outside. To cope with the growing demand for quality instruction, training departments are creating structures to support networks of internal and external training providers. An organization's training department is no longer seen as the sole provider of training; increasingly, it acts as a broker of learning services. Training professionals face a daunting challenge in having to ensure that purchased training meets specific needs and that it is available when and where it is needed, at a price that makes sense.

As reliance on external providers grows, trainers will become more responsible for managing training suppliers. They will need skills in contract negotiation and make-or-buy analysis. Trainers will take on internal consulting roles as the responsibility for training and development moves to line managers, supervisors and employees. Train-the-trainer course development will become more common, and more critical. Generally, training professionals will have to be ready to explore new ways to organize internal and external networks of experts and resources in order to get the job done in increasingly lean environments.

Outsourcing

Outsourcing is widespread, but not dominant, among ASTD Benchmarking Forum companies, which are some of the most successful companies in the world. In Forum firms, contract workers make up on average 23 per cent of the training design and development staff and 30 per cent of instructors. Outsourcing is less common for technical support, averaging 13 per cent of contract staff in Forum companies. The least outsourced function is administrative support. The management of suppliers creates a new role for training professionals. They must know how to select qualified suppliers and how to ensure that they provide effective, on-target services. The relationship between a buyer and a supplier involves more than the procurement of services based on a cost–benefit analysis. The buyer should be able to impart the larger mission and culture of his or her organization to the supplier.

Partnerships

Many community colleges and universities are developing departments to respond to the needs of businesses and their employees. The American Association of Community and Junior Colleges, based in Washington, DC, estimates that 90 per cent of its member colleges are, to some extent, in the business of training workers at companies, instead of just teaching subjects or trades. The Consortium for Supplier Training – made up of six US companies – has established formal ties with six community colleges and one university to provide training to the member companies' network of suppliers. The Consortium chooses the training courses, trains and certifies the colleges to provide the training, and makes the training available to the suppliers.

Many community colleges are also busy designing their services to be more amenable to the needs of businesses. For example, Kellogg Community College in Battle Creek, Michigan, provides just-in-time training, an open-entry/open-exit policy, and an open-registration procedure which lets companies send employees to the college's regional manufacturing technology centre at a moment's notice. Kellogg's curriculum lets employees choose only the skills they need to master, providing a more cost-effective service.

7. Training professionals will focus more on interventions in performance improvement

The relentless drumbeat of global competition has caused organizations to focus on every aspect of their operations, questioning how each function and process can contribute to strategic goals. Training departments are also under pressure to demonstrate their organizational value in the same terms. A paradigm shift is well under way in which training professionals must redirect their focus from traditional development inputs (classes, hours, and so forth) to outputs (performance at individual and organizational levels).

In the survey of training professionals at ASTD's 1996 International Conference, almost 89 per cent 'strongly agreed' or 'agreed' that a shift from training to performance improvement is one of the most important trends in the field. This shift is manifesting itself in changing titles, changing perceptions and changing skill requirements for training professionals. They now borrow from such areas as organizational development, industrial and organizational psychology and strategic human resources to provide performance improvement interventions, moving away from traditional training approaches. This, in turn, is resulting in more focus on aligning work practices and human resource management with high-performance work systems. The shift to performance improvement has great potential for transforming training and increasing its value to organizations. In this area, however, trainers still have a lot to learn.

Changing perceptions and titles

ASTD's 1993 National HRD Executive Survey (www.astd.com) asked about changes taking place in training. Sixty per cent of the respondents 'disagreed' or 'strongly disagreed' that the functions of a training department as we've known it would fade by 1995 or disappear by 2000. But when the same question was posed in 1995, 42 per cent of respondents 'strongly agreed' that the functions of the training department were already changing rapidly and that by 2000 training would balance with performance support.

When the ASTD's *Training & Development* magazine asked readers in the December 1995 FaxForum which term best described them professionally, 40 per cent of the respondents said, 'performance improvement specialist'. Among the Benchmarking Forum companies, many training departments have far from traditional titles. Here are just a few:

- Performance and Organizational Support Services;
- Skills, Strategy and Vitality;
- Learning Strategy;
- Learning Consultants;
- Strategic Requirements Group.

But does a title change mean a change in responsibility? Perhaps. Many HRD practitioners now actively promote a shift from training to improving employee performance. They acknowledge that training alone isn't likely to solve a performance problem. According to Joe Harless, a pioneer of performance technology, of the interventions that he and his associates have performed in more than 600 companies, 85 per cent of the time the performance problem was not related to a lack of skill or knowledge. This means that if the company had implemented a training fix, the performance problem wouldn't have gone away.

Changing competencies and skill requirements

An immediate implication of the move to performance support is that trainers and HRD practitioners must expand their competencies. In ASTD's 1995 HRD Executive Survey 73 per cent of the executives responding thought that training managers and staff were not prepared for performance support, up from 68 per cent in the 1993 survey.

Measurement and evaluation

One indication of being unprepared is the small amount of evaluation being done. Among the Benchmarking Forum companies, only Level 1 evaluations (based on Donald Kirkpatrick's four-level framework) are common, conducted for 94 per cent of all courses. Only 13 per cent are evaluated in terms of on-the-job performance; just 3 per cent are evaluated for financial impact. Two-thirds of the training departments don't perform any rigorous, quantitative studies to determine the return on their training investment. A possible reason for the lack of measurement is that the measures are not efficient. In *Performance Takes Training to New Heights* (Training & Development, September 1995), performance consultants James Robinson and Dana Gaines Robinson state that traditional training departments tend to be held accountable for the following kinds of measures:

- the number of instructor and trainee days per year;
- the number of different or new courses in a year;
- the overall results from trainee-reaction surveys;
- tests completed as part of a training programme;
- the number of training days per employee.

They advise that performance improvement departments should focus instead on the following measurements:

- the degree to which new skills transfer to the workforce;
- the degree to which individual and group performance improves;
- the degree to which training contributes to specific business goals;
- the quantity and quality of client relationships;
- the number of performance contracts agreed to and met in a year.

8. Integrated high-performance work systems will proliferate

Training departments – like all business units – are being forced to re-examine their role and to focus more on creating measurable results. The new emphasis will be on creating systems that align the separate efforts of functions, departments and people. Creating high-performance work systems is an ongoing, arduous task. The organizations that have initiated such efforts appear to be reaping rewards. But it is crucial not to underestimate the investment required. High-performance systems require, at minimum, that the people working within them be highly effective. That requires training. The evidence is clear: companies that use high-performance work practices provide more training than those that don't engage in such practices.

Within high-performance work systems, training will be aligned and integrated with actual work. Just-in-time and just-what's-needed training will be commonplace, as will be trainers with well-developed performance consulting skills. The extent of change required to implement high-performance work systems makes the role of trainers pivotal. They must be proactive in helping employees make the transition to new team-based, high-involvement structures and practices. Employees need training in group dynamics and interpersonal relations, and in systems thinking to understand better how all parts of their organizations fit together and affect each other. Trainers will also play a key role in providing feedback on employees' performance and the financial performance of their organizations.

9. Companies will transform into learning organizations

As more organizations become knowledge-based, it is essential that they promote and capture learning at the individual, team and organizational levels. This has fuelled considerable interest in the concept of the learning organization. Within a learning organization, training is integral to actual work, emerging as a by-product of work rather than something done in isolation. That fundamental change will result in the radical restructuring of the approach, content and level of training. Training professionals must develop ways to capture and share knowledge systematically, as work occurs and changes.

In a learning organization, a trainer's role is different from the traditional role. Learning is the daily responsibility of line managers and work teams; the work itself becomes the primary learning process. Within a learning organization, training professionals are responsible for facilitating learning and for tying it to organizational goals. Consequently, it is critical that they understand the business as a whole. They must ensure that all systems are designed to encourage, maximize and co-ordinate learning across all levels of the organization and that employees have opportunities to reflect on what they learn. Training professionals provide the mechanisms for cross-training among peers, and they help create reward systems to encourage employees to acquire new skills.

Most people use the term 'Learning organization' to refer to organizations which ensure that learning occurs by design and that new knowledge is used to direct the performance of individuals, teams and the entire company. No one model of a learning organization exists. All organizations can learn, but each will have its own style and way of learning. Most experts say that organizations identify their own learning styles and then seek ways to improve their learning capability and link learning to performance. A learning organization includes (but is not limited to) the following characteristics:

- A belief that systems thinking is fundamental.
- A climate that encourages, rewards and enhances individual and collective learning.
- A view that surprises, mistakes and failures are learning opportunities.
- Widely available access to information and resources.
- A desire for continuous improvement and renewal.
- Learning integrated with work.
- Opportunities for open dialogue and enquiry.

Models of the learning organization emphasize the importance of learning at different levels of a company. First, a learning organization should create an environment that promotes individual learning which is continuous and tied to work. Employees are allowed to make mistakes and challenge existing assumptions.

Team learning serves as an important step in moving learning from individuals to the organization, and a learning organization is often characterized by flexible team structures. Team learning occurs through active dialogue and enquiry, focusing on group development and building collaborative skills. Seventy-three per cent of the respondents to ASTD's 1995 HRD Executive Survey said that they encourage formalized team learning.

Perhaps the greatest emphasis in a learning organization is on systems and processes, in order to stimulate learning in a company so that it can overcome past mistakes and set a strategic direction for the future. Learning organizations develop systems to capture and store learning, making it resistant to erosion from employee turnover. A company wanting to become a learning organization must also examine and change its systems for communication, information and knowledge; its performance-management and support systems; its change-management processes; and its technology.

In the 1995 HRD Executive Survey, 94 per cent of respondents said that they thought it was important to build a learning organization; only 9 per cent thought their companies were not moving in that direction. The challenge for training professionals will be to put the concepts of a learning organization into operation. Listed below are some actions that training professionals and HRD practitioners can take to support and create a learning organization:

- Promote people who demonstrate a capacity to learn.
- Create forums for people to share what they learn and best practices.
- Change performance appraisals to assess learning activities and outcomes.

- Reward flexibility, new initiatives and risk taking.
- Enable people to take responsibility for their own learning budgets and opportunities.

Facilitating learning

With the increased emphasis on organizational learning, the use of assessment tools and surveys has boomed. The content of such instruments varies widely. Many offer the potential to put into action the aspects of a learning organization, but it is important to match the strengths of an instrument with a company's needs. For a learning organization to have its fullest effect, it must not become all things to all people. To avoid that trap, it is crucial to distinguish a move towards a learning organization from other management innovations. This requires training professionals to develop clear, practical guidelines. The first step is determining the appropriate assessment tool for an organization's particular situation.

10. Organizational emphasis on human performance management will accelerate

It is inevitable that more organizations will put into action the idea that people are their most important assets. Systems for managing and maximizing human performance will take on more significance. Training professionals will have much at stake in implementing systems to document and manage workforce skills and knowledge. They will need to hone their skills in such areas as job analysis, task analysis, evaluation and competency modelling. Employees' individual development plans will be important considerations, often tied directly to course offerings and training plans.

The move towards integrated performance-management systems challenges traditional training departments. Training professionals will have to adapt as the traditional barriers between HRD and training departments become fuzzier. They will have to be knowledgeable in such areas as employee selection and compensation systems, information management, skill standards and testing.

WBT: the future – the opportunity

WBT will be a particularly fast-growing market in the coming years as both IS and business unit managers increase their purchases of externally supplied Internet-based IT and applications software training. Training suppliers looking to offer corporate intranet-based training should target companies with an existing or planned intranet and should set their sights on business unit managers rather than IS managers as the greatest advocates of intranet-based training.

Research firm IDC believes that until training suppliers can provide full-motion video, rich graphics and simulations which are currently available on multimedia CD-ROM training tools, there will be a market for 'hybrid CD-ROM and Web-based training scenarios'. With hybrid CD-ROM and the Web, training suppliers can deliver more high-intensity bandwidth, but if they continue to develop multimedia CD-ROM training tools, the tools must have links to their Web training content. IDC expects future permutations of Web-based training to be more closely aligned with electronic performance support systems; that is, systems which offer data access, context-based retrieval with multimedia displays and user-friendly interfaces.

Web-based training has the potential to assist employees in 'learning as they perform' computer tasks. Systems are already in place whereby students can access online only the portions of classes that they need and IDC believes this capability will foster continuous learning. Long-term training customers will want more customization of course content and better tools for developing learning solutions that fit their individual needs. IDC expect that 'intelligent agents' – software that can travel over the network seeking out desired information – will enable customers to create their own personalized training and education Web curriculum. The key, then, for suppliers that plan to offer training over the Web is to make it possible for customers to tailor the site to their individual learning needs.

Social, economic and technological forces are coming together to change fundamentally the training and education worlds as we know them. Technological forces are being driven by the convergence of extremely powerful personal computer-based multimedia with the tidal wave-like adoption of the Internet. Education organizations, tools and technology are emerging and rapidly defining the look of training and learning via the Web.

The training potential of this new delivery system is enormous; in particular, the ability to provide tools that enable individuals to learn as needed means a giant leap forward for just-in-time, continuous learning in the workplace. The opportunity is for corporate, government and educational organizations to provide quality interactive learning to anyone, anywhere and at any time, which results in a better educated and more productive organization and society.

I trust that this book has provided you with the insight to chart your course for the future.

References and contact details

Laurie J. Bassi, George Benson and Scott Cheney, *Positioning Yourself for the Future: The Top Ten Trends*, American Society for Training and Development. Web: www.astd.com

Distributed Learning: The Opportunity for Training & Education, Asymetrix Corporation. Web: www.asymetrix.com

International Data Corporation, *Survey of Education Buyers' Needs & Requirements*, October 1997. Web: www.idcresearch.com

John A. Byrne, 'Virtual B-Schools', *Business Week*, 23 October 1995.

The Masie Center
E-mail: elliott@masie.com
Online Learning & Training Council
E-mail: oltc@masie.com

Tim Kilby
The Web Based Training Information Center
Web: www.webbasedtraining.com

Appendix: Useful information

WBT system providers

Integrated curriculum management systems

Advance (www.cpe.com.au/info/admin.htm)
Asymetrix Learning Systems Librarian (www.asymetrix.com)
CBTCampus (www.cbtsys.com)
Gartner Enterprise Learning Centre (shark.gartner.com/ggle/)
Global Knowledge Network Mentys (www.mentys.globalknowIedge.ca)
Learning Junction (www.teamscape.com)
LOIS (www.knowledgesoft.com)
Lotus LearningSpace (www.lotus.com)
NETg SkillVantage (www.netg.com)
OLI (www.empower-co.com)
Oracle OLA Online (ola-emea.oracle.co.uk)
Pathlore Software DLE (www.pathlore.com)
TopClass (www.wbtsystems.com)

Curriculum delivery systems

ASK International (www.askintl.com)
Aurora Interactive (www.aurora-int.com/)
BT CampusWorld (www.campus.bt.com)
CalCampus (www.calcampus.com)
Centra Symposium (www.centra.com)
Computer University (www.tlckinkos.com/computeru.html)
Cyberstate University (www.cyberstateu.com)
DigitalThink (www.digitalthink.com)
DOC Software (www.docsoftware.com)
Epson Knoware University (knoware.epson.com)

EveryOne's Computing (www.vquest.com/everyone/)
Gartner Group Learning (www.gglearning.com)
Global Knowledge Network Mentys (www.mentys.globalknowledge.ca)
Gymnasia Virtuales (www.cvbercorp.net/gymnv/)
IBM Global Campus (www.uk.ibm.com/learningtechnology)
IMG WebUniversity (www.imguniversity.com)
iNex Corporation (www.inexworks.com)
Infosourcenet (www.infosourcenet.com)
Internet Learning Systems (www.cybertravelspecialist.com)
Internet University (www.caso.com)
KnowledgePool (www.knowledgepool.com)
Lawrence Livermore National Laboratory (www-training.llnl.gov/wbt/)
Learning Base (www.learningbase.com)
Logical Operations' LearnltOnline (www.learnitonline.com)
Management Centre Europe (www.mce.be/wbt)
McGraw-Hill OnLine Learning (www.mhonlinelearning.com)
Microsoft Online Institute
   (www.microsoft.com/train_cert/html/online.htm)
NetSkills (www.netskills.ac.uk)
Netskills (www.netskills.ac.uk/TONIC/)
New School's Cyberspace Campus (dialnsa.edu/home.html)
NIITT NetVarsity (www.niitnetvarsity.com)
NovaNET (www.nn.com)
Omnitech (www.otcg.com/webtrain/matt/index.htm)
Online College Oxford (olco.ocx.com)
Online Training Center (www.iftech.com/otlc/)
Oracle OLA (ola-emea.oracle.co.uk or ola-us.oracle.com)
Outbound Train (www.outboundtrain.com)
Pebblesoft (www.pebblesoft.com)
Peritas Online (www.peritas.com)
Quicklearn (www.quicklearn.com)
Reality Interactive (www.realtools.com)
scholars.com (www.scholars.com)
Spectrum Virtual University (www.vu.org/classrooms.htm)
Street Technologies' Learning University (www.learninguniversity.com)
Sybase (dbcolon.sybase.com)
TCG (tcg.sask.com)
The eZone (www.waite.com/ezone/ezone/index.htm)
The Learning Centre (www.techwave.com)
The Mac Classroom (www.smithy.net/TMC/online.html)
The Open University (www.open.ac.uk)
Training Associates (www.damar.com)
UCLA Home Education Network (www.then.com)
Unipress Software (www.unipress.com/tutorial/html.html)
UOL Publishing (www.uol.com)

Utah Link Online Training
(www.kiz.ut.us/utahlink/public_html/online.html)
Virtual Online University (www.athena.com)
Virtual School (www.virtualschool.edu)
Wave Technologies' Online University (www.wavetech.com)
Web 101 (web101.com)
ZDNet University (www.zdu.com)

Wbt Course Authoring Software

Authorware (www.macromedia.com)
IBTAuthor (lbt.testprep.com)
IconAuthor (www.asymetrix.com)
Phoenix Internet (www.pathlore.com)
QuestNet+ (www.allencomm.com)
ToolBook II (www.asymetrix.com)

Further Information

American Society for Training & Development (www.astd.com)
Dyro's Web-Based Training Site (www.dvroweb.com/toc.html)
IT SKILLS magazine (www.training-source.co.uk)
ltcetera (www.Itcetera.com)
Multimedia & Internet Training Newsletter (www.brandon-hall.com)
Online Learning & Training Council (www.masie.com)
Technology for Learning Newsletter (www.techlearn.com)
The Masie Centre (www.masie.com)
Web Based Training Information Center (www.webbasedtraining.com)

Research on wbt

AST Computer (www.ast.co.uk)
Durlacher Quarterly Internet Report (www.durlacher.com)
International Data Corporation (www.idcresearch.com)
Spikes Cavell & Co (www.spikes-cavell.com)

Index

The Excellent Trainer

Putting NLP to Work

Di Kamp

Most trainers are familiar with the principles of Neuro-Linguistic Programming. What Di Kamp does in her book is to show how NLP techniques can be directly applied to the business of training.

Kamp looks first at the fast-changing organizational world in which trainers now operate, then at the role of the trainer and the skills and qualities required. She goes on to deal with the actual training process and provides systematic guidance on using NLP in preparation, delivery and follow-up. Finally she explores the need for continuous improvement, offering not only ideas and explanation but also instruments and activities designed to enhance both personal and professional development.

If you are involved in training, you'll find this book a powerful tool both for developing yourself and for enriching the learning opportunities you create for others.

Gower

Games for Trainers

3 Volume Set

Andy Kirby

Most trainers use games. And trainers who use games collect new games. Andy Kirby's three-volume compendium contain 75 games in each volume. They range from icebreakers and energizers to substantial exercises in communication. Each game is presented in a standard format which includes summary, statement of objectives, list of materials required, recommended timings and step-by-step instructions for running the event. Photocopiable masters are provided for any materials needed by participants.

All the games are indexed by objectives, and Volume 1 contains an introduction analysing the different kinds of game, setting out the benefits they offer and explaining how to use games to the maximum advantage. It is a programmed text designed to help trainers to develop their own games. Volume 3 reflects current trends in training; in particular the increased attention being paid to stress management and assertiveness. Volumes 2 and 3 contain an integrated index covering all three volumes.

Gower

Handbook of Management Games and Simulations

Sixth Edition

Edited by Chris Elgood

What kinds of management games are there? How do they compare with other methods of learning? Where can I find the most suitable games for the training objectives I have in mind?

Handbook of Management Games and Simulations provides detailed answers to these questions and many others.

Part 1 of the *Handbook* examines the characteristics and applications of the different types of game. It explains how they promote learning and the circumstances for which they are best suited.

Part 2 comprises a detailed directory of some 300 games and simulations. Each one is described in terms of its target group, subject area, nature and purpose, and the means by which the outcome is established and made known. The entries also contain administrative data including the number of players, the number of teams and the time required. Several indexes enable readers to locate precisely those games that would be relevant for their own needs.

This Sixth edition has been revised to reflect recent developments. And of course the directory has been completely updated. Chris Elgood's *Handbook* will continue to be indispensable for anyone concerned with management development.

Gower

Participative Training Skills

John Rodwell

It is generally accepted that, for developing skills, participative methods are the best. Here at last is a practical guide to maximizing their effectiveness.

Drawing on his extensive experience as a trainer, John Rodwell explores the whole range of participative activities from the trainer's point of view. The first part of his book looks at the principles and the 'core skills' involved. It shows how trainee participation corresponds to the processes of adult learning and goes on to describe each specific skill, including the relevant psychological models. The second part devotes a chapter to each method, explaining:

• what it is • why and when it is used • how to apply the core skills in relation to the method • how to deal with potential problems.

A 'skills checklist' summarizes the guidelines presented in the chapter. The book ends with a comprehensive matrix showing which method is most suitable for meeting which objectives.

For anyone concerned with skill development *Participative Training Skills* represents an invaluable handbook.

Gower

75 Ways to Liven Up Your Training

A Collection of Energizing Activities

Martin Orridge

Most of the activities in Martin Orridge's book require little in the way of either expertise or equipment. Yet they provide a powerful way of stimulating creativity, helping people to enjoy learning, or simply injecting new momentum into the training process.

Each activity is presented under a standard set of headings, including a brief description, a statement of purpose, likely duration, a note of any materials required and detailed instructions for running the event. In addition there are suggestions for debriefing and possible variations.

To help users to select the most appropriate activities they are arranged in the book by type or process. There are exercises for individuals, pairs and large groups and they range from icebreakers to closing events.

Trainers, managers, team leaders and anyone responsible for developing people will find this volume a rich store-house of ideas.

Gower

Successful Communication Through NLP

A Trainer's Guide

Sally Dimmick

Most professional trainers nowadays have some understanding of Neuro Linguistic Programming. They probably know that people take in information about the world through a 'preferred representational channel' and that we communicate better with people if we use their preferred channel - visual, auditory or kinaesthetic. Sally Dimmick's book goes further. It shows how NLP principles can be applied to every aspect of training and which particular aids and methods are the most suitable for each channel.

The first part of the text outlines the main concepts of NLP and explains how to identify a person's preferred channel. It also looks briefly at the significance of learning styles. Part II examines each representational channel in turn and relates it to the corresponding training methods and materials. The final chapter provides ways of combining the channels so as to maximize the transfer of learning. The text is enlivened throughout by anecdotes, examples and illustrations.

For teachers, trainers, managers and indeed anyone faced with the need to communicate in a professional way, Sally Dimmick's new guide will prove invaluable. It will be particularly welcomed by trainers looking for practical advice on how to use NLP.

Gower